PROCEEDINGS OF

THE
ARISTOTELIAN
SOCIETY

New Series—Vol. LXXX

CONTAINING THE
PAPERS READ BEFORE
THE SOCIETY DURING
THE ONE HUNDRED AND FIRST
SESSION 1979/80

Published by
The Aristotelian Society

First published 1980 by
The Aristotelian Society

© The Aristotelian Society 1980

ISBN 0 907111 00 9
ISSN 0066 7374

THE ARISTOTELIAN SOCIETY PUBLICATIONS

Proceedings: Old Series, in parts, and New Series begun in 1900, in
annual bound volumes.

Supplementary Volumes: annual bound volumes, Nos 31–51, 1957–1977.
(£7.50)

The Synoptic Index 1900–1949 (Basil Blackwell, £7.50) and Vol. II
1950–1959 (The Aristotelian Society, (£7.50), both edited by J. W. Scott,
and Vol. III 1960–1969 (Methuen, £7.50) edited by J. W. Scott
and Barrie Paskins, provide a complete guide to the contents of all volumes
from 1900 to 1969 inclusive. The current Continuation Volume is in preparation.

All prices are subject to revision without prior notice.

Most of the volumes out of print have been reprinted by the Johnson
Reprint Corporation, London Office at 24–28 Oval Road, London N.W.1,
New York Office at 111, 5th Avenue, New York, N.W. 10003, U.S.A., and
associated offices in Paris, Frankfurt, Bombay, Milan, Mexico, Athens and
Brookvale, New South Wales 2100, Australia.

Enquiries regarding any of the foregoing publications may be made of
the distributors: Element Books Ltd., The Old Brewery, Tisbury, Wiltshire.

Printed in England by
Bristol Typesetting Co. Ltd
St. Philips, Bristol

CONTENTS

I*—The Presidential Address

SHOOTING, KILLING AND FATALLY WOUNDING

by Alan R. White

I

Every item, including objects and actions, has or lacks various properties, features and relations; it exists or occurs in certain circumstances, and at particular times and places; it fulfils certain functions, plays some role and acquires or loses various further characteristics. As these objects are commonly signified by nouns and these actions by verbs, so the characterisations of the former are signified by adjectives and the qualifications of the latter by adverbs, and many features of both by relative clauses.

Thus, a man born to woman may have a sister, have written a book, acquired a job, been elected to an office and be possessed of a number of abilities and virtues. And an act, e.g. a shooting, must have been performed by someone, may have had various results, occurred at a definite time and place, have been done from certain motives and with certain instruments, have taken such a form and manifest different skills.

In virtue of certain of its characteristics or features, signified by the use of adjectives and adverbs, any item, whether an object or an action, is an instance of a certain *kind* and can be categorised accordingly. Such a categorisation is usually signified by a noun, verb or verbal noun. Thus, our man is a son and brother, author of a text-book and lecturer in the local technical college, Mayor-elect of the borough, a bit of a crank but certainly no fool. And our act of shooting may in virtue of

* Meeting of the Aristotelian Society at 39 Belgrave Square, S.W.1 on Monday October 8, 1979 at 6.30 p.m.

its different features be severally categorised; e.g., in virtue of its different agency as the act of a madman, of its motive as an act of kindness, of its legality as a crime, of its intention and result as murder, of its reason as rank disobedience, of its relation to its victim as treason, of its manner as a cock-shot or as a neat job, of its antecedents as a repetition of its consequences, as a dangerous precedent, etc. But just as a man who is a father, husband and uncle is several kinds of man, not several men, so, I shall argue, a shooting which is a killing, a piece of insubordination and a crime is several kinds of act, not several acts. And just as a father, an uncle or a husband is a man with certain relatives, not a man plus his relatives, so a killing, a piece of insubordination or a crime may be an act of shooting with certain relations, not a shooting plus its relations.

Whether anything can be characterised or qualified in a certain way, e.g., an object as to its condition, location, age, status, etc. or an act as to its antecedents, consequences, form, manner, reasons, time, etc. depends on what *kind* of thing it is an instance of, that is, on what features it already has. One kind of item, whether object or action, cannot be the same kind of item as another kind of item, but one item can be an instance of more than one kind. Therefore, one kind of item cannot have all the characteristics or qualifications of another kind of item, but the item which is an instance of both kinds can have the characteristics or qualifications of both the kinds it is an instance of. Thus, a man can be a natural or a step-son, but an author cannot be a natural or a step-author, while an author can be a plagiarising or a joint author, but a son cannot be a plagiarising or a joint son, though the same man can be both a step-son and a joint author. What is written on the board can be a column of Roman numerals and a series of even numbers, though numerals cannot be odd or even and numbers cannot be Roman or Arabic. What is written may also be an English sentence and a hypothetical proposition, though sentences cannot be true or false, believed or disputed, and propositions cannot be grammatical or ungrammatical, idiomatic or unidiomatic. The piece of rice paper I hand to you can be a harsh contract,[1] though contracts cannot be rice nor pieces of paper harsh. So one act of mine can be both a repeated shooting and an outright killing, though a shooting cannot be outright nor a killing repeated. To shoot someone might be to obey an order, though I could have shot him without hearing any order, but not have obeyed an order I did not hear. What characteristics, features, qualifications, etc. something can logically have is a function of what kinds of thing it is, and *vice versa*.

A failure to appreciate that the ways in which something can be characterised or qualified depends on the kind of thing it is— and, therefore, on some of the features it already possesses—has resulted in taking Leibniz's Law—that '$a=b$'=df. '$(F)(Fa=Fb)$'—in such a way that it seems to pose two equally unpalatable alternatives. It is, for example, argued, on the one hand, that propositions cannot be the same as sentences because propositions, but not sentences, can be true or false, believed or disputed, while sentences, but not propositions, can be English or Greek, grammatical or ungrammatical. On the other hand, it is argued that since propositions are sentences, sentences can be true or false, believed or disputed, and propositions can be composed of words. Similarly, it is argued, on the one hand, that the mind cannot be the same as the brain, because the mind, but not the brain, can be devious or salacious, while the brain, but not the mind, can be grey or weigh six ounces. On the other hand, it is argued that because the mind is the same as the brain, brains must be capable of being devious or salacious, and minds of being grey or weighing six ounces; or it is argued either that mental processes cannot be identical with brain processes because the latter, but not the former, are locatable, or that, because the two are identical, mental processes must be as locatable as brain processes.

The solution, I have suggested,[2] is that, e.g., a proposition is not of the same kind as a sentence, nor a mental process of the same kind as a brain process and, therefore, there is nothing— except a formal category such as *object*, *process* or *thing*—of which they could be either one or two instances; and, hence, they cannot be qualified or characterised in the same way. On the other hand, we can enquire in a particular case whether what we have is an instance of one kind, e.g. a proposition, and an instance of another kind, e.g. a sentence, or whether it is one instance which is of both kinds. So we can also ask, e.g., whether what appears in the footnote on page 7 is both an ungrammatical French sentence and a negative hypothetical proposition.

II

To-day I want to consider this problem in the setting of the current controversy whether, e.g., shooting and killing (or extending one's arm and signalling, springing to attention and obeying an order, pushing a door and closing it) are examples of two acts[3] or of one act with two descriptions.[4] And if they are examples of only one act with two descriptions, do they differ only in their descriptions?[5]

Clearly the words 'shooting' and 'killing' do not mean the same; there are many shootings which are not killings and many killings which are not shootings. Killing by shooting is something more than shooting; it is not merely shooting. The question is how this killing differs from this shooting. Is it an extra act or an extra description of the same act or, as I have hinted, an extra kind of the same act, i.e., a shooting which has resulted in the death of the victim.

It is a misunderstanding to argue[6] that this shooting and this killing cannot be identical on the ground that the relation between them is asymmetrical because, though the shooting *is* in these circumstances a killing, the killing *is not* in these circumstances a shooting. For the question is not whether the-killing-in-these-circumstances is a shooting—which would be absurd, for it would be the question whether a killing of a certain kind, namely one in which the victim died, was a shooting—but whether the killing is a-shooting-in-these-circumstances (namely, a shooting in which the victim died), that is, a certain kind of shooting. To which the answer is 'yes'. In other words, the relation between this killing and this shooting is quite symmetrical and, therefore, not incompatible with identity.

It is another misunderstanding to argue that the difference between the killing and the shooting can be one of only two sorts: Either the difference[7] between a shooting *plus* the victim's death and a mere shooting or only the difference[8] between two descriptions of what occurred.

The killing is not a shooting plus the victim's death, but—roughly and allowing for exceptions dependent on exactly how the shooting is related to the death—a particular kind of shooting, namely a shooting which has resulted in his death, just as a best-seller is not a book plus its record sales, but a particular

kind of book, namely a book which has achieved record sales
or just as a married man is not a man and his wife, but a particular kind of man, namely a man who has a wife. The killing
is the shooting which has this effect, not the shooting and this
effect. Similarly, though one's ear is certainly more than one's
ear lobe, *what* one pierces when one pierces one's ear need not
be something either more than or distinct from *what* one pierces
when one pierces one's ear lobe—nor need piercing the former
be distinct from piercing the latter. For to pierce one's ear is to
pierce a part of it, e.g. the lobe, which is attached to it; it is not
to pierce more of it than that attached part, e.g., the whole ear.[9]
To suppose otherwise is to make the same mistake as did Moore
when he argued that what we see when we see a table is not
what we see when we see its surface and that seeing the former
is not the same seeing as seeing the latter.

On the other hand, the killing differs from the shooting not
merely in its description, but also in what is described. For the
killing is not a mere shooting, but a shooting of a particular
kind, that is, a shooting which has resulted in a death, just as
a best-seller is not just a book, but a book of a particular kind,
that is, a book which has achieved record sales, and a married
man is not just a man, but a man of a particular kind, that is a
man who has a wife. What the first alternative confuses is not,
as advocates[10] of the second alternative suppose, 'a feature of the
description of an event and a feature of the event itself', but a
feature of the event and the conditions because of which it has
that feature.

Because what are identical are the killing and the shooting
which has this result, it is equally misleading either to say[11] that
the killing is not distinct from the shooting—because this gives
the wrong impression that the killing is not a different kind of
act from the shooting, but is just the shooting unqualified as a
cause of the victim's death—or to say[12] that the killing is distinct
from the shooting—because this gives the wrong impression that
as well as the shooting which resulted in death, the killer either
perpetrated another act or left unfinished part of his initial act.
The first view misleads us into thinking that whatever, e.g. time,
place, effects, reasons, etc., qualifies the shooting in itself ought
to qualify the killing, that is, the shooting which has resulted in
death; and *vice versa*. The second view misleads us into looking

vainly for either the supposed second act or the supposed second part of the initial act of the killer who may have had only a split second in which to shoot.

A shooting is the one and only act which is performed when a shooting results in a victim's death in such a way that a killing occurs. Moreover, it is one and the same shooting both before and after it resulted in his death, but it was not a killing unless and until it resulted in his death. Hence, the killing and the shooting—*viz.* the shooting which results in his death—are the same, namely, the same act, just as the best-seller and the book—*viz.* the book with the sales record—are the same object and the married man and the man—*viz.* the man with the wife —are the same object. There are no more two acts in the former than there are two objects in the latter. And, although killing is something more than shooting, *this* killing is no more than *this* shooting, because *this* shooting is a shooting which resulted in death.

Shooting and killing are different kinds of acts, though one and the same act may be of both kinds. Just as its antecedents can make something an act of one kind, e.g. bigamy, so its consequents can make it an act of another kind, e.g. the destruction of someone's happiness; but to be an act of different kinds is not to be two acts. An act that we perform a second time is thereby also an act of repetition, but that does not entail the performance of yet a third act. It is only sofar as it is a shooting which has resulted in the victim's death and not as a mere shooting that this shooting is a killing. What makes a shooting a killing is more than what makes a shooting a shooting.

Because shooting and killing, though they may on occasion be the same act, are, nevertheless, different *kinds* of act, it follows that not every feature of the one need be a feature of the other. Shootings, but not killings, can be lethal or non-lethal, through the heart or through the head, twice or five times; whereas killings, but not shootings, can be with a knife or a rope, against the sixth commandment or without any kind of gun.

Consider, further, the time and place of the shooting and killing. Those who identify the act by which the killing is done and the act of killing, those who separate them, and those who equate the act of killing with the instrumental act plus all the elements which make it a killing, all share[13] an assumption that acts must occupy the same time and space in order to be identical. Hence, the identifiers[14] claim, e.g. that a man who kills a space traveller by poisoning his water tank before he sets off from earth so that he dies when he takes a drink from it on Mars must have killed him on earth before he set off; the separators[15] insist that, since this is absurd, the killing must be a separate act from the act which caused the death; while those who propose a compositional analysis[16] suppose that the killing occupies the whole time and space from the poisoning of the traveller's water on earth to his death on Mars.

But, in order for a shooting to be a killing, the time and place of the killing need not be the same as that of the shooting, but only of the shooting that has resulted in death. A man can be shot many hours before he dies and far removed from the place where he dies, though he cannot be killed—as contrasted with being fatally wounded[17]—many hours before he dies[18] or in a different place from that in which he dies; for he could not have been shot to death before he dies or in a place different from where he died. Nor need he be killed at the time or place of his death, for a murderer can die before his victim dies, yet he cannot kill when he's dead. Soldiers who die in hospital after being shot on the battle field are not—except when a surgeon is careless—killed in hospital. *The Times* put the matter exactly right in a recent report of an accident in which one victim died immediately and the other later: 'A British soldier was killed and another fatally injured in a booby-trap explosion in the centre of Londonderry only a few hours after the Prime Minister had been there'.

Furthermore, a man who repents after he has shot someone, but before his victim dies, repents neither before, when, nor after he kills his victim; nor does he repent of killing him.

Similarly, if I write a review in April 1975 which hurts a colleague's feelings the following October when he reads it in a journal, then I have hurt his feelings. But, though I write the review in April and my colleague's feelings are hurt[19] in October, I do not hurt his feelings either in April or in October or in the interval between, but, at most, in 1975. Nor do I hurt them either in my study where I wrote the review, nor in the library where he read it with hurt feelings. In the same way, a book can be a best-seller, though the time and place of the book's publication need not be the time and place of its becoming a best-seller. What I did when I bought the book was not at the time buying a best-seller, though it has now become that.[20] There is nothing unusual in something's later becoming what it was not at the time.[21] It is precisely because something later acquires character-istics that it did not at the time possess that it has become what it now is. And one of the things that an action or event may either be at the time or later become is the cause of something else.[22] There is nothing inconsistent in saying that X which was an A has now become a quite different kind of thing, namely a B, and yet is the same X.

This is clearly recognised by the law courts which talk, e.g., of 'converting an act which has been completed ... into an assault'[23] or of 'the existence of other facts, not known to them, giving a different and criminal quality to the act agreed on'.[24] The courts recognise the possibility that 'There was an act ... which at its inception was not criminal ... but which became criminal from the moment ...'.[25]

The reason why the act of shooting and the act of killing with which it is identical can be dated differently is, therefore, that there was a time when they were not the same kind of act, namely before the former had the result which turned it into the latter. When the shooting resulted in death, it became, what it was not at the time of its occurrence, the cause of death and, therefore, a killing, just as when Miss Jones married Mr Smith she became, what she was not at the beginning of the wedding, Mrs Smith. And just as Mrs Smith and Miss Jones are the same person—though neither the same spinster nor the same wife—so the shooting and the killing are the same act—though neither the same shooting nor the same killing. And just as Miss Jones can be differently characterised from Mrs Smith, so the shooting and the killing can be qualified in different ways from each other.

If by doing what I now do I am going to save your life, cure your disease, avoid further trouble and bring happiness to your friend, then I *have not done* these at the time I do what I am doing because what I do has not yet had the effect of saving your life, curing your disease, etc. When and only when what I do can be qualified in those ways—and this will only be when its effects occur—then will it also become my saving your life, my curing your disease, my avoiding of further trouble and my bringing happiness to your friend; yet, of course, it will still be something which I did at the beginning. This is why I can repent my shooting of someone before he dies, but my killing of him only after he is dead.

By contrast, there are events, including deeds, whose being of a certain kind depends only logically and not temporally on the occurrence of subsequent events. Though such an event cannot be of this kind *unless* followed by a certain sort of future, its new character—as contrasted with our realisation of that new character—does not have to wait *until* that future. Thus, so-and-so cannot have been the beginning or the end of a series unless it was followed by other members or by none, and so, perhaps, it could not have been known to be either a beginning or an end until the presence or absence of other members was known. But whichever it was, if it was either, it was that when it occurred and not merely when it was known to be such. Hindsight enables us to see in the light of subsequent history what we often did not realise to have been so at the time. It is in this way that, e.g., so and so is my last or my worst act, a fatal or a fruitful move, a change or a continuation of policy, a shrewd or a mistaken concession, the peak or the trough of the birth rate. Hence, whereas a shooting would not be a *killing* unless and until the victim died, it would be a *fatal wounding* if, and not only when, the victim died. It is a confusion of these two to say 'we are not apt to describe an action as one that caused a death until the death occurs; yet it may be such an action before the death occurs. . . .'[26]

The difference between what something was and what it has become and, therefore, a confusion about *when* one thing is another, is often concealed by our proleptic use of words. Thus, to say that the Prime Minister's first speech was in the Mansion House in November on the subject of inflation may mean either that that was the time, place, and topic of his first speech as Prime Minister or of the first speech of his career. Analogously, though no schoolboy has been a Prime Minister, I could very well have been at school with the present Prime Minister. Similarly, we can say of the present Mayor that the Mayor was ill last year, when he was not yet Mayor; though our borough has never had an ill Mayor.

Philosophers often make difficulties for themselves in handling problems of identity by the way they put the question. Thus, instead of asking whether something can at one time lack a feature which it later acquires and, therefore, fail at one time to be what it later becomes—to which the obvious answer is 'yes' —they ask whether some thing with a certain feature can be identical with something else which lacks that feature. For example,[27] they ask whether an act which has occurred, e.g. a shooting, can be identical with an act which has not yet occurred, e.g. a killing, where the phrase 'an act which has not yet occurred' cannot fail to bring with it implications of its usual application to some completely fresh and separate event.

What holds for time and place holds also for other qualifications of action. It is equally no objection[28] to the identification of the act of shooting, which resulted in death, with the act of killing that, whereas to kill the victim can, perhaps, be said to be the result of shooting him, or killing him to have been done by shooting him, to shoot him cannot be said to be the result of killing him or shooting him to have been done by killing him. Contrariwise, whereas the reason for shooting him may have been to kill him, to shoot him cannot have been the reason for killing him. For, though shooting and killing are related in this way, shooting-which-results-in-death and killing are not. Equally, though the act of killing was performed by pulling the trigger —and, hence, the two are in this case the same act, though not the same kind of act—the latter, but not the former, may be the cause of one event, e.g. the gun's going off, while the former, but not the latter, may be the cause of another event, e.g. a fall in the stock market.

The difference in explanation is the difference between explaining the shooting simply as a shooting and explaining the shooting which, because it resulted in death, is a killing. This is analogous to the difference between explaining why an event took place at all, e.g., why the wood burnt, and explaining why it took place in such a way, e.g., why the wood burnt with a yellow flame.[29] There is no reason why an explanation of an act which takes account of certain of its features should be the same as an explanation of the same act which does not take account of those features. It is, therefore, unnecessary to adopt the heroic assumption that 'explanation is geared to sentences and propositions rather than directly to what sentences are about'.[30]

Similarly, 'we can know that a certain event is taking place when it is described in one way (sc. as a shooting) and not know that it is taking place when described in another (sc. either as a

fatal wounding or as a killing)' not merely because of the difference in description,[31] but because what we know is that the
given event has certain features and is of a certain kind and
what we do not know, or perhaps cannot at the time know, is
that this same event has certain other features and is of another
kind. This is simply an example of the well-known 'referential
opacity' of terms occurring in intentional contexts. I might know
or believe that a new student wished to see me without knowing
or believing that my nephew wished to see me, though the new
student is my nephew.

We can, in the same way, understand how one and the same
act can be both intentional and not intentional without having
to suppose either that there really are two acts or that intention
is really a characteristic of the description[32] of acts rather than
of acts themselves. For to say that, e.g., the action of killing
Polonius was intentional or unintentional is to say that it was
done with or without the intention of killing Polonius and to say
that killing the man behind the arras was intentional or unintentional is to say that it was done with or without the intention of
killing the man behind the arras. So Hamlet's killing of a man
in a room in Elsinore Castle, which was done with the intention
of killing the man behind the arras but not with the intention of
killing Polonius, was intentional as to one of its features but not
as to another, just as it could have been intentional as to its
manner but not as to its time. His one act was of at least two
kinds, of which one kind was intentional and the other not.

It would be easy to bring other examples under further classifications, such as 'the principle that not everything that is true
of the end is true of the means (and *vice versa*)'.[33] For example,
pumping poisoned water into a cistern can be the same act as
poisoning the inhabitants of a house who drink from it, yet it is
also a different kind of act, since the former is a means and the
latter an end. And as a means it can, unlike an (ultimate) end,
be justified or unjustified.

Again, if Xing is a *way* of Ying, then Xing *is* on this occasion
a Ying, even though Ying is not a way of Xing. Thus, if shooting
someone is a way of killing him, taking a plane a way of travelling from Boston to New York and giving tutorials a way of
teaching philosophy, then shooting him is on this occasion killing him, taking a plane is travelling from Boston to New York
and giving tutorials is teaching, even though killing is not a way

of shooting, travelling from Boston to New York not a way of taking a plane, nor teaching a way of giving tutorials.

The philosophical controversy about the identity of what one does when one does something by doing what *prima facie* is something else, as when one kills by shooting, has an exact parallel in jurisprudential discussions about the nature of the *actus reus*, e.g., of murder, assault or bigamy, and its relation to the accused's initial act, e.g., of poisoning someone's drink, setting one's dog on him, or going through a form of marriage with him. And just as some philosophers suppose that that which is done by doing something is either an additional act or is the original act plus its circumstances and consequences, so almost all jurists suppose that the *actus reus* is either the result of the initial act or the situation which is composed of the initial act and its circumstances and consequences. Since, moreover, both the courts and the text-book writers rightly agree that, in conformity with the celebrated dictum *Actus non facit reum nisi mens sit rea*, the necessary *mens rea* must be contemporaneous with the accused's act, the problem arises whether that act with which it is contemporaneous is the initial act or the *actus reus*.

The solution, I have argued elsewhere,[34] is, first, that the usual juristic analysis of the *actus reus* confuses the correct thesis that the *actus reus* is identical with that initial act which occurs in such and such circumstances and with such and such consequences, that is, it is a certain kind of initial act, and the incorrect supposition that the *actus reus* is the total situation composed of the initial act and its circumstances and consequences. This incorrect supposition derives ultimately, like much of contemporary English jurisprudence, from Austin's nineteenth century thesis that 'Most of the names which seem to be names of acts, are names of acts, *coupled with certain of their consequences*'. The court, on the other hand, rightly says 'the described conduct only becomes the defined crime if it is followed by particular consequences occurring after the completion of the physical acts done by the accused which constitute the described conduct.'[35] Thus, in assault 'the *actus reus* is the action causing the effect on the victim's mind'.[36] Secondly, the *mens rea* must accompany the initial act, since it is, e.g., setting my dog on someone, not assaulting him, that I do with intent to cause him apprehension or being reckless whether I cause this or not, and it is putting poison in his drink, not murdering him, that I do with intent to kill him. But, thirdly and most importantly, there is no more inconsistency in supposing that, though the initial act and the *actus reus* are identical, *mens rea* can accompany the initial act without thereby accompanying the *actus reus*, than in supposing that though stabbing the man behind the arras is identical with killing Polonius, I can intend the former without intending the latter.

Equally, the philosophical controversy about the time and place at which one does what one does by doing what is *prima facie* something else, as when one kills by shooting, has an exact parallel in jurisprudential discussions about the time and place of the *actus reus* in crime or the *tempus* and *locus delicti* in tort. In the light of my earlier suggestion that it is not necessarily logically possible to place or date precisely the killing in relation to the shooting, it is significant that the courts, who often, for jurisprudential reasons, have to assign such dates and places, seem fairly evenly divided in their choice, both in crime and in tort, in England and elsewhere, between the time and place of the initial act[37] and those of the result,[38] though some plump instead for a time and place which includes both the initial act and its result.[39] Thus, *George Monro Ltd v American Cyanamid and Chemical Corporation*[40] decided that the *locus* of the actionable tort was that of the act of selling, not of the harm done by, a dangerous substance. *Treacy v D.P.P.*[41] decided that the act of demanding money with menaces was to be dated and located to the time and place of writing and posting a letter, not to those of its reception. *Jenner v Sun Oil Co.*,[42] on the other hand, held that it was that of the place of reception, not of sending, of a libellous broadcast. Finally, *R v Burdett*[43] held that the place of a criminal libel included both the place of writing and the place of publication.

NOTES

[1] Cp. Lord Megaw in *R v Duru* [1973] 3 All E.R. 715, 'a cheque is a piece of paper; but also it's a piece of paper carrying with it a right to receive payment of a certain sum'.

[2] In 'Mind-Body Analogies', *Canadian Journal of Philosophy*, 1 (1972) 457–72 I have exemplified this by the controversy over the identity of mind and brain.

[3] E.g. J. Kim, 'On the Psycho-Physical Identity Theory', *American Philosophical Quarterly 3* (1966) 227–35; A. Goldman, *A Theory of Human Action* (1970) and 'The Individuation of Action', *Journal of Philosophy 68* (1971) 761–74.

⁴ E.g. G. E. M. Anscombe, *Intention* (1957); D. Davidson, 'Actions, Reasons and Causes', *Journal of Philosophy 60* (1963), 685–700 and 'Agency' in *Agent, Action and Reason*, ed. R. Binkley *et. al.* (1971), 1–25.

⁵ E.g. Anscombe and Davidson, *op. cit.*

⁶ E.g. Goldman (1971), 762–3.

⁷ E.g. J. L. Austin, 'A Plea for Excuses', in *Philosophical Papers*, (1961), 123–52; J. Feinberg, 'Action and Responsibility' in *Philosophy in America*, ed. M. Black (1965), at 146. L. H. Davis, 'Individuation of Actions', *Journal of Philosophy 67* (1970) 520–30; V. M. Weil and I. Thalberg, 'The Elements of Basic Action', *Philosophia, 4* (1974) 111–39. Cp. I. Thalberg 'When do Causes take Effect?', *Mind, 84* (1975) 583–9 at 585, who cannot see 'how the death can be what makes the "action" a killing, yet fail to be part of the total occurrence which is the killing', and J. J. Thomson, *Acts and Other Events* (1977), esp. 179 ff. But the sales which make the book a best seller are not part of the best seller lying on my table, nor is the previous marriage which makes this one an act of bigamy part of this act.

⁸ E.g. Anscombe, § 47 and Davidson, (1971) 21–2.

⁹ *pace* V. M. Weil and I. Thalberg, 122–3.

¹⁰ E.g. Davidson (1971) 22.

¹¹ E.g. Davidson.

¹² E.g. Kim.

¹³ E.g. Davidson, 'The Individuation of Events' in *Essays in Honor of Carl G. Hempel*, ed. N. Rescher (1969), 216–34; Davis, 521, 524–5; J. J. Thomson, 'The Time of a Killing', *Journal of Philosophy 68* (1971) 115–32 and *Acts and Other Events* (1977); Goldman (1971), 767–8; M. Beardsley 'Actions and Events: The Problem of Individuation', *American Philosophical Quarterly 12* (1975) 263–276.

¹⁴ E.g. Davidson (1969), 228–9.

¹⁵ E.g. Davis, Thomson (1971), Goldman.

¹⁶ E.g. Beardsley, 265, who quotes Dewey in support; Thomson (1977).

¹⁷ J. Bennett, 'Shooting, Killing and Dying', *Canadian Journal of Philosophy 2* (1973) 315–23 assimilates 'killing' to 'fatally wounding', while Thalberg (1975) conversely assimilates 'fatally wounding' to 'killing'.

¹⁸ *pace* Davidson (1969); contrast J. J. Thomson (1971) 117, 122.

¹⁹ We must not confuse the hurt (the death) with the hurting (the killing); a difference sometimes obscured by the transitive and intransitive use of the same verb, e.g. 'hurt', 'sink', 'melt', etc. It may be that every transitive hurting, sinking, melting etc. by the subject implies an intransitive hurting, sinking, melting, etc., of the object. Cp. Thomson (1977) Ch. IX.

²⁰ *pace* J. Perry, 'The Same F', *Philosophical Review, 79* (1970) 181–200 at 198, who denies that a statue and the piece of clay from which it is made can be identical on the grounds that the clay but not the statue was bought in Egypt in 1956. Equally the statue might be more, or less, valuable than the piece of clay.

²¹ Cp. Bennett, 316, 323, who yet, inconsistently (e.g. 316, 322), also holds that the killing must have occurred when the shooting occurred.

²² Cp. Weil and Thalberg, 125; Thalberg (1975), however, gets misled by a queer assumption, 588, that when X causes some later Y, there is a 'causing' in progress during the interval, into supposing that therefore an instantaneous X cannot be identical with the cause of Y. Davis 525, thinks that A cannot be B if it only 'becomes' or 'grows into' B.

²³ E.g. James J. in *Fagan v Metropolitan Police Commissioner* [1969] 1 Q.B. 439 at 445.

²⁴ *Churchill v Walton* [1967] 2 A.C. 244 *per* Lord Dilhorne.

[25] [1969] 1 Q.B. 439.

[26] Davidson (1969) 229–30; cp. Bennett, *op. cit.*, who wrongly—except at 321 where he follows Thomson—assimilates a 'fatal wound' to a 'famous insult'. The wound *was* fatal, though perhaps not known to be so, at the time, but the insult only later *became* famous. Bennett's two-fold classification of 'immediate' and 'delayed' characteristics fails to account for this intermediate class. Thus 'fatal' and 'fruitful' are neither immediate characteristics, like 'full' and 'feeble', nor delayed characteristics, like 'famous' and 'forgotten'.

[27] E.g. Thomson, 117.

[28] *pace* Kim and Goldman.

[29] *pace* Goldman (1970), 3; (1971), 767.

[30] Davidson (1969), 233; though contrast his more accurate, but inconsistent, view on 244, that 'it is not *events* that are necessary or support a cause, but events as *described* in one way or another'. B. Aune, 'Prichard, Action and Volition', *Philosophical Studies*, 25 (1974) 97–116 at footnote 14, who tries to account for the oddness of saying, e.g. that the act of killing, which was done by pulling the trigger, caused the gun to go off, by distinguishing a causal relation between events from an explanatory relation between propositions.

[31] E.g. Davidson (1971), 24.

[32] E.g. Anscombe, § 47, Davidson (1971).

[33] E.g. J. Annas, 'Davidson and Anscombe on "the same action" ', *Mind*, 85 (1976) 251–7.

[34] For discussion and references, see my 'The Identity and Time of the *Actus Reus*' in *Criminal Law Review* (1977).

[35] *Treacy v D.P.P.* [1971] A.C. 537 *per* Lord Diplock.

[36] *Fagan v Metropolitan Police Commissioner* [1969] 1 Q.B. 439; cp. *R v Morgan* [1976] A.C. 182 *per* Lord Simon of Glaisdale at 216.

[37] *George Monro Ltd v American Cyanamid and Chemical Corporation* [1944] K.B. 432, *Vancouver S.S. v Rice* (1933) 288 U.S. 445, *Caldwell v Gore* (1932) 175 La. 501, *Moore v Pyewell* (1907) 29 App. D.C. 312, *Anderson v Nobels Explosive Co.* (1906) 12 O.L.R. 644, *R v Peters* (1886) 16 Q.B.D. 636, *Bree v Marescaux* (1881) 7 Q.B.D. 434 *per* Bramwell J.

[38] *Bernstein v National Broadcasting Co.* (1955) 129 F Supp. 817, *Jenner v Sun Oil Co.* (1952) 2 D.L.R. 526, *Bata v Bata* W.N. 366, *Quinn v Kelly* [1945] Irish Law Times 143, *Albert v Fraser Companies Ltd* [1937] 1 D.L.R. 39, *Dallas v Whitney* (1936) 118 W.Va. 106, *Keeler v Fred T. Ley & Co.* (1931) 49 F. 2d 872, *Dunlop v Dunlop* [1921] 1 A.C. 367, *Otley v Midland Valley R.R. Co.* (1921) 108 Ken. 755, *Connecticut Valley Lumber Co. v Maine Central R.R. Co.* (1918) 78 N.H. 553, *Thomson v Kindale* (1910) 2 S.L.T. 442, *Joseph Evans and Sons v John G. Stein & Co.* (1904) 7 F. 65, *De Bernales v Bennett* (1894) 10 T.L.R. 419, *Alabama Great S.S.R. Co. v Carroll* (1892) 97 Ala. 126 *per* McClellan J.

[39] *Abbot-Smith v Governors of University of Toronto* (1964) 45 D.L.R. 2d 672, *R v Burdett* (1820) 3 B and Ald. 717.

[40] [1944] K.B. 432; contrast *Moran et al v Pyle National (Canada) Ltd.* [1974] 43 D.L.R. (3d) 239.

[41] [1971] A.C. 537, Lords Reid and Morris of Borth-y-Gest dissenting.

[42] [1952] 2 D.L.R. 526; Cp. *Bata v Bata* [1948] W.N. 366 on place of publication, not of writing, of libellous letters.

[43] (1820) 3 B. and Ald. 717.

For comments on an earlier draft, I am indebted to Monroe Beardsley, Peter Geach, Philip Peterson, Gilbert Ryle and Irving Thalberg.

REALISM

by Hartry H. Field

This lecture will be delivered at 19 Gordon Square, W.C.1, on Monday October 22, 1979, at 6.30 p.m. The text will not be published.

II*—THE PERSISTENCE OF MEMORY

by John Williamson

Identity continuity propositions are akin to theoretical postulates, in that they may be confirmed, falsified and underdetermined by evidence. They are unlike them in being entailed by a variety of types of proposition which it seems pretty easy for the man in the street to know to be true. I aim to show this in the special case of personal identity and continuity, especially in connection with sceptical theories about it.

In an appropriately unfinished novel, *The Sense of the Past*, Ralph Pendrel finds himself having lurched by unexplained magic into the past, partly but imperfectly in the persona of an ancestor. He has a troublesome time in conversation because he finds himself replying satisfactorily to questions to which he thinks at first that he doesn't know the answer, discovering in doing so that he has his ancestor's memories apparently mixed confusingly to his surprise among his own.

According to some radical theories of personal identity, this is not so strange a plight for a man. Except for the time travel it is an everyday situation, because personality does not endure for very long, and what we take to be memories are a mixed inheritance from the disappeared ancestral ghosts of ourselves of a short time ago. This contradicts the traditional supposition that the body's lifetime is also its normal persontime. That these radical theories are also sceptical is connected with the thesis mentioned earlier, that many propositions entail identity continuity propositions. Some of these concern knowledge and memory.

The possibility of inductive evidence for identity propositions in general may be explained by postulating a general equivalence, on the same level of abstraction as Leibniz' Law, and treating personal identity as a case under that law. Leibniz' Law is synchronic, but there is a general law for diachronic identity having the synchronic law as a special case. Let 'A at $t_1 = B$ at t_2' abbreviate 'A exists at time t_1 and B exists at time t_2 and A is at

* Meeting of the Aristotelian Society at 19 Gordon Square, W.C.1 on Monday November 5, 1979 at 6.30 p.m.

all times when it exists between t_1 and t_2 exactly identical with B'. Then for any individuals A and B:

(1) A at t_1 = B at t_2 iff at any time t at or between t_1 and t_2, if A exists at t or B exists at t, then A has every property at t that B has at t, and B has at t every property that A has at t.

This explains how there can be confirmatory evidence for diachronic identity. If we can establish that the Morning Star is the same size at a certain time as the Evening Star at that time, that goes some way but not all the way towards establishing that they are the same planet. It is in this respect of being confirmable and falsifiable by diverse underdetermining facts, that identity hypotheses resemble theoretical postulates.

The synchronic case, where t_1 = t_2, is equivalent to Leibniz' Law stated informally. The equivalence (1) is therefore a generalisation of the synchronic case. Diachronic sortal relative identity predicates are equivalent to a conjunction. 'Is the same X as' is equivalent, roughly speaking, to 'is an X and is the same as', where 'is the same as' may be replaced by its equivalent according to (1). Personal identity is a special case of that.

An equivalence may or may not be conscripted for use as a definition. The meaning of 'personal identity' has been sought in terms of memory and 'sameness of consciousness'. Whether or not that is right, conceptual connections between them exist, and this paper is an exploration of some of them.

That memory is a form of awareness of identity is obvious, in the sense that people normally have a sense of the past and of who they have been, and do so without requiring inductive evidence of the impersonal kind that a historian might use and which an amnesiac must resort to. Why this should be so is connected with there being diverse logically sufficient conditions of personal identity. That a man Sigmund is the same person as a certain person also called 'Sigmund' who existed at a certain earlier time is an implication of numerous miscellaneous propositions of varied types, which he and others may have varying reasons for supposing true; which may be true; which various people may know; and which Sigmund may know because he remembers. Facts concerning memory and knowledge of the past are logically charged with implied continuities of identity of all sorts, personal identity among them. That Sigmund is what Sigmund previously was is not a striking fact that he needs to ferret out or laboriously deduce. It is because it is implied, and by so much that he believes about himself and about the world, that it is a background belief, a common and obvious consequence of numerous elements in his ordinary picture of how the world used to be.

If its being a fact at all is put in question by some radical theory of identity, that puts in question for that reason not just one isolated fact, but a complicated and miscellaneous range of suppositions about the past, including some general apparent facts, such as that some human beings have known at least some things about the past. For this reason a radical theory comes under severe challenge except in a generally sceptical epistemology such as Hume's.

If successful reference to a certain object by the subject on presion of a sentence implies that the object exists at the time of utterance of the sentence, the true assertion of that sentence when in the past tense implies both that the object exists at the time of utterance, and also that it existed at some previous time. Consequently it must follow that it has existed continuously. I use 'continuously' here without meaning to imply that the continuity is uninterrupted, though interrupted continuity of existence would be an extraordinary matter to have to deal with. This kind of implication normally holds when the subject of a proposition is an egocentric demonstrative. For example, my uttering 'this is a piece of quartz' must, to achieve truth, succeed in referring to some piece of quartz at the time of utterance, and this could not be so if the piece of quartz successfully referred to, or some other, did not exist at the time of utterance. We cannot successfully refer in this egocentric way to what does not exist at the time of our referring to it. If so, then true propositions expressed by using such sentences as 'this quartz was found yesterday' imply that the quartz referred to both exists at the time of utterance, because of the egocentric nature of the demonstrative, and existed yesterday in order to satisfy the predicate. The statement made by uttering the sentence therefore implies the continuity of existence of the same piece of quartz. The case is generalisable, and the general form of the inference may be postulated to be as follows: Let e be some object referred to by means of an egocentric demonstrative, and let '=' used with time indicators be understood as diachronic absolute identity as before. Then

(2) (x)(that x truly asserts at t_1 using an egocentric demonstrative to refer to e that Fe at t_2 implies that $(\exists y)$ (y at $t_1 = e$ at t_2)).

It is assumed in this account that those are wrong who hold that 'I' is anomalous as an egocentric demonstrative in that it does not refer to anything. That assumption is commonly made, but if Miss Anscombe is right it is false, and this implication (2) would at least need some reformulation (G. E. M. Anscombe, 'The first person' in *Mind and Language*, ed. S. Guttenplan, Oxford, 1975; cf. also D. S. Clarke, 'The addressing function of "I" ', *Analysis*, *38*, 1978, 91–3). I do not comment on this controversy, as the issue cannot be done justice to incidentally, and it is not entirely central to this paper.

What is here asserted is that any past tense first person utterance that makes a statement implies continuity of personal identity. For example, the true assertion that I was in Nottingham last week implies the truth of '$(\exists x, \exists y)$ (x existed last week & y exists now & x is the same person as y)'. What the Anscombe thesis puts in question is whether one might explain this implication like that of other egocentric demonstratives where at least two implied propositions have a different time reference but the same object reference. What matters more here is the implication of continuity, rather than the way it is explained. It is an example of a sufficient condition of personal identity, but one where personality itself has no unique role, since it is just one of a range of similar principles of continuity of identity implied by past tensed statements referring to or speaking of presently existing things.

Further examples of implied continuity of identity are provided by propositions ascribing some property which it takes time to possess, and those describing some object in such a way that the description fits at a certain time, and what is ascribed is true of the same thing at some different time. For example, it necessarily takes time to move except at infinite speed, so that if a prophet on a camel goes from Mecca to Medina, there is some pair of times t_1 and t_2 such that some camel at t_1 is the same camel as some camel at t_2. Since we suppose people to move about, we must suppose various things which imply that someone at one time is the same person as a person at another time. Hume's question, as to why people believe that external bodies exist when unperceived invites this answer; they suppose it because they suppose, perhaps wrongly, that bodies move about behind obstacles to perception.

Time-fixed definite descriptions exist, such as 'the man who broke the bank at Monte Carlo in 1925'. They are time-fixed in the sense that if an object fits the description, its doing so implies possession at some time of some property which it had only for a limited time (e.g. that he is breaking the bank), and so implies that he existed at some relatively specific time. If the object also has some other property at some other time, any proposition making these facts explicit implies diachronic continuity of identity. Where the property also implies personality, personal identity is implied. That the man who broke the bank in 1925 went broke himself in 1929 implies that someone existing in 1925 is the same person as someone existing in 1929. Since we believe such things of ourselves, e.g. that we move about, that we have certain relations now with some person under past-time-fixed descriptions (e.g. that we finish sentences that we began, or forget things we once knew), it would be inconsistent not to believe that we are identical with people who, if the commonplace beliefs in question are true, are past versions of ourselves, and not somebody else.

There are then various miscellaneous reasons in the form of entailing beliefs for believing that I am the same person as a past version of myself. The implications are of a kind that provide similar reasons for believing in the continuity of various kinds of object, persons being just one kind of thing. This may seem platitudinous. I take it to be so, but there are those who have thought otherwise. Russell writes: 'there is no logically necessary connection between events at different times ... the occurrences which are called knowledge of the past are logically independent of the past'; and in a famous passage: 'there is no logical impossibility in the hypothesis that the world sprang into being five minutes ago, exactly as it then was, with a population that "remembered" a wholly unreal past' (*Analysis of Mind*, Ch. 9, 159–60). Again, on the same topic: 'no proposition about what

occurs in one part of space-time logically implies any proposition about what occurs in another part of space-time' (*Inquiry
Into Meaning and Truth*, Ch. 20). The example discussed here
is a counterexample to these claims. The man who went bank-
rupt in 1929 was the same person as a man who existed in 1925.
Had the world been created five minutes before his bankruptcy
it would not have existed in 1925, so something true of him in
1929 could not have been true of him. The 'recent creation'
hypothesis is logically contrary to a considerable range of propositions which, perhaps wrongly, we take to be true. A world
could be created, but it is not logically possible that it should
be *this* world, if what we believe about this world is true.

Knowledge of past truths about oneself is just another case of
something that implies continuity of personal identity. Knowing
something implies being a person; it implies that something is
true of the knower at the time of knowing (*viz.* that he knows
something); and it implies that some property or relation was
true of the same knowing subject at some earlier time; hence it
is implied that the knower at the time of knowing is the same
person as something that existed earlier. For example, if I know
now that I once lived in Yorkshire, it follows deductively that I
am the same person as a certain person who lived earlier in Yorkshire. The postulated general form of this inference is:

(3) (x)(x knows at t_1 that Fx at t_2 implies that x at t_1 is the
same person as x at t_2).

The implication depends on the implication of the truth of the
encapsulated proposition, for if 'knows' is replaced by a verb
that robs it of it, the implication of identity fails too. If x merely
believes or imagines that he once lived in Yorkshire, it doesn't
follow necessarily that he has previously been anybody at all.
If Russell is right in saying that the occurrences which are called
knowledge of the past are logically independent of the past, then
it is logically impossible that those occurrences should be what
knowledge of the past consists of.

Remembering that something is the case, often called 'factual
memory', implies knowing that it is so. It implies, too, knowing
it at the time of remembering. If someone never did know that
Caesar spoke Latin, and doesn't know it now, he cannot now
remember it; while if he once knew it but does not now know

it, he has forgotten, not remembered it. It is only if he now knows it that he can remember it. The general form is:

(4) $(x, y)(x$ remembers at t_1 that Fy at t_2 implies that x knows at t_1 that Fy at $t_2)$.

Putting (3)–(4) together gives:

(5) $(x)(x$ remembers at t_1 that Fx at t_2 implies that x at t_1 is the same person at x at $t_2)$.

Given transitivity it further follows that:

(6) $(x)(x$ remembers at t_1 that Fx at t_2 & x remembers at t_2 that Gx at t_3 implies that x at t_1 is the same person as x at $t_3)$.

This kind of point was first made by Grice ('Personal Identity', *Mind* (1941), 330–50), and it helps to explain why I should suppose, for example, that I am the same person as some child in a photograph with whom I have subjectively nothing in common that I can remember. We are linked by a chain of remembered yesterdays, but not by the survival of actual memories.

Having rehearsed that, it may be noted that attention has so far been restricted to a peculiarly impersonal form of remembering. If some teacher asks a pupil 'Do you remember the date of Waterloo?' he might very likely accept as a synonymous question in the context 'Do you know the date of Waterloo?' To remember is sometimes simply to know. There is no requirement in such a case of any personal involvement in the events of the past that are remembered. It is not perceptual memory (Broad's phrase in *The Mind and its Place in Nature*) which gives us the knowledge, but induction. We know the date of Waterloo on the basis of information and testimony, while the authority of our sources rests on documents, not presently experienced personal memories of the battle.

Personal memory may be of people, places, scenes or incidents that earlier were perceived by the rememberer. Remembering Churchill or remembering Prague does not commit me to knowing any specific fact about the object remembered. It is more like being able to imagine than like factual memory. Knowledge comes into the picture in a non-specific way, in that if I do not know anything at all about Churchill, I may better be described as having forgotten him, if I ever did know him.[1]

There are kinds of memory which are both personally involving and having specific epistemic implications. The forms of remembering seem distinguishable by their syntactic differences, or differences in implications. The first form was 'remembering that p', where 'p' stands in for sentences; the second was 'remembering x', where 'x' stands in for names; the third form to consider is 'remembering having F', where 'F' stands in for predicates representing actions done by the rememberer.

At first sight 'Nixon remembered having spoken to Dean about it' seems an ellipsis, spelled out as 'Nixon remembered that Nixon spoke to Dean about it', but this has been disputed (D. Wiggins, 'Locke, Butler and the Stream of Consciousness; and Men as Natural Kinds', in *The Identity of Persons*, ed. A. O. Rorty (U. California Press, 1976)). Factual memory is too impersonal for memory of one's past actions to be a case of it. The two sentences here differ in meaning because one implies something that the other does not, *viz.* that the rememberer knows that he is the same person as he who did the act. It belongs therefore to the list of sufficient conditions of diachronic personal identity.

To show this, consider a counterexample to the ellipsis theory. A person in this case has the relevant factual memory, but fails to remember his past action. Suppose a man calling himself 'Scrivener' has lost all memory of his past life prior to an assault when he was hit on the head. He begins to investigate his new amnesiac circumstances. He wants to know who now recognises him and who can give him information about himself, such as what his real name is and what his former profession was. He comes to hear during his inquiries about a certain man called Forsyth. He learns for example that Forsyth left Jamaica in 1966. He happens to be asked later whether Forsyth had ever travelled abroad. He remembers what he has been told about Forsyth leaving Jamaica. If Scrivener, unknown to himself, is in fact Forsyth, it is not true that he remembers having left Jamaica in 1966, for that is just the kind of memory he lacks because of his amnesia. It is true that Forsyth remembers that Forsyth left Jamaica in 1966, so this is a counterexample to the ellipsis theory. The key item lacking from his remembering having left

Jamaica is the knowledge that he, Scrivener, is the same person as Forsyth; the knowledge that the rememberer is the same as the one who did the action. It is therefore an implication of memory of past actions, of the form:

(7) (x)(x remembers at t_1 having done F at t_2 implies that ($\exists y$)(x remembers at t_1 that y did F at t_2 & x knows at t_1 that x is the same person as y)).

Since this kind of memory must be of what is past, t_2 is necessarily earlier than t_1, so the identity must be diachronic.

It is argued by Flew and Palma[2] about this kind of memory, that being identical with the person who did the past action cannot be part of the memory. The reason given does not apply to the present version of what they object to, because it turns on the alleged absurdity of being said to remember what is not past, *viz.* that x is the same person as y. This claim may be disputed for reasons given by Malcolm, who argues that factual memory of the present or future or of tenseless generalizations is quite possible and usual. I think Malcolm is right, but in any case there is no absurdity in knowing that x is the same person as y, which is all that is here in question. There is a clear sense in which the identity must be part of what is remembered, given by (7), which is in part why amnesiac loss of memory is necessarily associated with a crisis of identity, but merely forgetting things is not.

Some reason for objecting to (7) is based on an example of Malcolm's[3], of a man who has a recurring apparent fantasy of being kidnapped by three men in a green car, and who does not know that this actually happened to him as a child. Some have taken it to show either that he remembers being kidnapped without knowing that he remembered;[4] or that he remembers having been kidnapped but does not remember that he was kidnapped.[5] On the second view, (7) is falsified. Malcolm's view and mine is that it is not a clear case of remembering anything. Possibly what persuades some to think that it is, is a causal theory of memory. For this an empirical assumption needs to be added to the story; that the recapitulatory experiences were caused by the actual kidnapping. They might not have been. Even so, it is at best a kind of unconscious memory, since the man himself does not think he was ever kidnapped, does not think he remembers it, and knows nothing of the actual events. Memory is normally to be contrasted with unconscious states such as oblivion, forgetting, amnesia, sleep. The example is better cited as a case of forgetting a kidnapping than of remembering one.

The causal theory relies on the idea of memory experiences, and it may be doubted whether this is a well defined class when there are epistemological implications. Russell's phrase 'knowledge experiences' surely does not pick out any class of a distinctive type of experience; likewise some forms of memory are not essentially accompanied by any specific type of experience at the time of remembering.

A further sufficient condition of identity concerns the remembering of experiences. To remember having earlier had an experience may mean any of three things: to remember having been in certain circumstances (e.g. having the experience of going down the Cresta Run); to remember having perceived something (e.g. having heard Callas sing); or to remember having felt some sensory or emotional feeling not directly felt by others (e.g. having a toothache). The sufficient condition relates to the traditional doctrine of the privacy of experiences of the third type. The privacy thesis is expressible as a principle of personal identity as follows:

(8) $(x)(y)(x$ feels or felt sensory experience E_1 at t_1 & y feels or felt experience E_2 at t_2 & E_1 at t_1 is the same token experience as E_2 at t_2 implies that $t_1 = t_2$ & x is the same person as y).

Among the derived consequences of this, given (7), are:

(9) $(x)(y)(x$ remembers at t_1 having felt E_1 at t_2 & y remembers at t_3 having felt E_2 at t_4 & E_1 at t_2 is the same token experience as E_2 at t_4 implies that x is the same person as y).

That is to say that if x and y remember having felt the same experience, they cannot be different people.

Mackie writes: 'I see no reason for saying that it is part of the meaning of the words "memory", "remember", and so on that a man can remember only that same man's experiences'.[6] He goes on to say that if this were to be denied, one could nevertheless give a Lockean account of personal memory in terms of 'q-remembering' instead of 'genuine remembering'. All that is probably true, but it is not decisive support for his suggested thesis that someone could remember somebody else's experiences, in the precise sense of that which conflicts with (9). Of course, I might remember his having them, or seem to remember my having experiences which I have some reason to suppose that somebody else actually experienced, as one might suppose that Céline and Julie do in the film 'Céline and Julie go boating'. Thesis (9) is not a consequence of a thesis about the meaning of 'remembering' alone, but of a composite doctrine of which such a thesis is part. The meaning thesis is not that the privacy of remembered experiences is part of the meaning of 'remembering'; and does not concern privacy. It is that one kind of memory is a form of knowing, thesis (7). It is only when coupled with the quite separate and general thesis of the privacy of sensory experiences (8) that it implies the privacy of remembered experiences in particular.

The privacy thesis has usually been considered as a condition of conceivability, i.e. that it is inconceivable that a felt experience should be somebody else's, not mine. Likewise, if so, it makes no sense to claim to remember having felt someone else's sensory experiences, except that I can feel a different token of the same experience type. Nothing we can remember or experience will count as remembering the same token experience. Among the reasons for saying so is that it would follow from (7) that it implies remembering that I felt someone else's experiences; and by (4) it follows that I felt someone else's experiences. The absurdity of this consequence according to (8) implies the absurdity of whatever implies it.

The claim that we can q-remember other people's experiences has different possible meanings. On some interpretations it is no doubt true. It does not conflict with what I have argued, but it has been defended on a ground that does conflict, so it remains to try to clarify why a harmless thesis has been thought true for a wrong reason. Arising out of this is a question, not of the truth of what I have argued, but of its usefulness, for it has been said that the concept of memory can be 'dropped' in favour of q-memory.

The distinctions between different kinds of memory carry over to q-memory, presumably, though discrimination in this respect has not always been the first preoccupation of those who

see philosophical work for q-memory to do. It may be true
that I can q-remember that someone else felt ill; that I can
q-remember how someone else felt (e.g. touched by grief); that
I can q-remember someone else's action; that I can q-remember
someone else's having perceived some public object. All these
things can be remembered. Of things belonging to someone else,
what cannot be remembered is my having felt some private token
experience which someone else experienced. Can I q-remember
it?

Parfit gives as his reason for thinking so, that my q-remembering an experience does not imply my identity with the owner of
the experience. His reason for that in turn is that it cannot be
part of what I seem to remember (or q-remember), that I am
the owner, and he alludes to Palma's discussion in support.[7] Since
the latter discussion is otherwise not relevant, he presumably
thinks that my identity with the owner cannot be part of what
I actually remember. If talk about parts is a way of talking
about entailments, my reasons for disagreeing with that have
already been given. Nothing else is disputed here, for 'I seem to
remember' clearly does not imply the same things as 'I remember', and it seems in itself obvious that that I seem to remember
having felt an experience does not imply that I am the person
who felt it. If I know for a fact that I am not the real owner,
it must seem to me that I do not remember having felt it, but
that, I should say, is compatible with it also seeming to me that
I do remember it.

Q-remembering is somewhat complex. I understand Parfit's
account of it to be equivalent to the following schema:

(10) x q-remembers having felt a private experience token
    E iff (i) x believes that someone felt E; and
    (ii) it seems to x that x remembers having felt E; and
    (iii) someone felt E; and
    (iv) that someone felt E brings it about that x believes
    that someone felt E.

This account, which may perhaps elaborate a little on Parfit's,
helps to clarify why there is no inconsistency in someone
q-remembering having felt E without actually having done so,
and without being the same person as the one who did. Equally,
it does not imply that the q-rememberer is a surviving version

of the person who originally felt E, or that the original owner became a different person who retained the memory. It may be supposed that some future technology may enable two people's heads to be joined together by wires in such an ingenious way that the experiences of one person A cause, by suitable electric currents, the other person B to seem to have subsequent memories of having felt those same experiences, although he never felt them at the time. Then it may be that A believes that someone felt an experience E; that it seems to A that he remembers having felt E (though he may believe that he did not, or suspect it in view of the wires sticking out of his head); that someone B, did actually feel E; and that B's feeling E causes A to think that someone felt E. In such an event, A q-remembers having felt E, but no one has any reason to suppose that A is a surviving version of B, any more than they have for supposing him to be identical with B.

Should q-memory replace memory? The question is puzzling, for while the background motivation is perhaps complex, concerning problems about fission or fusion of human bodies, or the possibility of a 'stream of consciousness' version of Locke's theory of the meaning of personal identity, or a causal theory of memory, or all of these; nevertheless the only immediate reason I know of is simply that all memories are q-memories, so that we are free to talk about q-memory instead of memory. So we are, but if the suggestion is that we simply pay no further attention to memory claims, the same reasoning tells us there must be a loss of content in what we claim. Q-memory seems not so well defined for types of memory other than the rather uninteresting case of memory of particular sensations, but even so the suggestion of concept revision seems baseless. It may be that all squares are shapes, but that is no reason for giving up the concept of squareness in favour of the concept of shape. Perhaps the parallel is wrong, but there seems no greater reason in the case of memory and q-memory to give up a concept, on the ground that its instances belong to a wider genus.

This paper has been concerned with the implicative content of various types of memory claim. The list of implications considered looks miscellaneous, for logic provides little theory to decide whether they hold or not, or to systematise them. My chief claim is that that $(\exists x,\ \exists y,\ \exists t_1,\ \exists t_2)(x$ at t_1 is the same person as y at t_2 & $\neg$ ($t_1 = t_2$)) is among the implications of a wide family of complex propositions of quite different types, including first person past tense assertions ('I sneezed yesterday'); assertions with person reference and a time-consuming predicate ('Smith went home'); time-fixed descriptions with a predicate having a different time fixture ('the man who spoke spoke again'); knowledge of past truths about oneself ('I know I was in Glasgow yesterday'); factual memory about oneself ('I remember that I was in Glasgow yesterday'); memory of past actions ('I remember running for the train'); memory of past experiences ('I remember that headache').

This so far theoretically unregimented network of logical connections constitutes in general the conceptual connection between our hypotheses about the detailed nature of the world and what is going on in it, and our hypotheses about what stable particulars occur in it, persons included. Radical theories of personal identity which claim that personal identity does not endure, or does so for brief time spans only, have complex ramifications if these implications are valid, for the falsity follows of all those members of the family of propositions mentioned.

NOTES

[1] Malcolm defends this thesis in 'Three forms of memory' in *Knowledge and Certainty* (Cornell, 1963).

[2] A. G. N. Flew, 'Locke and the problem of personal identity', *Philosophy* (1951); A. B. Palma, 'Memory and personal identity', *Australasian Journal of Philosophy* (1964).

[3] *op. cit.*

[4] This view is taken by C. B. Martin and M. Deutscher 'Remembering', *Philosophical Review* (1966).

[5] S. Munsat, 'Does all memory imply factual memory?', *Analysis Supp.* (1965); D. Locke, *Memory* (Macmillan, London, 1971), pp. 55–6.

[6] J. L. Mackie, *Problems from Locke* (Oxford, 1976).

[7] D. Parfit, 'Personal identity', *Philosophical Review* (1971).

III*—THE ORIGINAL CHOICE IN SARTRE AND KANT

by Thomas Baldwin

It is well known that in his account of human action in *Being and Nothingness*[1] Sartre assigns a central place to the thought that in his actions a man expresses that fundamental project in choosing which he chooses himself. What came as a surprise, to me at least, was the fact that in *Religion Within the Limits of Reason Alone*[2] Kant subscribes to a view which is in many ways similar to Sartre's. For Kant here maintains that the maxims under which a man's actions are determined are grounded in an ultimate disposition which is itself chosen. In the first part of this paper, therefore, I shall discuss the similarities between the views of Sartre and Kant on this topic. But I should first make it clear that I am not claiming to have uncovered a Kantian 'source' for Sartre's views. Sartre never openly refers to Kant's *Religion*; what one does find in Sartre is a passing critical reference to what he calls Kant's notion of a 'choice of intelligible character' (*B&N* 480), which is not, I think, a phrase Kant ever uses, combined with the use of this phrase by Sartre himself to describe his own conception of the original choice of fundamental project (*B&N* 563). Essentially, I wish to draw attention to the striking similarities between one of Sartre's central doctrines and the views propounded by Kant in one of his later works. This helps in two ways: it shows a tradition into which Sartre's thought fits, and it enables one to identify one way in which some of the tensions in Kant's philosophy lead to the development of something altogether unKantian.

I

Sartre's theory of action includes the following propositions:

(S1) A man's actions are fully intelligible only in the light of his fundamental project.

---

* Meeting of the Aristotelian Society held at 19 Gordon Square, W.C.1 on Monday November 19, 1979 at 6.30 p.m.

(S2) The identity of a man's fundamental project is a necessary and sufficient condition of his identity.

(S3) The fundamental project is chosen in an original choice of oneself.

(S4) No transformation of one's fundamental project can be voluntary.

(S5) We can have no knowledge of our own fundamental project.

(S6) What makes a man's actions free is that they derive from his fundamental project.

The background to these propositions is a complex 'ontological' theory about the concepts employed in the understanding of action, and I shall describe some aspects of this theory in order to elucidate the claims (S1)–(S6) I have set out. We can begin with a familiar thought: that what distinguishes actions from bodily movements is that in some respect the former are intentional. But what is distinctive about Sartre's theory is the claim that a man's intentions and desires are elements within a single project which gives a unique volitional structure to his life. His argument starts from the recognition that in our ordinary understanding of action we refer not only to a man's intentions but also to apparently causal factors, to states of affairs (*motifs*) to which an action is a response, and to subjective attitudes (*mobiles*) which prompt this response. But, Sartre argues, this level of understanding is not self-sufficient, for no state of affairs can by itself move us to action. Rather, we can only grasp the motivational role of these apparently causal factors when we recognise that a man has a deeper project in the light of which he apprehends some state of affairs in a way relevant to his ends. This both accounts for his response to this state and for the role of his subjective attitude, which we unreflectively take to be a separate element in the motivational story, since it is revealed as no more than the agent's implicit ('non-thetic') consciousness of his project in so far as it is manifest to him in his consciousness of the state of affairs to which he responds.

So far the argument has only been that our ordinary understanding of action requires reference to a deeper project which informs an agent's assessment of his situation and his response

to it. To see how this leads on to the thought of a unique fundamental project we need to follow Sartre's thought that our life
has an organic structure which entails that we can only understand its elements when we can see them in relation to the total
structure. This thought is a consequence of Sartre's account of
the internal structure of consciousness; in his view every act
of consciousness has within itself an element of implicit self-
consciousness, and it is through this element of self-consciousness
that acts of consciousness cohere in a single, personal, life. Thus
far Sartre has not departed much from the Kantian theme of
the transcendental unity of apperception; but where Sartre de-
parts radically from Kant is in his account of self-consciousness.
For Sartre, the self-consciousness that accompanies every act of
consciousness makes reference to an ideal self which both
specifies some way in which one's life would have intrinsic value
and indicates the inadequacies of one's present life, thereby
'nihilating' it.

There is much here that is obscure and contentious; but what
matters for the moment is that the unity of a person is given,
in the light of this account of self-consciousness as in some way
teleological, by reference to that ever implicit ideal self. Since it
is precisely the pursuit of this ideal which constitutes one's
fundamental project, the project provides the total structure
within which one's ordinary intentions and motives become
comprehensible. Thus (S1) a man's actions are fully intelligible
only in the light of his fundamental project. Further, since the
project informs all acts of consciousness, the identity of the project determines the identity of the person (S2; cf. *B&N* 468–9).
The next proposition (S3), that the fundamental project is itself
chosen, is probably the hardest claim to understand, let alone
accept. Sartre holds that this original choice of self is no familiar, self-conscious, act of choice; nor is it an early, unconscious,
act of choice (*B&N* 563–4). There is no time within a man's life
when he makes this choice; rather, his whole life is the choice:
'choice and consciousness are one and the same' (*B&N* 462).
It is clear enough here what Sartre wants to disavow: the view
that each man's fundamental project is just given to him in
such a way that his life's orientation to that end is just his des-
tiny, or a natural fact about him. For Sartre wants to insist that
men are responsible for the course of their lives, much more so

than they like to think, and his talk of an original choice is, in part, an expression of this insistence. Yet there is more to it than this: the project that is chosen involves the creation of the values constitutive of an ideal self, for Sartre holds a voluntarist conception of value. Value, he writes (*B&N* 38) 'can be revealed to an active freedom which makes it exist as value by the sole fact of recognising it as such'. It follows from this that one's relation to one's fundamental project must include an act of will, and the conception of the original choice meets this need. This voluntarist conception of value also underpins the account of motivation discussed above, since in creating our own values, we choose our reasons for action.

Since through our original choice we create the only values that are our values, we will never find any reason for altering our chosen project, despite the fact that we apprehend at some implicit level of anguish that we might have chosen some other project. Hence although a transformation of one's fundamental project is always possible, it can never be voluntary (S4; cf. *B&N* 475). Further, self-knowledge, in the sense of knowledge of one's project, is impossible (S5). For, in order that something should become an object of knowledge, it is necessary that it should be possible to separate it out within one's experience as a figure standing out against a ground. This is not possible where one's own fundamental project is at issue, since it shapes and informs the whole of one's life. It is easy to mistake Sartre's point here, and it is worth quoting his statement of this point (*B&N* 570–1):

> But if the fundamental project is fully experienced by the subject and hence wholly conscious, that certainly does not mean that it must by the same token be *known* by him; quite the contrary ... We are not here dealing with an unsolved riddle as the Freudians believe; all is there, luminous; reflection is in full possession of it, apprehends all. But this 'mystery in broad daylight' is due to the fact that this possession is deprived of the means which would ordinarily permit *analysis* and *conceptualization.*

Finally, the connection between the fundamental project and freedom (S6) needs elucidation. At one level one can say that since what makes actions free is that they be determined by choices ('the technical and philosophical concept of freedom, the only one which we are considering here, means only the autonomy of choice' *B&N* 483), the thought that our actions derive from a fundamental project which is itself chosen in an original choice of self vindicates their freedom. Sartre has also, however, a more ambitious argument which relies on giving the concept of freedom a metaphysical interpretation as nihilation, which means not merely the ability to stand back in thought and action from any putative characterisation of one's future life, but the *necessity* that one should be thus disengaged from oneself (hence the futility of any attempt to be sincere). This difficult concept of nihilation, which is central to Sartre's account of human life, is linked to the idea of a fundamental project *via* the teleological account of self-consciousness which I mentioned above. According to that account, every act of consciousness includes an inner reference to that ideal self whose pursuit constitutes our fundamental project, and, Sartre holds, it is because of this inner reference that in every conscious state we find ourselves lacking and disengage ourselves from ourselves. Hence it is through our fundamental project that we nihilate ourselves and sustain our freedom. There is must that is questionable in this line of thought, but since it is the concept of choice, and not that of nihilation, with which I shall be concerned here, I shall say no more about it.

II

In *Religion Within the Limits of Reason Alone* Kant makes the following claims:

(K1) A man's actions are fully intelligible only in the light of his disposition.

(K2) The identity of a man's disposition is a necessary condition of his moral identity.

(K3) This disposition is chosen in an original act of choice.

(K4) No transformation of one's disposition can be voluntary.

(K5) We can have no certain knowledge of our own disposition.

(K6) What makes a man's actions free is that they derive from his disposition.

Obviously, I have formulated these claims in such a way that they parallel the Sartrean claims (S1)–(S6). Essentially, in place of a Sartrean fundamental project one should now think of a Kantian disposition (*Gesinnung*). As before, these claims presuppose a great deal of theory which I shall not discuss. But in order to see that the similarities between (S1)–(S6) and (K1)–(K6) are not just the result of artful phrasing, more needs to be said.

In his discussion of the Third Antinomy in the *Critique of Pure Reason* Kant had argued that in so far as the actions of men manifest their intelligible character, the actions are free; and it is with his development of this argument in *Religion* that I am here concerned. In *Religion* Kant argues that we can ask for the reason whereby the will is determined under one maxim rather than another, and that we will thereby be led back to some ultimate reason, or ground, which accounts for the adoption of maxims. This 'ultimate subjective ground of the adoption of maxims' (*Religion* 20) Kant here calls a *disposition*, and this embraces part of what was previously called intelligible character. The disposition is not just an ultimate maxim, in the sense of a first principle; it is, Kant says (*Religion* 21), a 'property of the will', and we can think of it as constituting the basic structure of the will, which, as *Willkür*, is allowed to be both free and heteronomous. Since actions are, for Kant, intelligible only in the light of the maxims under which they are determined by the will, it now follows that for a full understanding of a man's actions, we must have a grasp of his disposition, which alone will account for the maxims adopted (K1).

Since the disposition constitutes the basic structure of the will, it is clear that it must be a necessary condition for the identity of the moral subject: any change of disposition will create, morally speaking, a new person (K2). Kant writes, of a man whose disposition has changed from evil to good (*Religion* 68):

> Although the man (regarded from the point of view of his empirical nature as a sentient being) is *physically* the selfsame guilty person as before ...; yet, because of his new disposition, he is (regarded as an intelligible being) *morally* another in the eyes of a divine judge ...

Whether the identity of the disposition is a sufficient condition for the moral identity of a person is less clear. It would be neater if this was Kant's view, and one could identify disposition with intelligible character. But many of his remarks contradict it; e.g.

he says that all men start out with the same evil disposition, though one might take this as the claim that all men start out with dispositions which, being evil, are of the same kind. I think, however, that one is forcing Kant in reading him this way; on the other hand, there is a natural development of his theory in which this view belongs, and it is this, I suppose, which is signalled by Sartre's attribution to him of the thesis of an original choice of intelligible character.

Despite the fact the disposition is a constitutive property of the will, Kant holds that it must itself have been adopted by a free choice (K3). For otherwise it would be merely a given, natural, feature of men, and to suppose this would be to subvert the imputability of actions. This original choice of disposition, like the Sartrean original choice, must be quite unlike all ordinary choices whereby the will determines itself in accordance with its disposition; hence the original choice is said to be 'intelligible action, cognizable by means of pure reason alone, apart from every temporal condition' (*Religion* 26–7), whereas our ordinary choices are 'sensible action, empirical, given in time' (27). Both choices, however, can be acts of will (*Willkür*), because the will is the point of contact between phenomenal and noumenal domains.

Just what Kant meant by intelligible action is as unclear as his general talk of noumena. Sartre takes him to be invoking literally another world within which intelligible action takes place (*B&N* 480), and de Beavoir complains[3] that 'as the choice of his character which the subject makes is achieved in the intelligible world by a purely rational will, one cannot understand how the latter expressly rejects the law which it gives itself'. But this is, I think, to ascribe transcendent metaphysics to Kant, and it seems better to aim to interpret his view in terms of an *a priori* condition for the imputability of action: that only where the ultimate ground for the adoption of maxims is itself chosen are the actions thus determined imputable. This need not entail that the disposition be chosen in a separate, non-empirical, act of choice; it will be sufficient if each choice itself counts as an endorsement of the disposition in which it is itself grounded.

So far I have explained (K1)–(K3); (K4), the claim that no transformation of one's disposition can be voluntary, seems to follow readily from what has gone before. If my disposition is

the ultimate subjective ground for all my acts of will, no reasons
for changing my disposition can appeal to me, although, Kant
insists, a change from evil to good disposition is always possible.
The result is a situation of some paradox: Kant writes (*Religion*
43):

> If a man is corrupt in the very ground of his maxims, how
> can he possibly bring about this revolution by his own
> powers and of himself become a good man? Yet duty bids
> us do this, and duty demands nothing of us which we can-
> not do. There is no reconciliation possible here, except by
> saying that man is under the necessity of, and is therefore
> capable of, a revolution in his cast of mind, but only of a
> gradual reform in his sensuous nature . . .

(K5), the claim that our disposition is not known to us, is not
one that Kant maintains absolutely; for example, we know
enough about men to know that all men have started their lives
with an evil disposition. Nonetheless, because the disposition is
the ultimate subjective ground for the adoption of maxims, any
inference from the actions of a man to his disposition is uncertain. In particular, no one can be certain that he has enjoyed
that change of heart which is the casting off of his original evil
disposition and its replacement by a good one.

There remains, finally, the claim (K6) that what makes a
man's actions free is that they derive from his disposition. In
ascribing this claim to Kant it is, of course, only his negative
concept of freedom that is relevant, and in *Religion* Kant interprets this in terms of absolute spontaneity, that is, the ability of
the agent to determine his actions in accordance with the maxims
he has adopted (cf. fn. to p. 45). Since it is precisely the determination of action according to maxims that is, in *Religion*,
grounded in their derivation from a disposition, that they be so
derived is sufficent to make them free in this sense.

It is, of course, no part of my thesis that Kant and Sartre have
exactly the same conception of human nature, and what has been
said already shows some of the differences. I cannot forbear,
however, from mentioning one other respect in which Sartre's
views turn out to be identical with, in this case, consequences of
Kant's position. It is very important to Sartre that the original
choice of myself is the choice of a world. This claim is not quite

as strange as it may sound; Sartre's conception of a world is taken from Heidegger, and is, roughly, a situation conceived from the perspective of the practical, and not theoretical, interests within which we conduct most of our lives. Thus his thought is that through my original choice of myself I make myself a person with specific interests and desires; hence concepts such as 'useful', 'tool', and 'route' not only acquire significance for me, but their application is fixed by the specification of my interests and desires; he writes (*B&N* 463) 'we choose the world, not in its contexture as in-itself, but in its meaning by choosing ourselves ... The value of things, their instrumental role, their proximity and real distance (which have no relation to their spatial proximity and distance) do nothing more than outline my image'. This thought matters to Sartre because it supports his account of the motivation of action which I described earlier; it is because my choice of myself is a choice of a world that there are always reasons (*motifs* and *mobiles*) for my actions. But what I now want to note is one other consequence of this thought which Sartre draws: that in choosing a world, we make ourselves responsible for it. This is undoubtedly one of the most strange features of Sartre's philosophy, for it is hard to see why in choosing the world 'in its meaning' we should make ourselves responsible for what has happened. But Sartre is unequivocal on this point: 'the Jewish blood that the Nazis shed falls on all our heads' (*Anti-Semite and Jew* 136; cf. *B&N* 553–6).

Does Kant make a similar claim? Certainly not explicitly; nonetheless, it is arguable that something similar is required by Kant's two-standpoint theory. What Kant needs is a 'soft libertarian' position which assigns conceptual priority to the idea of a free moral subject, but nonetheless finds a niche for empirical determinism. I am persuaded by Wolff[4] and Walker[5] that the only way to effect such a reconciliation is to make the causal laws under which the empirical world is determined contingent upon the free will of the moral subject, so that Kant is committed to the proposition that the original choice of disposition is also a choice of the order of nature. Hence a radical extension of responsibility, such as Sartre endorses, seems to be also a consequence of Kant's theory; and Walker's argument at this point[6] provides a close parallel to Sartre's rhetoric (though, of course, for Walker this is intended as a *reductio*): 'I can be blamed for

the First World War, and for the Lisbon earthquake that so
appalled Voltaire. Gandhi is no less guilty than Amin of the
atrocities of the Ugandan dictator'.

III

It is not easy to separate out from these theories of original
choice those features which can be assessed out of their context.
But I want to focus on the thought that in the understanding of
a man's actions we should reach towards a specification of his
original choice of himself. As I have already indicated, this
choice is not to be conceived of as taking place at some determinate time (e.g. childhood) and then having causal consequences
for some ensuing period of a man's life. Instead, the concept of
self-choice should be taken to apply to a structural feature of
human life such that, in some way, our ordinary choices can be
legitimately viewed as endorsements of a deeper project, disposition, or character, with which we identify ourselves. This
proposal is, I think, best articulated in the context of a holistic
account of human life, such as is implied by Sartre's insistence
that man is a 'totality'. Sartre holds both that a fundamental
project is presupposed by each of a man's actions and that the
project is nothing more than its expression in all of them (cf.
B&N 565: 'there is not first a single desire of being, then a
thousand particular feelings, but the desire to be exists and
manifests itself only in and through jealousy, greed, love of art,
cowardice, courage, and a thousand empirical expressions . . .').
He provides a helpful analogy here (*B&N* 567): the relation
between project and particular action is like that between physical object and its sensible aspects on a Husserlian view of the
latter. Husserl held both that our concept of a physical object is
no more than the concept of that which gives meaning to its
sensible aspects, and also that the sensible aspects are themselves
given to us essentially as aspects *of* something. Whether this is
a defensible position, I am not here interested in: it does, nonetheless, illustrate Sartre's holistic account of human life, according to which our actions are aspects of ourselves, though we are
nothing more than the projective structure of our actions. And
in the light of this account, which can easily be applied within

the Kantian approach, it is easy to make some sense of the doctrine of original choice as the view that, through the constituent role of a man's actions as aspects of himself, in choosing them, he is choosing himself. There are not here two choices; it is rather that the holistic account legitimates the interpretation of our ordinary choices as self-choices.

The question that now arises is how well this modest interpretation fits in with the rest of the theories of Kant and Sartre. In the case of Kant, I think, the fit is fairly easy as long as one drops the two-standpoint theory. The resulting account is one according to which the adoption of maxims under which the will is determined both has a significance in relation to a man's disposition, or character, and yet also adds its own aspect to that disposition. Thus conditions (K1), (K3), and (K6) are here still satisfied. But one modification of Kant's account seems desirable: it is, I think, a presupposition of (K4), the proposition that no transformation of disposition can be voluntary, that a man's disposition be, at a certain point in his life, determinate and consistent. For it is only in relation to such a determinate disposition that one could identify a different disposition as ruled out. Hence one can remove the resulting paradox about the call of duty by rejecting this presupposition, and taking it that a man's disposition is never wholly determinate; that is, the significance of an action can always be extended by later actions which, by revealing further aspects of a man's character, tell us more about his earlier life as well. Another analogy of Sartre's is helpful here (B&N 469-70): he compares a project to a painting, and our actions to the brush strokes. This meets the holistic requirement that the significance of each brush stroke can only be grasped in relation to the whole painting, though the painting is still nothing more than the totality of the brush strokes. It can also be developed to meet the new indeterminacy requirement, by supposing that we have, not a finished painting in a frame, but one whose boundaries can always be extended in a way which may modify the pictorial significance of any brush stroke.

This indeterminacy of disposition removes, I think, the grounds for (K4). It also modifies the account to be given of personal identity; for if one retains (K2) the link between disposition and personal identity, then if the former becomes indeterminate, so must the latter. But it reinforces the grounds for (K5), in that the nature of a man's character is not now even a possibly determinate object of knowledge.

Some of the same considerations can be applied to Sartre, but his theory differs, of course, from Kant's in respect of its intimate connections with the teleological account of self-consciousness and the account of consciousness as a nihilation. In assessing his theory I propose to abstract from these points, and to concentrate on the further point, which Kant, of course, does not share, that the choice of project is the creation of one's values and interests, and thus that the analysis of motivation leads one directly back to the chosen project. It is this view which Merleau-Ponty criticizes in the final chapter of *The Phenomenology of Perception*,[7] and Merleau-Ponty's critique has been recently repeated by Charles Taylor.[8] Merleau-Ponty puts the core of his critique as follows, deliberately characterising Sartre in Kantian terms (*PP* 438): 'the choice of intelligible character is excluded, not only because there is no time anterior to time, but because choice presupposes a prior commitment, and because the idea of an initial choice involves a contradiction'. Merleau-Ponty is not here attacking the view that there is some timeless original choice of self which is distinct from our ordinary choices; for he knew as well as anyone that this was not Sartre's view. Rather, he is attacking the view that we can ground all our reasons for action in an original choice (however we understand this) of values. In the terms of the holistic account of human nature I have ascribed to Sartre, the point is this: we can view our ordinary choices as endorsements of a deeper project, only so long as we do not undermine their status as choices. Yet it is precisely this which Sartre does by claiming that the choice of self is the creation of values; for a choice can only be made where we are drawn in two ways as once, and thus presupposes 'prior commitments' which are not the products of that choice. Even though our choice will reveal which commitment we felt most strongly, it cannot create that commitment in the first place. Hence, as Merleau-Ponty argues, it cannot be that all our commitments, or reasons for action, are the products of choices. This point is well exemplified by Taylor by reference to Sartre's own example of the young man described in *Existentialism and Humanism* who had to choose between staying to look after his mother in Occupied France and leaving France to join the Resistance. If that choice is to be a real choice at all, then we must suppose that the young man is genuinely drawn both ways, and thus that, from the perspective of this choice, these incompatible commitments were not subject to his will.

It is, on reflection, no surprise that Sartre's view of the original choice as a creation of values undermines his view of it as a choice of self. For since, in accordance with the first view, he takes the view that the motivation for action is itself always chosen, all our ordinary choices, whereby we may appear to be choosing ourselves, are just a shadow play by which we deceive ourselves. 'The result' he writes (*B&N* 450) 'is that voluntary deliberation is always a deception'. And, in a similar vein, he says of the young man described in *Existentialism and Humanism* (p. 70): 'if he comes to ask your advice, it is because he has already chosen the answer'.

There is no doubt that, in rejecting Sartre's account of the motivation of action, one is committed to rejecting much of his theory. In particular, his view that in choosing oneself one chooses one's world, which I mentioned above, now falls away, as Merleau-Ponty notes (*PP* 439): 'my freedom does not draw the particular outline of this world'; and with this, there also falls away his account of our responsibility. But one can nevertheless retain his theory of an original choice of oneself (as the example of the more modest Kantian theory shows) and, within the context of his holistic account of man, retain (S1) and (S3). By introducing indeterminacy into the fundamental project, in the way I suggested before, one can reinforce (S5), the thought that our project is not known to us, but weaken the grounds for (S4), the thought that no change of project can be voluntary, though this rejection of (S4) is also contingent on rejecting Sartre's account of motivation, since if my choices were to create, however indeterminately, the only values that will appeal to me, it is clear that I could have no reason for breaking away from my project. (S2), the connection between my project and my identity, can remain here; if my project is in some respects indeterminate, then so am I. Finally, (S6), the connection between freedom and self-choice, is only strengthened at this stage. In Sartre's theory this connection was undermined by the thought that all my reasons for action are chosen, for it is hard, on such a view, to distinguish between the aims of my fundamental project, my 'involuntary spontaneity' as Sartre calls it, and those of an unconscious will which plunges on ahead of me

44 THOMAS BALDWIN

beyond any voluntary control and leading me to some unknown fate. Once the theory of motivation is dropped, all this falls away, and at least the conception of freedom as the 'autonomy of choice' is now made consistent, although its application to us is not thereby vindicated.

NOTES

[1] All page references to the translation by H. Barnes (Methuen pb. 1969). I will abbreviate the title as *B&N*.

[2] All page references to the translation by T. Greene and H. Hudson (Harper pb. 1960). I will abbreviate the title as *Religion*.

[3] *The Ethics of Ambiguity* (Citadel, 1948) p. 33.

[4] *The Autonomy of Reason* (Harper, 1973) pp. 208–9.

[5] *Kant* (Routledge, 1979) pp. 148–9.

[6] *op. cit.* note 5, p. 149.

[7] All page references to the revised translation by C. Smith and F. Williams. I will abbreviate the title as *PP*.

[8] 'Responsibility for Self' in *The Identities of Persons* ed. A. Rorty (California, 1976).

IV*—THE MOST EXTENSIVE LIBERTY

by Onora O'Neill

Introduction. I want to explore some difficulties in the notion of a most extensive or maximal liberty. These difficulties seem to me to be grave. If my argument succeeds it will show that the notion of maximal liberty is indeterminate. There is no general procedure for identifying a largest (or a larger) set of liberties. This result should prove embarrassing to any political theory which aims to identify such maximal liberty.

The theories I have in mind are a variety of liberal theories. In the first place there are theories which not only require that we identify a most extensive set of liberties, but pose this as the first requirement of a just society. Recent examples include the political theories of both Rawls and Nozick. Rawls' claim that liberty has priority over other social goods implies that a maximal set of liberties can be identified and that justice requires that securing these should take priority over securing any other social goods (at least in reasonably prosperous societies). Nozick's argument that only a minimal state and so maximal liberties can be just commits him also to holding that the notion of maximal liberty is determinate. In the more distant past there are passages both in Rousseau and in Kant which can be read as claiming that justice requires not merely universalisable (hence equal) but maximal liberty.

In a second category there are theories which assign liberty no general priority over other social goods but nevertheless use the notion of maximal liberties in certain contexts. John Stuart Mill may serve as exemplar here. He assigns liberty no general priority since he derives its value from its utility and holds that it may justly be restricted when required to protect or even to benefit others. But within the sphere of self-regarding action—action which does not affect others substantially—Mill too uses the notion of maximal liberty. When he claims that 'the sole end for which mankind are warranted, individually or collectively, in interfering with the liberty of action of any of their number, is

---

* Meeting of the Aristotelian Society at 19 Gordon Square, W.C.1 on Monday December 3, 1979 at 6.30 p.m.

46 ONORA O'NEILL

self protection"[1] he must either hold that it is possible to identify
a greatest set of liberties of self-regarding action; or admit that
his theory cannot determine which set of such liberties should be
preferred. This naming of some positions I shall seek to undermine is only illustrative.

There have, of course, been many attacks on the priority of
liberty; and also on attempts to identify maximal sets of liberties
of particular sorts. I shan't review these attempts here, but will
say why I think it worth mounting another attack. Critics of the
priority of liberty have often set out from premisses which might
be disputed by advocates of the priority of liberty. For example,
some criticisms of Rawls' theory of justice have claimed that he
does not justify the priority he assigns liberty, because it is not
possible to separate the distribution of liberties from the distribution of other social goods; or that his whole separation of
liberty from other social goods is based on an unwarranted re-
striction of the notion of liberty, which fails to view the exercise
of economic power as liberty restricting. On the other hand some
criticisms of Mill's *On Liberty* have concentrated on the difficulty of identifying self-regarding action or the alleged incompatibility between his claims about liberty and their supposedly
Utilitarian foundation. Such criticisms lead one into Rawlsian
or Millian exegesis (which I want to avoid) or into disputes over
the merits of rival views of liberty (which I hope also largely
to avoid). To join battle closely with theories which advocate
maximising liberties, or maximising liberties of some sorts,
it would be better to start from a premiss which any advocate
of maximal liberty must accept. I shall not be contending that
justice as a matter of fact does not require us to seek the greatest
possible liberty, but that no serious account of justice *can* require
us to do so, since the notion of the greatest possible liberty is
indeterminate.

I shall therefore start from an assumption which any advocate
of maximal liberty accepts:

> Liberty may be restricted only for the sake of securing a
> more extensive liberty.

Those who do not advocate maximal liberty, but do demand
that liberty of some particular sorts be maximised, would rely on
a restricted version of this premiss:

Liberty (of sort x) may be restricted only for the sake of securing a more extensive liberty (of sort x).

The hope of theorists who accept such premisses is that one can then work out what the most extensive or maximal set of liberties (or of liberties of type x) would be. To do this would require one to specify different sets of co-possible liberties, and then to identify one of these sets as more extensive than any other. This, I shall argue, is not generally possible. We can in general identify neither maximal sets of co-possible liberties nor maximal sets of co-possible liberties of a specific sort. If this claim is correct then any refurbished liberal political theory would have to place at least some restrictions on liberty over and above those needed to secure liberty itself. I shall not try to investigate systematically what these sets of additional assumptions might be, nor whether the theory or theories they would lead to are recognisably liberal political theories. However, I shall fire the odd shot into the dark.

Definitions of Liberty. One might object that there is no generally accepted liberal starting point from which this attempt to undermine the notion of maximal liberty can get going. For different liberals have worked with different conceptions of liberty, hence a given argument can undermine some (but not all) accounts of maximal liberty. I shall deal with this by starting from a very spare, schematic account of liberty which I think would be accepted by any liberal—and also by many others. Following MacCallum and Rawls and many others I shall interpret liberty triadically: A is free from x to do y.[2] As it stands this is too schematic to provide any principle of individuation for liberties. To complete the schema one has to decide how 'x' and 'y' may be instantiated.

Here is where disputes about the definition of liberty arise. Can 'x' range only over physical restraints or physical restraints imposed by particular others which literally prevent A from doing y? Are laws which prohibit A from doing y to be construed as restricting A's freedom to do so? Are threats to harm A should he do y, or offers to benefit him if he refrains or their combination restrictions of A's liberty? Can one draw some distinction between 'internal' and 'external' obstacles to A's doing y, and if so is there reason to think that external obstacles are liberty restricting while internal obstacles are not? Is there any worthwhile distinction between negative and positive conceptions of liberty? Without answers to questions such as these we cannot hope to deal with important questions such as whether (some) economic disabilities are restrictions of liberty. However, I don't believe that the particular answer one gives to these questions about the instantiation of 'x' affects the argument that I shall use to show that the concept of maximal liberty is indeterminate. I shall assume that any particular form of liberal political theory takes *some* position on the permissible instantiations of 'x'; but it does not matter for my arguments which position is taken. It is enough that the position taken makes it possible to individuate liberties and so to raise and answer questions about whether distinct liberties are co-possible.

Similar considerations apply to the view one takes about the permissible instantiation of 'y' in the schematic definition of liberty. Some position must be taken up on what 'y' can range over, in order for it to be possible for liberties to be individuated. Some liberals might wish to construe 'y' as ranging over particular bodily movements which make use of specifiable spaces and objects at specifiable times.[3] If one takes this sort of interpretation of 'y', then the individuation of liberties is given by principles for individuating spatial and temporal regions and material objects. But the project is implausible because the whole point of a system of liberties is to coordinate permissible uses of a shared material world. Many such uses cannot be specified by listing exclusive rights to control differen tobjects and spaces. If we are all to have liberty of access to some public place we must be free to move in ways which take account of the movements of others and any listing of the spaces an individual may occupy can be given only by reference to the actions he and others are engaged in.

More commonly liberals might want to construe 'y' as ranging over types of action, so that the individuation of liberties will be as hard as the individuation of actions. If 'y' is interpreted in this way, then it may not be immediately clear whether two liberties are co-possible: for example the liberty of association may be incompatible with some liberties of access to public places. Or again, it may be that some liberties which can be specified by putting in an act description for 'y' turn out on reflection to be liberties which could not be generally possessed. For example, we can all be free of curfew laws to stay out late at night; but we cannot all be free of such laws to stay out later than others. However, I shall take it that there are no insuperable problems in individuating liberties to do types of actions. If there were, either we would have to think of liberties as liberties to move our bodies in specified places and times, or the argument could stop here. For if liberties cannot be individuated and enumerated, then we cannot form sets of co-possible liberties and if we cannot form sets of co-possible liberties we shall not be in a position even to ask which of these sets is maximal.

Maximal Liberties. Assuming that we have some sufficiently determinate conception of liberty for us to individuate liberties, we can then raise questions about the compatibility of distinct liberties. Evidently there will be many distinct sets of compatible liberties. For there are many ways in which the liberties of a set of persons can be restricted to make them mutually compatible. Any one of these sets of restrictions might therefore be compatible with the principle that liberty may be restricted only for the sake of liberty. For example, this principle would permit any of various restrictions on the liberty of assembly for the sake of liberty of access to public places. Again, it would permit any of various possible restrictions on freedom of speech in public contexts for the sake of securing others' like liberty. Or again, many distinct sets of liberties for car drivers and for pedestrians can be identified each of which restricts liberty only for the sake of liberty.

Analogous problems arise in identifying a maximal set of liberties of a specific sort. Consider, for example, Mill's claim that for self-regarding action liberty should be maximised. Self-regarding actions do not, by definition, harm others. But liberties for self-regarding action do require of others that they not interfere. Such liberties too impose corollary restrictions. Hence there are many distinct possible sets of co-possible liberties of self-regarding action. There are various ways in which to reconcile the right to privacy with freedom of information; various ways in which to reconcile liberty of expression or worship or lifestyle with others' like liberty even when the possibility of harm is not relevant.

To identify one of these sets of co-possible liberties as maximal requires not merely that liberty be restricted only for the sake of liberty—that condition is met by each of many co-possible sets of liberties. It requires that liberty be restricted only for the sake of a more extensive liberty. But how is one set of co-possible liberties to be shown larger than others? It is not enough to claim that the set of co-possible liberties can be identified as the one with most members. If liberties are liberties to do certain actions, and actions can be individuated in diverse ways, then liberties can be individuated in diverse ways. If so it would always be possible to show that any given set of liberties was as numerous as any other merely by listing the component liberties more specifically. We can, if we want to, take any liberty—e.g. the liberty to seek public office or the liberty to form a family—and divide it up into however many component liberties we find useful to distinguish—or for that matter into more than we find it useful to distinguish. But if we cannot rely on picking out the set of co-possible liberties with most members in order to determine the most extensive possible liberty, what method are we to use?

Rawls in *A Theory of Justice* tried to give a procedural solution to the problem of identifying the most extensive liberty. He appealed to the standpoint of 'the representative equal citizen' whose progressively shrinking veil of ignorance left him able to make successive choices of liberty-securing institutions in the light of increasing information.[4] Hart has discussed this procedural approach sympathetically but concluded that:

> I do not understand except in very simple cases what sort of argument is to be used to show what the representative's rational preference would be and in what sense it results in a greater liberty.[5]

The charge points to a defect of any revised procedural solution: only if we already had criteria for identifying greater (and so maximal) sets of liberties would it be possible to show that certain procedures would reliably select the more extensive of two sets of liberties.

Any theory which holds that liberty or liberties of a specific sort should be maximal faces a problem for which no merely procedural solution seems adequate. Yet a substantive solution to the problem also appears to be unlikely since the very claim to identify a most extensive liberty assigns liberty priority over other social goods, so rules out appeal to any of these in assessing which of two or more sets of co-possible liberties is more extensive. But if sets of liberties are to be judged greater or less without such appeal, how is this to be done?

One case in which it would be possible to determine which of two sets of co-possible liberties is the greater is when one set includes all those liberties which are in the other set plus some further liberties. But we have no reasons to suppose that there will always be such a dominant set of co-possible liberties, and good reason to suppose that there will not be. For if we can instance any two liberties, to do y_1 and y_2, which are not co-possible for a set of persons, then we know that there can be no dominant set of co-possible liberties. For any set of liberties which dominates a set of liberties which includes the liberty to do y_1 cannot dominate any set of liberties which includes the liberty to do y_2.

This consideration suggests the following fallback position: though it is not plausible that we can identify any set of co-possible liberties which is dominant with respect to all others, there may be a set of co-possible liberties which though not maximal is the largest basic set. Such a largest basic set of co-possible liberties would have to be a subset of every non-dominated set of co-possible liberties, and would not itself be dominated by any other set of co-possible liberties which is included in every non-dominated set of liberties. We might call such a largest set of basic liberties a *core* set of co-possible liberties, and might transfer some of the considerations advanced in favour of the priority of liberty (or of maximal liberties of a particular sort) in favour of the priority of core liberties or core liberties of a specific sort. We might imagine, for example, that certain rather elementary liberties of the person would be part of any non-dominated set of co-possible liberties, so would be core liberties. If we decide that a search for the most extensive liberty must be fruitless then we might try instead to identify the core set of liberties.

However this search too will lead nowhere. For it is a search which supposedly begins from the identification of alternative sets of co-possible liberties each of which is dominated by no other set of co-possible liberties. The core liberties are supposed to be the intersection of these non-dominated sets of co-possible liberties. However it will turn out that there are no liberties which are members of every non-dominated set of liberties. For, given some set of co-possible liberties which is dominated by no other, we can form a counterpart set consisting of precisely those liberties to restrict others' action which are ruled out by the first set. For example, if we start with a set of liberties which includes the liberty to vote, hence precludes the liberty to prevent others from voting, the counterpart set will include the liberty to prevent others from voting, so restrict the liberty to vote. A counterpart set of liberties formed on this principle will share no members with the set of liberties of which it is the counterpart. Further such a set of liberties will itself be either a dominant set, or will be dominated by some set which also includes no member of the original set of liberties. We have here a method which shows that for any dominant set of co-possible liberties there will be another set of liberties containing none of the same liberties which is also a dominant set. Unless there is some general reason to suppose that all sets of liberties constructed on this principle will contain non-co-possible liberties, the quest for a core set of liberties can bear no fruit.

The Importance of Liberty. If no set of liberties is Pareto optimal, and there is no core set of liberties, then it seems that we cannot identify a maximal or a basic set of liberties and that attempts to give liberty priority must lead to indeterminate results. Yet we feel quite reasonably that some liberties are much more important than others, and that some liberties are more important at some historical stages than at others. (What use had cavemen for freedom of the press; what good use have we for the right to bear arms?). We might therefore reasonably look for additional premises which would make it possible to identify a most important (if not strictly maximal) set of liberties.

However such additional premises must be selected with care if they are not to amount to a rejection of the very enterprise of picking out some set of liberties or of liberties of a specific sort without referring to other social goods, so giving up on the priority of liberty. For this reason, for example, one cannot use a Utilitarian principle to choose the optimal or most important set of co-possible liberties. For the whole point of the idea that liberty can have priority, or that liberty of a certain sort can be restricted only for the sake of liberties of that sort, would be undermined by using Utilitarian criteria to select among sets of co-possible liberties.

Nor can appeal be made to some account of the worth of liberty such as Rawls proposes. Rawls defines the worth of liberty in this way:

> liberty and the worth of liberty are distinguished as follows: liberty is represented by the complete system of the liberties of equal citizenship, while the worth of liberty to persons and groups is proportional to their capacity to advance their ends within the framework the system defines.[6]

As here defined the worth of liberty presupposes a determinate complete system of liberties, so cannot help to determine what an optimal set of co-possible liberties would consist of.

What other grounds might be invoked, compatibly with a commitment to the priority of liberty, or of liberties of a specific sort, for regarding one set of liberties as being, if not strictly maximal, still the most important? Perhaps one plausible consideration is a very restricted claim about what liberties are good for. At the very least liberties are good for autonomous action. Whether or not some set of liberties could be justified in terms of other goals, such as maximising utility or equality of some sort or social solidarity, any set of liberties is at least a necessary condition for those who have the liberties to act autonomously in certain respects. It is in the first place because we can use liberties to do or to refrain from various acts that we value liberties. Hence an appeal to autonomy does not appear to concede that liberty does not have priority, as would an appeal to utility. However if an appeal to autonomy is to be of any help in identifying some set of liberties as more important than others, we need a clear account of autonomy.

Historical and Ahistorical Views of Autonomy. Different liberals have held quite different views of autonomy. On one view

autonomy is something that persons have regardless of their particular historical situation or education or economic circumstances. This quasi-Kantian view holds that rational beings are
inherently autonomous. (They may act on heteronomous principles but in choosing to do so they still exercise their autonomy.)
If this view is correct then liberty is of equal value to all rational
beings, since all are autonomous to like degree.

But another liberal account of autonomy is that it is developed
and fostered by particular historical and educational circumstances, so is not the equal and unavoidable heritage of all
rational beings, but something which different persons may have
to different degrees and which some may entirely or almost
entirely lack. John Stuart Mill takes this view in *On Liberty*
when he argues not only that liberty is of greater value to persons of greater autonomy ('Genius can only breathe freely in
an atmosphere of freedom') but that liberal institutions and
laws encourage persons of strong individuality or autonomy,
while other institutions create deferential or submissive persons.
In Mill's view there is a virtuous spiral here. Liberal institutions
create autonomous persons who use and value liberal institutions. On the other side there are historical circumstances in
which some classes of persons—women, slaves, colonised peoples
—are so lacking in autonomy that they may not desire liberties,
nor if granted them be able to use and enjoy them.[7] Rawls too
assumes that there have been and perhaps are historical circumstances in which the value of liberty is slight and when it would
be reasonable to trade off liberties for other social goods.[8]

The view that persons are inherently autonomous cannot help
to select among different co-possible sets of liberties. If autonomy
is an ahistorical characteristic of all persons (or of all rational
beings) and is the grounds for conferring equal and maximally
extensive liberties, then the liberties of all persons, to whichever
epoch or generation they belong, should be the same. But it is
then not determinate which set of liberties is optimal or most
important.

So if we value liberty because it permits autonomous action
and want to use this premiss to determine which is the most
important set of co-possible liberties, we cannot view autonomy
ahistorically. If we view autonomy historically then we are confronted with very wide variations in the amount and types of

autonomy which persons of different sorts and epochs typically have. We may retain a Kantian flavour by contending that despite these variations persons have, apart from their historical circumstances, an equal capacity to become autonomous—though it would be very hard to specify the truth conditions for this belief. In any case this background Kantianism will not be of any more help in establishing which set of liberties is most important than can straightforward Kantianism. But if we are to determine which set of liberties is most important for a particular group of persons by considering the respects in which those persons are autonomous, then we will presumably conclude that different sets of liberties are important for sets of persons with different patterns of autonomy.

For persons who have particular difficulties in resisting certain sorts of social pressure it may turn out that guarantees of privacy are particularly important for autonomous action. For persons living in feuding times it may be that certain liberties of a more basic sort—the right to bear arms, *habeas corpus*—are important guarantees of some sphere of autonomous action. For late twentieth century persons in developed economies, there is no general agreement which liberties contribute most to autonomous action. Is our autonomy more likely to find expression amid institutions which permit or foster the widest possible variety of associations or endeavours, even though these may produce a very uneven distribution of other social goods, especially wealth and power—or in institutions which curtail such possibilities to prevent the formation of powerful and intimidating agencies which may reduce the liberties of individuals? Will we be more able to exercise autonomy if we have varied economic opportunities or if we have guaranteed economic minima?

Arguments to identify the most important or optimal set of co-possible liberties for a given set of persons at a given time are undoubtedly difficult and tentative. But they become even more intricate when we try to extend them to identify the optimal set of liberties for a set of persons for an extended period. For the institutions which implement that set of liberties will also have effects on the capacities for autonomous action of the persons who live with and under those institutions. And if we take an historical view of persons' autonomy such an extension is presumably unavoidable. It would be artificial to take the capacities

for autonomous action of a set of persons at some arbitrary
starting date as given for an extended perod if we have reasons
to think that the very institutions identified as offering those persons the greatest chance to act autonomously may as time goes
on alter the capacities they and their successors have for autonomous action.

Further, we do have good reasons for thinking that the sorts
of institutions necessary to secure optimal liberties for a set of
persons with given capacities for autonomy may over time
change those persons and their descendants in ways which would
make another set of liberties optimal. Though we lack any detailed theory of what makes persons autonomous and what makes
them conformist or other-directed, we probably have reasons for
thinking that there are certain 'formative' institutions—including
but certainly not limited to familial and educational structures
—which affect capacities for autonomy in one way or another.
But we do not have reasons for believing that those institutions
which provide optimal liberties for persons at t_1 will generally
be the institutions which provide optimal liberties for persons
who have lived with and through those institutions from t_1 to t_2.
Some forms of compulsion have historically helped rather than
restricted the capacities of persons for autonomous action, including, for example, compulsory schooling and taxation used
to improve the health and welfare of persons who might otherwise suffer the paralysis of extreme poverty. On the other hand
some forms of liberty may produce more conforming, dependent
people. Mill in *On Liberty* laments the dearth of strikingly independent or autonomous persons in his own time and links this
dearth to the partial realisation (for example through the free
circulation of books) of the liberties which he then perversely
argues are necessary for the development of persons of flourishing
independence.

When the institutions which define liberties and restrictions
for a particular society themselves help form the capacities of
members of that society for autonomous action, it is no longer
possible to use a premise about the capacities for autonomous
action of persons in that society in working out what the optimal
set of liberties is. For we do not know whether to determine
which are the liberties which will be optimal for persons as they
are now, or whether to determine which are the liberties which
will be optimal for persons as they may be in the long run under

various assumptions about the institutional arrangements for the interim period, of whatever length.

This problem is one that has not been fully faced even by those liberal theorists who have had a very strong sense of the historical development of human capacities. For example, Rousseau's Lawgiver was to select the laws and institutions which would best secure and express the autonomy of which a particular people was capable.[9] But if the capacities for autonomous and independent action of persons or of peoples are constantly developing, then there is no single transformation from natural to moral existence which even the most exalted Lawgiver could achieve. The Lawgiver's task is worse than Sisyphean. No choice of laws and institutions is final, and at each choosing he may be faced with distinct sets of co-possible laws and institutions *each* of which is optimal for the capacities for autonomous action which the people may be expected to have at *some* future time. There is no way of determining which liberties are optimal.

The problem must be faced even if we lack the advantage of a Rousseauian Lawgiver. Should we settle for less than optimal liberty at t_1 for the sake of capacities for autonomous action and so the liberties of t_2? If future generations will or may be more autonomous if we settle for less than optimal liberties, would it be illiberal to fail to secure future liberties, or illiberal to fail to secure present liberties? For example, if some methods of child-rearing and some sorts of schooling produce more conforming and submissive persons, should parents and schools be prevented from using those methods? Or if some present uses of liberty, for example those which increase population faster than resources, are likely to produce future scarcities which in turn damage the autonomy and the confidence of future persons, should we be concerned to restrict our own consumption to avoid those future scarcities and so the impact on future liberties: or may we justify risking future restrictions on liberty as suitable to, indeed optimal for, the reduced autonomy of those future persons? Have we harmed the liberty of our descendants if we use our own liberty so that they will or must become persons for whom many liberties we can use are useless?

There are some circumstances—I can see two—under which it can be made reasonably clear what a *long run* policy of restricting liberty only for the sake of present and future capacities for autonomous action would amount to. First, there is John

Stuart Mill's virtuous spiral. If more liberal institutions and practices will produce more autonomous persons, then we may reasonably hold that establishing optimal liberties for the present generation is always the way to establish optimal long-run liberty. Each generation by seeking the most liberal institutions it can make use of produces a next generation capable of more sorts of autonomy, so able to enjoy still further liberties. Secondly there is a pessimistic analogue; if each generation by choosing sets of liberties which are optimal for its own exercise of autonomy stunts or reduces the capacities for autonomous action of the next generation, then successive generations will have grounds for seeking a more and more reduced set of liberties, even while following a determinate policy of seeking whatever liberties are optimal for the autonomy and individuality of present persons.

But if the effects on the autonomy of future generations of choosing an optimal set of liberties for the present generation are mixed, then it is not clear that there is any way of determining an optimal set of liberties, which is not merely optimal for a set of persons who are falsely assumed not to change their capacities for autonomous action over time. In short it seems that a serious and determinate liberalism must take a historical view of autonomy but that in taking a historical view of autonomy liberalism becomes once more indeterminate.

Conclusions. These arguments don't show that a refurbished liberal political theory is impossible. But they do show that it would have to rest on stronger foundations than an appeal merely to liberty and the autonomy of persons. Theories which assign liberty priority over all other social goods, or which assign liberties of specific sorts priority over other goods, cannot establish which set of co-possible liberties is maximal, nor even which is optimal. Liberty cannot then be the first, nor the only, virtue of social arrangements.

NOTES

[1] J. S. Mill, "On Liberty" in *Utilitarianism* (ed. M. Warnock, Collins, London and Glasgow), 135.
[2] G. MacCallum, "Negative and Positive Freedom", *The Philosophical Review*, 76, 1967, 312–345; J. Rawls, *A Theory of Justice*, (Harvard Univer-

sity Press, Cambridge, Mass.), 171, 201–5. For a survey of recent disputes about the analysis of liberty see W. A. Parent, "Some Recent Work on the Concept of Liberty", *American Philosophical Quarterly, 11,* 1974, 149–67. Parent argues that these disputes are disputes within the very weak characterisation of liberty on which I here rely.

[3] For example, H. Steiner, "Individual Liberty", *Proceedings of the Aristotelian Society,* 1974–5, 33–50, esp. 44ff.

[4] *A Theory of Justice,* 195–201.

[5] H. L. A. Hart, "Rawls on Liberty and its Priority", 242–3, reprinted in *Reading Rawls,* (ed. N. Daniels, Blackwells, Oxford, 1975), 230–252.

[6] *A Theory of Justice,* 204.

[7] J. S. Mill, *op. cit.,* 135–6 and also *The Subjection of Women.*

[8] *A Theory of Justice,* 126–30.

[9] J.-J. Rousseau, *The Social Contract,* Book II, Chs. VII and VIII.

The
Journal of Philosophy

Subscriptions at $12.00/year; $9.00 to students

$16.00/year to libraries

Students price extended to retired and unemployed philosophers. Published bimonthly 1904 to 1976, monthly thereafter. Complete volumes and all separate issues available back to January 7, 1904 (volume I, number 1); prices as follows :

VOLUMES I–LX (1904–1963)

32-page issues, $1.50; 64-page, $3.00. Volumes, $30.00 each.

VOLUME LXI (1964) AND LATER

32-page issues, $1.00; 64-page, $2.00; 96-page or over, $3.00.
Volumes (unbound, volume indexes included), $20.00 each.

ALSO AVAILABLE

Cumulative Fifty-year Index, 1904–1953; articles classified by subject and author, 452 p.; cloth, $12.00. Ten-year Supplement, 1954–1963 : 98 p.; paperbound, $2.00.

720 PHILOSOPHY HALL, COLUMBIA UNIVERSITY, NYC 10027

V*—MORAL REALISM AND MORAL DILEMMAS

by Samuel Guttenplan

The question I shall consider in the paper is this: does the existence of moral dilemmas constitute a special problem for that view of ethics which is, I think, best described as moral realism? That moral dilemmas do create special problems for realism—that their existence can be used as the beginning of an argument against realism—is a view I attribute to Williams.[1] It will be my contention that a realist account of morality and moral discourse cannot be undermined by appeal to features of moral dilemmas. Even further, I shall suggest that a particular account of moral realism, one which seems most plausible on grounds independent of the present issue, can best support some basic intuitions we have about moral dilemmas.

A word of caution must be inserted here. It would not be difficult to find philosophers who think any account of ethics which goes under the rubric 'realist' can be rejected out of hand; though I believe that the well-known anti-realist arguments will not stand up to close scrutiny. My aim in this paper, though, is the fairly narrow one outlined above. I do not intend my arguments to provide general support for realism; they will certainly fail to convince the confirmed anti-realist for whom Williams' arguments are at best only a small part of the case against realism.

Suppose some act x of Smith's to be a paradigm case of a fully deliberate moral action. Here is what one sort of moral realist would say about this case: the state of mind which led Smith to do x is fully specifiable as a belief (or beliefs) of Smith's about the world. Using Murdoch's phrase, the world, for Smith, was 'compulsively present to the will'.[2] This state of mind *may* be expressed by Smith, for example, by a judgement of the form 'I (Smith) ought to do x' but this is neither the only nor the obviously correct form of words for this purpose. (I shall discuss this shortly.) In those cases where the motivating states of mind

---

* Meeting of the Aristotelian Society held at 5/7 Tavistock Place, W.C.1 on Monday January 7, 1980 at 6.30 p.m.

are expressed we are to take these expressions as acts of assertion; acts whose component claims are suitable for truth ascription.

I take it as obvious why this view, even in the schematic form here presented, is accurately describable both as moral realism and as moral cognitivism; and it is this view, though not exactly this formulation of it, which Williams thinks vulnerable to arguments based on features of moral conflict.

My formulation of the realist position begins with the states of mind of agents whereas Williams seems most concerned with the verbal expression of these states. I think my formulation preferable for the following three reasons: (i) agents can find themselves in moral dilemmas (and deal with them) without at the same time being able to express what, on the realist view, are those beliefs which define the dilemmas; (ii) by focussing on the putative truth or falsity of moral judgements (as Williams does) one runs the risk of mistaking the 'cognitivism' of naturalist views such as that of Mrs Foot for the cognitivism outlined above. For Mrs Foot an agent's moral judgements are about the world and are straightforwardly either true or false but these judgements are not the full expression of that state which, in the above-mentioned paradigm case, led Smith to do x; Smith's desires, needs or interests, in Foot's view, are a crucial part of that state.[3] Though it would be a complicated matter to spell out (and I haven't the space here), Foot's inclusion of a conative state in the full specification of Smith's reason for doing x makes her attenuated cognitivism less susceptible to Williams' arguments. For example, from her perspective it is difficult to see the point of Williams' contrast of moral conflict with belief conflict and his parallel between moral conflict and desire conflict. In any case, the real target of Williams' arguments is full-blooded cognitivism and this is obscured by the attention he gives to the verbal expression of moral judgements. (iii) Williams' worries about realism and dilemmas are independent of the questions whether 'ought' is that word most suitable to express what the moral realist sees as the beliefs that prompt action. Yet Williams' reliance on 'ought'-judgements confuses both this independence and, at places, the structure of his argument.

In outline, and against the background of the above remarks, Williams' argument (hereafter called 'A') is as follows.

(A) (1) For the realist the structure of moral conflict[4] must mirror the structure of belief conflict.

(2) Moral conflict has features, partially reflected by desire conflict, that are incompatible with our understanding of belief conflict. In particular, moral conflicts are soluble, if at all, with 'remainders'; agents continue to think of the 'rejected' moral demand as applicable whereas they do not so think of the rejected belief after the resolution of a belief conflict.

Hence, moral realism is false.

I shall discuss this argument in detail in Section IV after a necessary detour in Sections II and III. In what remains of this section I should like to make some remarks about that part of Williams' paper where he discusses, in a quasi-formal way, what he calls 'the logic of moral thought'.[5] I do not think I am alone in finding this part of Williams' paper unclear and much of what I say later depends, crucially, on getting these matters sorted out.

Williams' discussion centres on an argument which purports to show conflicting 'ought' judgements to be formally inconsistent. This argument is as follows:

(B) (1) I ought to do *a*   premise
    (2) I ought to do *b*   premise
    (3) I cannot do *a* and *b*   premise
    (4) I ought to do *a* and *b*   from (1) and (2) by the deontic equivalent of a principle of modal logic: in Williams' words 'the agglomeration principle'.

    (5) It is not the case that   from (4) by the principle '*cannot* I ought to do *a* and *b*   implies *not-ought*'—a corollary of the more common '*ought* implies *can*'.

(B) is rejected by Williams after he adduces some evidence (by counter-example) for the invalidity of the agglomeration principle, though he accepts its use of 'ought' implies 'can'. (Interestingly, Lemmon accepted agglomeration and rejected (B) because of what he saw as the unacceptability of 'ought' implies 'can'.[6]

I shall say nothing against Williams' (or Lemmon's) rejection of (B); my interest is in the place of that rejection in the argument against realism. It can seem that Williams' rejection of (B) is intended as an argument against realism independent of (A); though I am unsure that this was what Williams himself fully intended. Part of the reason for this appearance is the space Williams devotes to his attack on agglomeration; an attack which is largely independent of (A).

Let us suppose first (and merely to see where it gets us) that the rejection of (B) is meant to tell against realism independently of (A). The logic here might be as follows: when I know that beliefs of mine conflict there can be some plausible argument to show that the retention of these beliefs leads to a formal contradiction. Since (B) fails to show this of (1), (2) and (3), (1) and (2) cannot be just like conflicting beliefs.

Aside from the question of whether one can construct the requisite argument in the belief case, I would urge that nothing in the above is unduly troublesome for the realist. He is committed (at least insofar as my formulation of his position is accepted) to seeing the expression of motivating moral requirements as the expression of beliefs; in cases of moral dilemmas this requires him to view the conflicting moral requirements as inconsistent. He is not, however, committed to accepting 'ought' as the word suitable to fully capture such requirements and nothing prevents his claiming that the rejection of (B) merely shows the unsuitability of 'ought' to that task. Williams cites Ross as a realist who thinks (B) (1) and (2) inconsistent but this only converts the present line into an *ad hominem* against Ross; perhaps realists would be better advised to use 'must' since, as Lemmon argued, conflicting 'must' judgements seem incompatible.

There is, of course, another way to look at the rejection of (B); one which is closer to what I think were Williams' intentions. He thought that the acceptance of (A) showed that the structure of belief conflict could not be projected onto moral conflict. He may also have thought that if (B) was unshakeably valid then this told against the acceptance of (A). At one point Williams says of the agglomeration principle: 'I want to claim only that it is not a self-evident datum of the logic of *ought*, and that if a more realistic picture of moral thought emerges from abandoning it, we should have no qualms in abandoning it.[7] This suggests that Williams sees the rejection of (B) as in some way a necessary condition for maintaining that view of moral thought which acceptance of (A) entails.[8] This is a very different motive for rejecting (B) than that canvassed above but there are, I think, problems here too.

It just isn't necessary for Williams to challenge (B) or any similar argument that purports to show that the verbal expressions of conflicting moral requirements are incompatible. *If (A) is accepted* then it shows that, whatever else it is, moral conflict cannot be assimilated to the model of belief conflict; in a moral dilemma the verbal expression of moral requirements may be opposing or in some sense incompatible, but they cannot be *inconsistent* in the way that conflicting beliefs are. Given this it is open to Williams to see (B) as merely establishing whatever form of incompatibility is appropriate (against the background of (A)) to what are, after all, described as *conflicting* moral requirements. (B) alone can never show (1), (2) and (3) to be inconsistent in the way that beliefs can be; for that one must begin by seeing (1) and (2) as appropriate candidates for truth ascription and that is precisely what (A) is meant to undermine. One could view (1) and (2) as expressions of approval and still accept (B) after suitably reinterpreting the conclusion along emotivist lines.

Logical flaws in (B) are no threat to the realist—he must simply make sure that the moral requirements involved are suitably expressed. On the other hand, the acceptance of (B) or similar, by itself, is no threat to Williams' main anti-realist argument. In the end everything turns on the question of whether the realist can answer (A) and worries about (B) only confuse the issue.

II

Examination of (A) comes in Section IV. I have first to consider a proposal which, if correct, would defuse the difficulties which dilemmas pose for realism without the need for my later arguments. This proposal has received most detailed treatment in Wiggins' *Truth, Invention and The Meaning of Life* and it is this work that will serve (even if at points loosely) as my text.[9]

The proposal which I have extracted from Wiggins' paper is essentially concessionary to Williams' argument: it is by and large (if implicitly) accepted but a version of the realist doctrine comes out unscathed. The key to this lies in Wiggins' distinction between what he calls 'evaluations' and 'deliberations'. The distinction can be understood *both* as a distinction between what I shall for the present, and neutrally, call 'attitudes' *and* as a distinction between our understanding of linguistic judgements that express those attitudes. If this distinction is to be fully grasped it must be explained in both ways.

Roughly, to evaluate some object, action, character or state of affairs (this list is meant to be representative not exhaustive and I shall use *actions* in what follows) is to believe or, less often, to know of the action that it possesses a certain property or properties of which 'honesty', 'goodness', 'maliciousness' and 'corruptness' are typical. An evaluative attitude is cognitive; it is an attitude whose natural description is in terms of the idioms of belief or knowledge about the world.

For someone to adopt a deliberative or practical attitude toward some action is for him to be disposed to perform that action. Evaluations are exercises of our specifically cognitive abilities; practical attitudes or deliberations are not.[10]

Shifting from the material to the formal mode gives us further necessary insight into the above distinction. An evaluative judgement, a claim of the form 'x is corrupt', is to be treated as an assertion whose assessment is in terms of what Wiggins calls 'regular truth'. Regular truth is characterised by the following 'truisms': (1) every regular truth is compatible with every other regular truth; (2) regular truths answer to evidenced argument and converge upon agreement; (3) regular truths are such independently of our wills and of our limited means of recognising them; (4) every regular truth is true in virtue of something; (5) every candidate for regular truth is determinately either true or false.[11]

On the other hand, deliberative judgements, judgements such as 'I ought to do such-and-such', are seen as inappropriate to the extension of regular truth; though they may nonetheless be assertions apt for the extension of some truth predicate. Wiggins says: '[i]f there were practical truth it would violate the third truism [and hence the fourth] of regular truth'.[12]

What I have so far said about Wiggins' distinction between evaluation and deliberation should be treated with caution. In particular, my remarks about cognition may make it sound as though I see him as adopting, for practical judgements, some banal non-cognitivism. Also, at the point in his essay where the above remark comes it is not clear whether Wiggins is himself arguing for a position or merely expounding one someone else might hold. I hope that what I am about to say shows that I have not misunderstood him.

Wiggins takes himself to have argued that our judgements about values (pure evaluations) can be seen as appropriate candidates for regular truth and, therefore, as apt for expressing attitudes we may have about what is or is not the case—cognitive attitudes. Our claims about value can be understood as claims about the 'world',[13] and it is because of Wiggins' views here that I think he is a realist at least about evaluations and, hence, about moral evaluations.

Practical attitudes or deliberative judgements, however, cannot be understood as characterising the world. They are not candidates for regular truth and as Wiggins notes: '. . . the world is not what they purport to characterise.'[14] Nonetheless they can be understood as 'objective' in a sense full enough to rule out various shallow forms of non-cognitivism such as emotivism. This I take to be the point of his analogy of ethics and Wittgenstein's philosophy of mathematics. Insofar as one is tempted to identify the objectivity of a judgement or attitude with its susceptibility to regular truth Wiggins is an opponent. Whether Wiggins ultimately intends the separation of objectivity from regular truth to be a reason for 'tampering in certain ways with the received truisms of regular truth'[15] or, less radically, as something we shall just have to live with, is a question he explicitly does not answer.

It is against this background—the possible objectivity of evaluation *and* deliberation though the realism of only the former— that Wiggins grounds both his attack on the fact/value distinction and his defense of the is/ought gap. And it is here that one can see the outlines of his answer to the subject of this paper: the reconciliation of realism with the existence of genuine moral dilemmas. What follows is an admittedly crude and schematic picture using aesthetic evaluations as an example which should make these features of Wiggins' account clear.

Wandering around a museum, Smith notes the following

about two paintings: painting A is representational, contains a predominance of grey and black pigment, lacks focus, is not painterly; painting B is non-representational, uses mostly primary colours, is full of motion, is delicately painted. Some would say that these judgements make use of both descriptive and evaluative predicates. I take Wiggins' view to be that 'it is either false or senseless'[16] to deny to any of these judgements assessment in terms of regular truth; and his resistance to the fact/value (or descriptive/evaluative) distinction is grounded on that denial.

Suppose, though, that Smith is a painter himself and, while working on a specific painting, he wonders whether to fill out a portion of his canvas in one of two ways—call them C and D. Smith can imagine what each of these options will look like and he can make about them the sort of evaluative judgements he did about A and B. However, there is no specific reason for believing that his evaluation of C and D will force on him either the judgement 'I must realise C' or 'I must realise D'. They *may*. The evaluation of C and D may be so one-sided (or of a sort Wiggins calls 'practically focussed') as to lead Smith to make one or other of the above practical judgements; but this will not in, general be the case. This is where the gap between 'is' and 'must'[17] opens up. It could very well happen that Smith can truly predicate certain positive values of C and D, respectively, but that the exigency of his having to fill out the canvas in *one* way makes it impossible for him to realise jointly the values he sees in C and D. In such a case, Smith cannot think of his evaluations ('is' statements) as fixing his practical judgements ('must' statements). The treatment of valuations is realistic; but it is, in a sense to be discussed, pluralistic and this latter feature, in providing a rationale for the is/must gap, allows us to cope with a most important feature of moral dilemmas—what Williams sees as their being resoluble, if at all, with remainders. Smith's dilemma was an aesthetic one but it need not have been. C and D could have been morally significant states of affairs which he foresaw as the result of his doing either *c* or *d*. A positive moral evaluation of C *and* D could have been accurate without Smith's seeing himself as morally compelled to do either *c* or *d*; and if he chose, say *c*, this would in no way constitute a rejection of his evaluation of D. On the contrary, his belief that he was correct in seeing value in D serves as the 'remainder' after he did *c*.

Somewhat metaphorically, one can put it like this: realism

seems to require, at least in principle, a firm connection between reality and our beliefs or judgements about it; this is so in virtue of the truisms of regular truth. On the other hand, in order to appreciate what moral dilemmas are like we seem to require 'slack' somewhere between our cognitive encounters with reality and our practical judgements. Recognising that truths about values are bound by the truisms of regular truth is perfectly consistent, Wiggins thinks, with recognising that circumstances often arise in which we cannot simultaneously realise all that we think valuable. The plurality of values in the world allows us to have the needed slack between evaluation and action. Of course, on this view, practical judgements are denied a fully realistic treatment inasmuch as they are denied candidature for regular truth. Williams' argument (A) is accepted as valid but, in loosening the connection between moral evaluation and action, Wiggins' form of realism is no longer correctly character ised by (A)(1). What we are offered is a form of moral (evalu- ative) realism which *seems* to cope with the problems posed by the existence of moral dilemmas. The question is whether this is, after all, only an appearance.

III

Consider the following claim which Smith might make (as a moral and not aesthetic agent):

(1) State of affairs C is more valuable than D.

(For the purposes of what follows I shall assume that Smith is in a position where he feels compelled to act and where his only options are *c* and *d*—actions which would realise C and D, respectively.) If it is reasonable to treat (1) as a candidate for regular truth—as a claim no less realist than the attribution of value to C and D—then it is difficult to see why Smith's belief in the truth of (1) would fall short of necessitating (in some way) the judgement 'I (Smith) must do *c*'. But if claims about reality of the form given in (1) are available, in principle at least, to agents (and we do make such claims all the time), then the slack needed to accommodate dilemmas is taken up.[18] The version of realism adumbrated in the last section collapses into a realism more like that under threat from Williams' argument.

There are two sorts of move one might make in an effort to

regain the slack between an agent's evaluations of moral reality and his determination to act: one consists in denying to claims such as (1) the status of regular truth; the other in allowing them this status but treating genuine moral dilemmas as cases in which such claims are not true. As will be seen, these moves are not completely disjoint. I shall begin by discussing the second of them.

The claim (1) could fail to be true in three ways: (a) it may, in fact, be the case that D is more valuable than C; (b) it may be the case that C and D are equally valuable; or, (c) it may be the case that the values in C and D are, in some sense, incommensurable so that (1), while not strictly false, is nonetheless not true.

The first of these options is clearly of no help in the present issue: we have assumed that Smith believes (1) true and its being, in fact, false goes no way to allowing Smith to retain his qualms about doing c rather than d.

The second option, however, does at least offer us some account of these qualms. If C and D are of equal value—are 'tied'—and Smith appreciates this, then he cannot see himself as required to do one action as against the other. The disposition of values in the world, though known, does not force a unique practical judgement and, hence, does not force the rejection of other such judgements. Of course, that moral dilemmas are occasioned by ties between evaluations is a 'solution' that needs only to be raised to be dismissed. But the various specific grounds for dismissal are important. That it is *ad hoc* and, to that extent implausible, is one such ground. Even more importantly, and plausibility aside, it fails to do more than superficial justice to the very features of dilemmas it was invoked to explain. If an agent really did believe that moral dilemmas occurred only in cases where the values he might realise were equal, then he could never see his dilemmas as more serious than that of Buridan's ass. Regret or moral distress for doing one thing and not the other would arise, in *every* dilemma, if indeed it could, because an agent believed the option not chosen was just as valuable as the one he did choose. Yet, as Williams rightly points out, moral distress is no less appropriate in those cases of conflict where the agent is convinced that one option is morally preferable and the tied value proposal goes no way to meeting this point.

Discussion of option (c) calls for some preliminary remarks. It is not an unfamiliar thought that the values (moral or otherwise) we attach to things are, in some sense, incommensurable. Indeed some would think that only monistic prejudice supports the idea that claims such as (1) are, in every circumstance of choice, true or false and, hence, that our values can be, in principle, completely ordered.[19] Rejection of such an ordering is what the pluralism implicit in Wiggins' account consists in.

Of course, it is apparent that in embracing pluralism and its attendant thesis of incommensurability one is giving up, for the comparative idiom embodied in (1), truism (5) of regular truth. Instances of this idiom are no longer seen as determinately either true or false. This, in turn, may make it unclear why I have considered this option here and not as part of the move which consists in denying regular truth status to comparative claims.

There are two reasons for this. First, though I have so far spoken of the realistic treatment of moral judgements as, in part, requiring the applicability of regular truth, I have nowhere held a brief for the particular conception of truth imposed by the truisms listed earlier. In fact, I think it perfectly acceptable for someone, given good reason, to abandon truism (5) for all or some classes of assertion and still to consider his treatment of those assertions as realist; though abandoning, say, truisms (1) and (2) would rule out this possibility. This means that if the reasons for incommensurability are strong enough and if the pluralism that results from realism *sans* truism (5) allows room for moral dilemmas, then we will have found a form of realism which is not threatened by Williams' argument (A). However, I think that applying realism *sans* (5) to the comparative idiom does *not* yield an acceptable account of moral conflict and since my thinking so is connected with my rejection of the tied value solution, this is my second reason for considering option (c) here.

It is clearly not incumbent on me to reject the thesis that, due to incommensurability, value comparisons may fail to be determinately true or false; I need only show why accepting this thesis still leaves us without a full enough account of the problems of moral conflict. Even so, I should like to at least note what seems to me a mistake that might lead some to accept the incommensurability thesis too hastily.

The comparison of values made in (1) was intended to be

specific. I did not indicate which values C and D were thought to possess but, even in its schematic form, we are to think of (1) as comparing these values in the completely particular circumstances Smith found himself; nothing follows from (1) about Smith's general ranking of whatever values he saw in C and D. If this specific/general distinction is overlooked, incommensurability might seem forced on us. For example, it would generally be accepted that wisdom and gentleness were valuable though we might find it senseless to be asked to rank them. Nonetheless, it just does not follow from this that we would be unable to rank two particular acts one of which exhibited gentleness and the other wisdom. The question whether Englishmen are heavier than Frenchmen (except on a certain reading) is unanswerable, but it is nevertheless true that we expect to be able to decide whether any given Englishman is heavier than any given Frenchman.[20]

Continuing with the main line of argument, let us suppose that even in the particular contexts of moral decision values can be incommensurable. This means that, in some cases, claims such as (1) can fail to be true and an agent might well find that he is *not* forced to accept one or another practical judgement. Such is the picture of moral conflict which we get by adding incommensurability to the realist treatment of evaluation discussed earlier. The trouble is that this picture suffers from the same defects as the tied value opion. It is true that in some moral dilemmas the agent finds that his moral commitments (beliefs) do not take him to a decision and the above picture handles this well enough. However, the really difficult cases for the realist are those in which the agent does think one course of action right though his not doing the other is a source of regret and moral distress. In these cases an agent may actually judge that one value overrides the other so that the appeal to incommensurability completely fails to explain why regret and moral distress are in place; the possibility of a plurality of incommensurable values can account for the uncertainty of decisions, not the distress we feel when we judge our actions right because we have compared values and found one more compelling. There is more to be said about moral realism and these sorts of dilemma—that is the business of the next section. Here I want only to point out that the pluralist realism which follows from the acceptance of the incommensurability thesis does not, *merely as a result of its pluralism*, take us any further to answering Williams' arguments.

What then of the second strategy? Can we escape the troublesome consequences of judgements such as (1) by seeing them as deliberative or practical and, hence, as inappropriate candidates for regular truth? I think it must be admitted that we can but the price paid for this account of dilemmas seems too high.

Remember first that abandonment of regular truth here does not involve only truism (5); that possibility has already been canvassed. The move under discussion consists in the refusal to see the assertibility predicate of practical judgements as captured by some or all of the other truisms of regular truth. Thus, in a particular case, an agent could see both 'I must do *a*' and 'I must do *b*' (where *a* and *b* are not compatible) as applicable, that is, as assertible in the circumstances. Similarly, it could be the case that someone accepts the applicability of 'I must do *a*' though another could, without irrationality, not disagree and yet assert that he would feel compelled to do *b*. Wiggins says:

> When we judge that this is what we must do now . . . we are not fitting truths . . . into a pattern where any discrepancy proves that we have mistaken a falsehood for a truth. Often we have to make a practical choice which another rational agent might understand through and through, not fault or disagree with, but (as Winch has stressed) make differently himself.[21]

Comparative claims such as (1), if seen as candidates for regular truth, threaten the above account of practical judgements. If someone thinks that *c* will result in a more valuable state of affairs than *d* and that the converse is false, it is difficult to see how he can rationally think that both 'I must do *c*' and 'I must do *d*' are applicable. (Abandoning only truism (5) for the comparative but rejecting regular truth completely for these latter judgements will not suffice. We would still be left without an account of dilemmas in which the agent thinks his decision the right one because of his acceptance of one or the other comparative claim.)

The threat is removed, however, if we think of (1) as more practical than evaluative and, hence, as an inappropriate candidate for regular truth. Smith can then accept both 'C is more valuable than D' and 'I must do c' though another agent (or, in tragic dilemmas, Smith himself) could, without irrationality, not disagree with Smith while asserting 'D is more valuable than C' and 'I must do d'.

Against this I have a number of points though no one of them is completely knock-down. In any case, as I shall argue in the next section, a realist need not take such drastic steps to counter Williams' arguments.

First, it seems to me just implausible that the judgement 'state of affairs C has such-and-such a value' is a candidate for regular truth (with or without truism (5)) while 'C is more valuable than D' is not. Surely if evaluations are given a realist treatment then so should comparative evaluations.

Secondly, while it is true that practical judgements have purposes other than characterising a world, this does not show that they do not also have that purpose. A general may, in telling his troops the likely course of tomorrow's battle, try to inspire them. This does not show that his discourse does not also consist of fitting truths into a pattern. Without spelling it out fully here, it is crucial to the realist account that I favour that moral beliefs both are genuine beliefs about the world and are motivating; whether or not one accepts that this view is correct, it is far from obvious that these two features are incompatible.

Finally, the target of Winch's article is the *usefulness* of universalisability in moral reasoning; he never claims that two cases which are known to be *exactly* alike can be resolved differently.[22] His point is simply that, when all the evidence is considered, few if any cases will be alike and this is because the character of the agent is a significant element in our understanding of the concrete reality of moral cases. I can understand a man's decision 'through and through' in a case like one I am faced with and yet decide differently but since I am not just like the other man the cases and thus the realities are different.[23]

IV

The verbal expressions of the states of mind of an agent in a moral dilemma must be seen as in some way conflicting. This much is necessary to our viewing the agent as someone in a dilemma. However, our acceptance of (B) or any similar argument in no way forces us to view such conflict as logical, i.e., as establishing the *inconsistency* of the relevant verbal expressions. The task of this section is to show that the Williams argument I outlined as (A) fails to establish that we *cannot* treat that conflict as logical. Before attempting this, though, I must insert a brief note about 'ought'.

I earlier canvassed an interpretation of Williams' use of argument (B) which saw it as an attack on realism independent of (A). Understood this way it cannot be cogent but what did emerge was that there may well be grounds for considering 'ought' unsuitable to capture the conflicting demands which characterise moral dilemmas. If this is so the use of 'ought' in what follows is bound to lead to unnecessary difficulty, so to avoid this I shall dispense with this word and speak instead of *moral requirements*. An agent is in a dilemma when he has reason to see himself as morally required to do *a*, morally required to do *b* and knows he cannot do both *a* and *b*, where 'morally required' satisfies whatever logical or quasi-logical principles are needed to make argument (B) acceptable.

I shall begin by describing a highly schematic fourfold classification of moral conflicts. This classification is not intended as one which would be of use to general moral discussions; its purpose is merely to allow us to gauge the form and seriousness of the attack on realism contained in (A).

(i) The Resoluble: A believes that he is morally required to do *a* and morally required to do *b*. He then discovers that he cannot do both. After deliberation that we would accept as cogent, he decides that he was wrong, in the circumstances, to believe that he was morally required to do *b*, so he does *a* without experiencing moral qualms about his failure to do *b*.[24]

(ii) The Uncertain: B's dilemma, in form, is like that of A but no amount of deliberation convinces B that one or other course of action is morally required. Circumstances are such that B has to act but his doing, say, *a* in no way shows that he believes that *a* is morally required. Action, in this case, is in the dark and precisely because of this B has moral qualms about the course he takes.

Cases (i) and (ii) are not only unproblematic to the realist/cognitivist position, they are just those sorts of cases which might incline one to adopt such a position. The realist is committed to construing moral claims as apt for truth ascription in just the way that so-called 'factual' claims are; but it need be no part of his position that it will be an easy matter to actually decide the truth of these claims. Further, I think a sensitive handling of what might be called 'moral epistemology' will make it plausible that the most true-to-life cases of moral dilemma fall under the rubric of (ii).[25]

(iii) The Resoluble with Remainder: C, unlike B, is convinced that *a* is the better thing to do and he sees himself as morally required to do *a*. However, unlike A, doing *a* is accompanied by moral distress and regrets for what he has left undone, that is, *b*.

(iv) The Tragic: D is forced by circumstances to choose between *a* and *b* though he realises that either action will be the occasion of moral distress and he firmly believes that neither presents a stronger moral case.

Type (iii) cases are those which, given argument (A), are most difficult for a realist. I shall return to them shortly. Tragic cases embody *two* problems for the realist: first, if D believes that it is simply false that he is morally required to do *a and* false that he is morally required to do *b*, it is unclear why he feels the way he does about each course of action; and secondly, it may seem unclear how a realist could allow it to be rational for D to be convinced that neither course could be supported by stronger moral arguments.

The second of these worries might be met in a number of ways: (a) one could see tragic conflicts as a reason to adopt the realism less truism (5) discussed in section III, thereby making the existence of this feature of such conflict perfectly intelligible. On the other hand, (b) one could see the above schematic account of tragic cases as misleading: D might be seen as convinced not of the ultimate incompatibility of *a* and *b* but of his (our) inability to understand the situation that confronts him in a way that will lead to the appropriate evaluation. This would have the effect of making tragic conflict a species of (ii) and (iii) though it is open to us to see the epistemic problems in tragic cases as substantially different from those of (ii).

Either way, however, leaves us with the first of the above-mentioned worries—that involving regret—and this is also the pressing difficulty for the realist account of (iii). So, if a realist can give a plausible account of (iii), he need make no further provision for tragic conflict which, given the above discussion of the second worry, is either a species of (iii) or, upon suitable revision of the realist account of truth, is subject to the same objection as (iii).

The place to begin is with a brief consideration of Williams' remarks about belief conflict: I think that his account of such conflict is apt to mislead and that when it is replaced the way will be open to a convincing yet realist account of type (iii) cases. According to Williams someone is in a state of belief conflict when he believes that p, believes that q, and also recognises some empirical truth which is inconsistent with p and q. Contrasting the moral case with it, he says of belief conflict:

> ... my concern to get things straight is a concern both to find the right belief ... and to be disembarrassed of the false belief ... whereas in the moral case my concern is not in the same way to find the right item and be rid of the other ... In the moral case I do not think in terms of banishing error. I think, if constructively at all, in terms of acting for the best, and this is a frame of mind that acknowledges the presence of both the two *oughts*.[26]

On this view of belief conflict we are rather like fastidious hosts and a false belief is a piece of crockery which we totally reject from use at table because it is flawed. There is, however, another view.

In many cases our beliefs are based on an articulable body of evidence though, in any given case, we may be only partially able to articulate it. If we learn of some fact r which forms an inconsistent triad when added to two of our other beliefs, p and q, the appropriate reaction is to suspend belief in both p and q pending a re-examination and possible augmentation of evidence. (Exceptions here are possible. The fact that r may be, and often is, such as to specifically undermine one or the other of p and q. Nonetheless, it can happen that r itself does not offer us a clue as to which of the original beliefs is false and, for obvious reasons, this is the appropriate case to focus on here.) On the present view, our goal in having beliefs is not to rid or 'disembarrass' ourselves of any we might suspect as false, but rather accommodate our beliefs in a consistent way to the evidence we have—to our understanding of the way the world is. At the point of belief suspension and with evidence behind them, both p and q have claims on us: one might say that thinking for the best is a frame of mind that acknowledges the presence of both beliefs.

When the examination and collection of evidence allows us to decide which of p and q is false, there is a whole spectrum of reactions possible. At one end is that described by Williams: a vital piece of evidence may have been overlooked or misinterpreted and we may come to reject, say q, comprehensively. Less drastically, however, we may come to realise that, while q is strictly false, the evidence for it remains and can be accommodated by our entertaining belief in some variant of q. The detective who discovers that two of his hypotheses about a crime are inconsistent with a further incontrovertible piece of evidence, may 'retain' the one he thinks false by altering it slightly. He had believed (inconsistently with all the facts) that the murderer met the victim the day before the crime at 8 o'clock; after reviewing the evidence he now realises that he can account for it consistently by believing that they met at 7.00.

Williams remarks that a rejected desire can survive the point of decision 'in one or another guise' and I see no reason why the same does not apply to cases of belief conflict. The beliefs we come to hold after the resolution of conflict may be so closely related to the original beliefs that 'survival' seems the appropriate notion; in other cases, if not survival, then some recognisable ancestor relation may be more appropriate. However described, there will be a range of cases where the new belief—the one needed to accommodate the evidence without inconsistency—bears a worth-remarking-on relation to the old. I have now to say how this, and the above account of belief conflict out of which is grows, helps with the problem of moral conflict.

On the realist view, the fully virtuous agent's perception of a situation leads to beliefs which result in his performance of the appropriate action. In type (i) cases this action is that which follows from A's belief in the truth of 'I am morally required to do a'; he came to accept that 'I am morally required to do b' is false and had no claim upon him. In type (iii) cases the pattern of truth and falsity is the same but the agent, C, experiences moral distress at not doing b and, perhaps, is led to make it up to those persons affected by this omission. Such distress and such further behaviour, Williams argues, must seem irrational to the realist and, hence, the realist picture of the fully virtuous agent must represent him as radically different from 'a decent human being' or as ineliminably irrational. I think that we can remain realists and yet paint a very different picture.

C originally entertained the belief that he was morally required to do a and to do b as a result of his then best view of the situation. The realisation that a and b conflict changed that view and his further thought is that a is, and b is not, morally required. However, C's earlier view of the situation included considerations in favour of doing b—evidence for the truth of 'I am morally required to do b'—and the later recognition of conflict would not, by itself, destroy this evidence. Given this we can see C's behaviour and feelings as themselves morally required by the undismissed evidence which originally, and it turned out mistakenly, made it appear that he was morally required to do b. The behaviour and feelings constitute the survival, or perhaps more plausibly the 'offspring' of the thought, 'I am morally required to do b'.

On the realist view then, the difference between type (i) and type (iii) cases turns out to be a difference in the concrete circumstances which generate them; regret, and any remedial behaviour which follows a decision in type (iii) circumstances, are reactions required of the virtuous agent by those circumstances; in this respect they resemble the requirement to do a.[27] The agent who is genuinely in such a situation but who has no such reactions is neither rational nor fully virtuous. He is someone whose grasp of reality is deficient and whose behaviour and feelings are less than admirable because of this deficiency.

Moral realism offers us a way to understand each of the different types of conflict and though I haven't spelled this out, it does so in a way which makes what Williams calls the 'unavoidability' of such conflict completely intelligible. Further, it is difficult to imagine any other account's coping so well with the epistemological issues of type (ii) cases. None of this proves that realism is correct but that has not been the object of this paper.

NOTES

I have benefited from comments on this paper by David Hamlyn and Ian McFetridge. John McDowell read an almost complete earlier version and I am most grateful to him for his help.

[1] 'Ethical Consistency', Aristotelian Society Sup. Vol. (1965).

[2] *The Sovereignty of the Good* (1970) 39.

[3] See especially the 'Postscript' to 'Reasons for Actions and Desires' in her *Virtues and Vices* (1978).

[4] In what follows I use 'conflict' in the semi-technical sense described by Williams in the above-mentioned essay.

[5] Williams, *op. cit.* 117–123.

[6] E. J. Lemmon, 'Moral Dilemmas', *Philosophical Review* (1962) 150 fn.

[7] Williams, *op. cit.* 122.

[8] He as much as says this. *Op. cit.* 122–3.

[9] *Proceedings of the British Academy* (1976). Wiggins nowhere *explicitly* makes a proposal to deal specifically with Williams' qualms about realism and moral conflict; I have abstracted one from his very interesting piece.

[10] Care should be taken here: Wiggins' distinction is between *pure* evaluation and deliberation; he allows all sorts of grades in between.

[11] See Wiggins *op. cit.* 357.

[12] *Ibid.* 367.

[13] 'Whatever that is' is Wiggins' own remark about this word, 370.

[14] *Ibid.* 370–1.

[15] *Ibid.* 370.

[16] *Ibid.* 372.

[17] 'Must' is a temporary replacement for 'ought' given that 'ought' can be misleading in ways discussed in Section I.

[18] I do not mean to suggest that judgements such as (1) have to be part of the actual reasoning of agents in or out of dilemmas; it is just easier to put my point in such terms. The most general way of making it would be to say that the nature of reality was such as to make judgements like (1) true or false and that this could, in principle, be perceived by agents whether or not they could make the judgements.

[19] Values perceived and ordered in *concrete circumstances*. This will be taken up later on.

[20] See Wiggins *op. cit.* 367n. where he seems to be careless about the general/specific distinction.

[21] *Ibid.* 367.

[22] P. Winch, 'The Idea of Universalizability', *Monist* (1965) especially 213-4.

[23] In that this paper is primarily about dilemmas I have only been concerned with Wiggins' essay from that point of view even though dilemmas play no explicit role in the essay. I hope to deal more directly with Wiggins' views in another place.

[24] Williams gives a realistic example of this type in 'Conflicts of Values' in *The Idea of Freedom: Essays in Honour of Sir Isaiah Berlin* (1979).

[25] Some enlightening remarks about such epistemic difficulties can be found in Murdoch, *op. cit.*

[26] *Op. cit.* 110.

[27] Some may find difficulty in thinking of emotions such as regret as the result of an agent's perception of what is morally required. I do not find this difficult though I admit the story will be a complex one. Given his remarks in 'Morality and the Emotions' (in *Problems of Self* (1973)) I would guess that Williams would be on my side in this matter.

VI*—IS IDENTITY A RELATION?

by C. J. F. Williams

1. The question which is my title is one which Frege asks at the very beginning of "On Sense and Reference". Reasons for a negative answer, or at least for denying that identity is a relation between objects, are what he immediately proceeds to give. However, he believes that eventually he is able to circumvent these reasons. The distinction between sense and reference, with which his famous paper is concerned, is introduced precisely with these credentials: it is only by distinguishing between the sense and the reference of the proper names that name them that identity can be regarded as a relation between objects. Frege believes, of course, that the distinction between sense and reference is sound, and his final answer to our question is an affirmative one.

Russell, who pruned the category of proper names so severely that scarcely any expressions were left in it, believed that a proposition which attached "— is the same as . . ." to a brace of genuine proper names was condemned to be either false or tautological. The *raison d'être* of the concept of identity was to be found only when the sign of identity was inserted between quantified variables. Roger White, in a recent paper delivered to this society,[1] has shown how Wittgenstein, in the *Tractatus,* put forward a thesis in the theory of identity which moved it forward from the uncomfortable half-way house at which Russell had left it. For Wittgenstein identity is not something which needs to be expressed by the introduction of a special sign; it is something which is shown by repetition of signs already in use, names or variables. "Identity of object I express by identity of sign, and not by using a sign for identity. Difference of objects I express by difference of signs" (5.53). And he goes on, in no uncertain terms, to give a negative answer to our question: "It is self-evident that identity is not a relation between objects" (5.5301).

---

* Meeting of the Aristotelian Society held at 5/7 Tavistock Place, W.C.1 on Monday, January 21, 1980, at 6.30 p.m.

F

The view for which I am going to argue concurs with Wittgenstein in this negative point, but dissents from his positive claim that the concept should be expressed by identity of sign, not by a sign for identity. The contrast, in fact, is one which does not stand up to examination. Clarity is achieved, and distinctions which have to be made can only be made, by having a sign for identity. But the syntactic category of that sign is not that of a relation, but another category, or family of categories, for which, as far as I am aware, there is at present no established name.

Wittgenstein regards a proposition of the form "$(\exists x).f(x,x)$" as a proper expression of identity, and in this he does not disagree with Russell. It is not when they are affirming identity but when they are denying it that they part company. "$(\exists x,y).f(x,y)$" suffices for Wittgenstein as an assertion of difference, but for Russell this would have to be written "$(\exists x,y).f(x,y). \sim x=y$" (5.532). Wittgenstein does not state explicitly his rules for the variation of variables, but makes his point simply by examples. I shall not attempt to supply this deficiency, although such rules would be as necessary if my own emendation of Wittgenstein's suggestion were adopted, as they would be if his own system were fully to be explained. We can avoid this necessity by considering only the affirmations of identity and forgetting for the moment about denials.[2]

I hope to show that paradox is generated by accepting Wittgenstein's suggestion about the correct way of expressing what is normally expressed by an affirmation of identity, if that is not accompanied by acceptance of his ban on having more than one name for one object. What this paradox is designed to demonstrate is that we require something more for the expression of identity than the reoccurrence of a variable bound by a single quantifier.

2. Consider this proposition

    (1) Abyssinia was once invaded by Mussolini and Ethiopia is now at war with Somalia.

Since Ethiopia *is* Abyssinia and (1) suffers from none of the hazards of referential opacity, we can infer

(2) Ethiopia was once invaded by Mussolini and Ethiopia is now at war with Somalia.

One of the premisses of this inference, as I have stated it, uses the so-called " 'is' of identity", and it may be objected that I am not entitled to this premiss, given my intention of restricting myself to expressions of which Wittgenstein would have approved. The objection can be met, up to a point, by expanding "Ethiopia *is* Abyssinia" to "For some *x*, both 'Ethiopia' in (1) names *x* and 'Abyssinia' in (1) names *x*". But Wittgenstein, of course, would not have allowed a proposition like (1) in the first place. Difference of signs is not to be allowed where there is no difference of objects. So what I am asking you to consider is a language in one respect like our own but unlike Wittgenstein's, namely, in that the same object can have different names, but in another respect like Wittgenstein's and unlike our own, namely, in that it contains no sign for identity other than identity of sign.

From (2), by existential generalisation, we can pass to

(3) For some country *x*, *x* was once invaded by Mussolini and *x* is now at war with Somalia.

This, on the Wittgensteinian view, is the same proposition as one which misleadingly contains a sign for identity, namely

(4) A country once invaded by Mussolini *is the same as* one now at war with Somalia.

Now someone who believes that (1) may easily not believe that (4), given that he does not know that Ethiopia is Abyssinia. But someone who believes that (1) can, in one sense at least, be said to believe that (2). Even Quine, who invented the terminology of referential opacity, allows that there is a transparent sense of "believe". For a belief construction to be transparent just is for propositions like

(1A) Mark believes that Abyssinia was once invaded by Mussolini and Ethiopia is now at war with Somalia[3]

to entail propositions like

(2A) Mark believes that Ethiopia was once invaded by

Mussolini and Ethiopia is now at war with Somalia,
given the identity of Ethiopia and Abyssinia.

Now (2), it is agreed, entails (3), which is its existential
generalisation. The fact that (2) entails (3) is not, of course, by
itself able to guarantee that (2A) entails

> (3A) Mark believes that, for some country x, x was once
>   invaded by Mussolini and x is now at war with
>   Somalia.

Mark may not, as Quine would put it, be enough of a logician
to be relied on to believe everything that is entailed by anything that he believes. But Mark does not have to be much
of a logician to be relied on to believe the existential generalisations of what he believes. If he believes that Jane is coming to
supper, how can he fail to believe that someone is coming to
supper? If he believes that two is an even prime number, is
it intelligible to suggest that he does not believe that some
number is both even and prime? *Some* entailments of our
beliefs are so evident that failure to believe what is entailed in
such an obvious manner is a criterion for denying that the
entailing proposition is really believed at all. So it looks as
though (3A) is after all entailed by (2A); not, however, merely
in virtue of the fact that (3) is a proposition entailed by (2),
but in virtue of the fact that it is the existential generalisation
of (2).

We said that (4) was the same proposition as (3)—that is
indeed the point Wittgenstein is concerned to make. If so, (3A)
will be found to entail, and for that matter to be entailed by,

> (4A) Mark believes that a country once invaded by Musso-
>   lini is the same as one now at war with Somalia.

It is precisely this sort of mutual entailment that, some would
say, constitutes the identity of propositions. On Wittgenstein's
view, (3A) simply states perspicuously what (4A) states misleadingly.

Now we have a chain of *prima facie* entailments leading from
(1A) to (4A). But (1A) says that Mark believes that (1) and (4A)
that he believes that (4), and the first of these is just what it
seemed could be the case without the second being the case.

Mark could quite well believe that Abyssinia is a country once invaded by Mussolini and Ethiopia a country now at war with Somalia without believing that a country once invaded by Mussolini is the same as one now at war with Somalia. One of the links in the chain of entailments which stretches from (1A) to (4A) must be weak. Which is it?

To challenge the entailment of (2A) by (1A) would be to challenge the possibility of a transparent interpretation of the "believes" construction. To challenge the entailment of (4A) by (3A) would be to reject the Wittgensteinian point about the correct way to express facts about identity. We wish to hold these two positions rigid. What then of the entailment of (3A) by (2A)?

8. A first look at the two propositions might lead us to wonder whether a confusion had arisen between (3A) and

(5) For some x, Mark believes that x was once invaded by Mussolini and x is now at war with Somalia.

Ex hypothesi, the verb "believes" in these sentences is being given the transparent interpretation; and just as this interpretation licences us to infer (2A) from (1A), so it allows us to quantify into the positions occupied by "Ethiopia" in (2A) from outside the belief context, thus producing (5). Just so, when "believes that" is understood transparently, from "Philip believes that Cicero deounced Catiline" we can infer that there is someone of whom Philip believes that he denounced Catiline; but when "believes that" is understood opaquely this inference is invalid. When "believes that" is understood opaquely, on the other hand, from the fact that Philip believes that Cicero denounced Catiline we do seem to be able to infer that Philip believes that someone denounced Catiline. The transparent interpretation allows the quantifier wider scope, the opaque interpretation allows it narrower scope. But these are not exclusive alternatives. The transparent interpretation allows the quantifier wider scope *as well as narrower*. The opaque interpretation drives the quantifier inwards, but it does not follow that the transparent interpretation drives the quantifier outwards. Indeed, with "believes that" construed transparently, "There is someone whom Philip believes to have denounced Catiline" seems actually to entail "Philip believes that someone denounced

Catiline" : how could he believe of someone that he did it, if
he did not believe that someone did it? So (5) seems to be a
red herring. If (2A), (3A) and (5) behave like the Catilinian
examples, (5) will entail (3A); and so far from our having to
choose between (5) and (3A) as the proposition entailed by (2A),
we cannot have (5) without (3A). We could in any case get to
(3A) from (2A) via (5); so we cannot be prevented from getting
to (3A) direct by the fear that we are confusing it with (5).

4. But do (2A), (3A) and (5) behave like the Catilinian examples? Someone who believes (transparently interpreted) that
Cicero denounced Catiline believes of Cicero that he denounced
Catiline. Does someone who believes that (2) believe of Ethiopia
that it was once invaded by Mussolini and is now at war with
Somalia? Is what (2A) asserts, with "believe" there understood
transparently, tantamount to saying that, in Mark's view, the
predicable

> (6B) . . . was once invaded by Mussolini and is now at
> war with Somalia[4]

is truly applicable to Ethiopia? If that is what (2A) asserts,
it looks as though the same must be asserted by (1A), since the
transparent interpretation of (1A) and (2A) makes each entail
the other, given that Ethiopia *is* Abyssinia. But surely it would
be intolerable to attribute to Mark, simply on the strength of
(1A), the view that (6B) is truly applicable to anything at all.

We must distinguish here between (2A) and

> (6A) Mark believes that Ethiopia was once invaded by
> Mussolini and is now at war with Somalia.

There need be no hesitation in inferring (3A) from (6A). That
case is on all fours with the Catilinian example. We need, then,
to focus on the difference between the sentences which express
the content of Mark's beliefs as stated in (2A) and (6A), namely
(2) and

> (6) Ethiopia was once invaded by Mussolini and is now
> at war with Somalia.

Propositions like (6) are formed by attaching a proper name
to a complex, in this case conjunctive, predicable, as here to

(6B). Two strategies have been employed by logicians for explaining the structure of conjunctive predicables. Take the predicable " . . . is old and wise". Those who favour the notion of satisfaction as the key to explaining the structure of propositions would explicate this predicable by saying that an object satisfies the predicable ". . . is old and wise" iff it satisfies the predicable " . . . is old" and it, the same object, satisfies the predicable " . . . is wise". Those, on the other hand, who use the notion of truth for this purpose would explicate the complex predicable by saying that a proposition formed by attaching it to a proper name, say, "Catherine", is true iff the proposition "Catherine is old and Catherine is wise" is true. There is an important difference between these explanations. The satisfaction-type explanation includes in the truth-conditions the phrase "it, the same object" (whose rôle we shall be looking into at a later stage). The truth-conditions provided by the truth-type explanation, on the other hand, contain no expression whose rôle is specially tied to identity. Suppose we explain what it is for someone to believe that a given proposition is true by saying that he believes this if he believes that the truth-conditions for the proposition are satisfied. On the satisfaction-type explanation, therefore, someone believes that Catherine is old and wise if he believes that Catherine satisfies the predicable " . . . is old" and she, the same person, satisfies the predicable " . . . is wise". This gives rise to no *inconvéniont*. On the truth-type explanation, however, someone believes that Catherine is old and wise if he believes that Catherine is old and Catherine is wise. This is a recipe for trouble, as we shall see if we apply the same procedures to (6A). Thus, on the satisfaction-type interpretation, (6A) is true if Mark believes that Ethiopia satisfies the predicable " . . . was once invaded by Mussolini" and it, the same country, satisfies the predicable " . . . is now at war with Somalia". Nothing amiss so far. On the truth-type interpretation, however, (6A) is true if (2A) is true. This would have the undesirable consequence that it is true also if (1A) is true, given that "Mark believes that" is interpreted transparently throughout.

Prior once described as the most plausible way of defining propositional identity a definition of it as the propositional counterpart of indiscernibility.[5] By this he meant the law expressible by "$p = q \to (\delta) (\delta p \equiv \delta q)$", where "$\delta$" is an operator which forms propositions from propositions. Whether or not this formula counted as a definition, Prior was sure it was true. Substituting "Mark believes that" for "δ", it can be used to show the non-identity of (2) and (6), given the non-equivalence of (2A) and (6A). It would also show that the explanation of the meaning of a complex predicable like (6B) cannot be given via the identity of the truth-conditions for (6) and (2). (6) contains no proper name that (2) does not contain. (6) and (2) are both propositions about Ethiopia. In this they do not differ. If they are distinct propositions, the difference must lie, not in what they are about, but in what they say about it. We shall have, therefore, to examine the structure of the predicable (6B). And we shall not be helped in this by noting the material equivalence of (6) and (2).

5. A proper appreciation of the structure of (6B) is, I believe, achieved by ignoring (2) and following a route direct from (1) to (6B). (This need not surprise us. If both (1) and (2) are transparent contexts for the proper names which occur in them, (2) does not in fact take us any further on our journey than (1). What we need first is to form a two-place predicable

(1B) — was once invaded by Mussolini and . . . is now at war with Somalia

by omitting the proper names "Abyssinia" and "Ethiopia" from (1), or, equivalently, both occurrences of "Ethiopia" from (2). From this we can form a one-place predicable, which is manifestly equivalent to (6B), by inserting the words "it, the same country" in the second gap in (1B). This yields

(6B*) — was once invaded by Mussolini and it, the same country, is now at war with Somalia.

It would be a mistake to regard the one-place predicable (6B*) as formed by making "it, the same country" one of the arguments of the two-place predicable (1B), as "Ethiopia" is argument to this predicable in (1) and (2). Rather, we should see "it, the same country" as simultaneously filling up both argument places in (1B) to form the one-place predicable (6B*). In this respect (6B), which means the same as (6B*), is less misleading than it, because it does not have the appearance of filling an argument-place in (1B), but rather of closing up one of the gaps, which would otherwise leave room for an argument, to leave a one-place predicable. But not all two-place predicables of ordinary language can be converted to one-place predicables by the simple device of closing a gap. The analogous way of converting "— admires . . ." into a one-place predicable is by filling the second gap by the word "himself". Peter Geach has argued that here too "himself" should be regarded, not as supplying one argument to "— admires . . .", leaving the other argument-place empty, but as simultaneously filling up both argument-places to form a new one-place predicable.[6] Indeed, the view I have been advancing about the relation of (6B*) to (1B) can be seen as a generalisation of Geach's doctrine about the relation of "— admires himself" to "— admires . . .". Geach goes on to introduce a notation which represents the logical form of "— admires himself" better than ordinary language or classical quantification theory (ibid., §84). Geach writes:

> What we might well have is a more perspicuous symbolism than "$F(x,x)$" for "x bears the relation F to itself"—a symbolism showing clearly how a one-place predicable is here formed from a two-place one. Let us use the symbol "$(—; u, v)$" for this purpose; this symbol, which may be read (say) as "— being both u and v", will form a one-place predicable "$(—; u, v) F(u, v)$" from the two-place predicable "$F(—, —)$", "u" and "v" being of course bound variables.

Geach's notation makes it clear that "$(—; p, v)F(u, v)$" is produced from "$F(—, —)$" by making "$F(—, —)$" argument to "$(—; u, v) — (u,v)$" rather than vice versa, just as "$(\exists x)F(—, x)$" is produced by making "$F(—, —)$" argument to $(\exists x) — x$" rather than vice versa. In "— admires himself" "— admires" is to "himself" as "— admires" is to "someone" in "— admires someone", not as "— admires" is to "Albert" in "— admires Albert". Geach's notation may be used to form

(6B^g) $(—; u, v)$ u was once invaded by Mussolini and v is now at war with Somalia from (1B). (6B^g) presents in a perspicuous form what is expressed misleadingly by (6B) and (6B*).

Geach introduced his symbolism to deal only with reflexive predicables like "— admires himself". I have generalised it to cover the formation of predicables like (6B) from (1B). But Quine, some years ago, drew our attention to a symbolism, derived from Combinatory Logic, which performed the task performed in all contexts by the repetition of variables. In this system "$F(x, x)$" is replaced by "Ref $F(x)$". Quine, as might be expected, provided translations only for expressions involving quantifiers and variables, and made no provision for proper names; but we need not follow him in this, and where "a" is a proper name we may write "Ref $F(a)$" in place of "$F(a, a)$".[7] This symbolism makes it abundantly clear that "Ref" is an operator on predicables, that "Ref" is function to "F" as argument, rather than vice versa.

Geach's operator "(—; u, v) — (u, v)" and Quine's operator "Ref" thus perform, or are capable of performing, the function that is performed both by the English word "self" in "— admires himself" and by the English word "same" in (6B*). The French have a single word for it: "*même*"; and the Greeks used "*autos*", in various combinations, to do both jobs.

We are now in a position to explain the difference between (6) and (2). (6) is formed by attaching (6B) to the proper name "Ethiopia". (6B) is formed by closing the second gap in (1B), and this produces the same result as filling that gap by "it, the same country", as in (6B*). This operation is more perspicuously exhibited in (6B^g) by the use of Geach's operator (which we may call the identity operator) to operate on (1B). So where (2) and (1) are formed by attaching occurrences of a proper name or names as arguments to the predicable (1B), (6) is formed by first attaching (1B) as argument to the identity operator, to form a one-place predicable, and then attaching the proper name "Ethiopia" to this one-place predicable. The structure of (2) and (1) is given by the two-place predicable (1B) and occurrences of proper names. The structure of (6) is given by (1B), the identity operator, which has the rôle of forming a one-place predicable out of a two-place predicable, and the single occurrence of a proper name. The conceptual content of (6) is thus greater than that of (2), although it contains fewer English words. They are therefore distinct propositions. The equivalence of (1A) and (2A) is explained by the fact that the only difference between them is the substitution of one name for another name of the same object. Leibniz's Law applies here. The non-equivalence of (2A) and (6A) is explained by the fact that the substitution of (6) for (2), which is what differentiated them, is the substitution of a materially equivalent, but not identical, proposition. Leibniz's Law does not apply.[8]

6. The fallacious reasoning which took us from (1A) to (4A) has now been exposed with the help of (6A). It was the move from (2A) to (6A) which tempted us; but we have seen now that it should not be made, and why it should not be made. To nail down the mistake more firmly still, Geach's symbolism can be used to display the move from (2A) to (6A) as a case of the operator-shift fallacy. (2A) is equivalent to

(2A^g) (Ethiopia; u, v) Mark believes that u was once invaded by Mussolini and v is now at war with Somalia.

But we cannot from this infer

(6A^g) Mark believes that (Ethiopia; u, v) u was once invaded by Mussolini and v is now at war with Somalia,

which is the same proposition as (6A). The transition from (2A) ($=(2A^g)$) to (6A) ($=(6A^g)$) involves a failure to notice a scope distinction. In (2A) ($=(2A^g)$) the identity operator has wider scope than the belief operator; in (6A) ($=(6A^g)$) it is the belief operator that has wider scope.

7. It may still be asked why (3A) is not inferrable directly from (2A). Is not (3) the existential generalisation of (2), and have we not seen reason to maintain that anyone who believes a proposition to be true will believe the existential generalisation of that proposition to be true? The answer to this, I think, lies in refining our notion of existential generalisation. In the system described in Quine's "Variables Explained Away" (op.cit.), the equivalent of "$(\exists x) F(x, x)$" is obtained in two moves. The

object of the exercise is to get rid of variables. The first move is to use the operator "Ref" which I have already described. This allows us to reduce the variables in "$(\exists x)\ F(x,\ x)$" by one, by rewriting it as "$(\exists x)\ \text{Ref}\ F(x)$". The next move is to substitute for the existential quantifier the operator "Der" which provides for the deletion of the last variable in the formula on which it operates. In place of "$(\exists x)\ \text{Ref}\ F\ (x)$" we thus obtain. "Der Ref F" as the combinatorial equivalent of "$(\exists x)\ F(x,\ x)$". Armed with an identity operator, such as Geach's operator or "Ref", we may eliminate open sentences which have more than one occurrence of a given variable. Existential quantification will then be exactly representable by Quine's "Der", which corresponds to an existential quantifier binding a single occurrence of a single variable. If we use the identity operator, as in ($2A^g$) and ($6A^g$), to eliminate repeated occurrences of proper names in the same way, we shall be able always to represent existential generalisation by the removal of the name and the prefixing of "Der" to the resultant expression. The move from (2) to (3) will not be a case simply of existential generalisation, in the strict sense in which we are now using this term. It will involve the successive performance of two operations: first, the application of the identity operator, next, existential generalisation. The first operation converts (2), which is of the form "$F(a,\ a)$", to (6), which is of the form "Ref $F(a)$". The second converts (6) to (3), which is of the form "Der Ref F". It is only the second operation which is properly describable as "existential generalisation" in our new, restricted, sense of the term.

Provided we adhere to this new, restricted, sense of "existential generalisation", we can continue to maintain the principle that, if a person believes a given proposition to be true, he must believe the existential generalisation of that proposition to be true. The principle, thus amended, legitimises the move from ($6A^g$) ($=(6A)$) to ($3A$). It legitimises the move from "Mark believes that Jane is coming to supper" to "Mark believes that someone is coming to supper". "Someone" here can be represented by "Der". But it does not legitimise the move from ($2A$) to ($3A$). For this we need not only "Der" but "Ref". And this we are not entitled to. Interpreted transparently ($2A$) is equivalent to ($2A^g$). It is a fallacy to regard this as equivalent to (6A^g), from which we could indeed infer (3A). Mark may believe about a country that it was once invaded by Mussolini, and believe also about what is in fact the same country that it is now at war with Somalia, without realising that the two countries are the same. I may believe that John Paul II voted for Wojtyla, without believing that the Pope voted for himself. But I cannot believe that the Pope voted for Wojtyla without believing that he voted for someone. It is, so to speak, the opacity of the identity operation, compared with the transparency of existential generalisation, which compels us to separate them out from each other. and to insist on a restricted sense of "existential generalisation", one which is captured by Quine's combinator "Der". Only in this way are we able to block the move from (2A) to (3A), while preserving the principle that a man who believes that p believes also that q, where "q" is the existential generalisation of "p".[9]

8. The detection of the fallacious reasoning involved in the alleged derivation of (4A) from (1A) may thus be said to have enforced recognition of the identity operator, seen as an operator which forms a one-place predicable from a two-place predicable. As my references to Geach and Quine and to Combinatory Logic show, this operator is not unknown. What is not generally accepted is that this operator is the proper expression of the concept of identity. I mean by "proper" here what would be meant by someone who said that the particular quantifier was the proper expression of the concept of existence. Russell would say, and I would agree, that it is a mistake ever to construe "— exist" as a predicate of objects. Wittgenstein thought that, in the same way, it was a mistake to construe "— is the same as . . ." as a two-place predicable of the first level, as expressing a relation between objects (or a relation in which an object could stand to itself). Wittgenstein concluded that there was no need of a sign for identity, that we should express this instead by identity of sign. My argument is supposed to show that this too was wrong. There are contexts in which identity of sign is not enough: (2A) contains a repetition of "Ethiopia", but this is not enough to entitle us to ascribe to Mark the identity-involving belief ascribed to him in (4A). (6A)(= (6A^g)) is enough to entitle us to do this; but this is because (6A^g) has

the identity operator occurring within the scope of "Mark believes that". This operator is a sign for identity, and Wittgenstein was wrong to think we could do without such a sign. He was right, however, to wish to dispense with a sign like "— is the same as . . .", construed at face value as a two-place predicable of first level.

9. In giving "it, the same country" as an ordinary-language expression of the identity operator I wished to call attention to two points. The first was that we use the word "same" in the natural language, not only as part of what has the superficial appearance of a two-place predicable, "— is the same as . . .", but as part of an expression for forming a one-place out of a two-place predicable. The second was that I wished to recall that the ordinary pronouns, "it", "him", "her", etc., perform this same task. I need not have used the bulky phrase "it, the same country" to provide a natural language expression of our operator : either "it" or "the same country" would by itself have done the job, if I had not wished to make as many points as I could as soon as possible. But let us now concentrate for a moment on "it".

The doctrine that the pronouns of natural language, in one of their most frequent uses, correspond to the bound variables of quantification is a familiar one, associated with the names of Quine and Geach. It has recently been challenged by Gareth Evans.[10] Evans wishes to substitute a doctrine, favoured it seems by linguists, that this use of pronouns is to be explained in terms of "coreferentiality". On the coreferentiality view

> (6ᵉ) Ethiopia was once invaded by Mussolini and it is now at war with Somalia,

which attaches to "Ethiopia" the same predicable as (6B*), except for the omission of the redundant "the same country", has the same meaning as (2). The rôle of "it" in (6ᵉ) is the same as that which would be performed by its antecedent, "Ethiopia", if we repeated it by substituting "Ethiopia" for "it" in the sentence. But our argument for a difference of meaning between (2) and (6) can be run through again to establish a difference of meaning between (2) and (6ᵉ). If Mark believes that (6ᵉ), he believes of Ethiopia that it was once invaded by Mussolini and is now at war with Somalia; so he believes that some country was once invaded by Mussolini and is now at war with Somalia. But this last belief is what is attributed to him in (3A), which is not, as we have seen, entailed by (2A). The content of the belief attributed to him in (2A) cannot therefore be the same as (6^e); so (2) and (6^e) are distinct.

Geach has an argument against the "coreferential" interpretation of the pronoun "himself" which is in fact of the same form as the argument we have been using.[11] Geach points out that there is an intuitive difference between "Only Satan pities himself" and "Only Satan pities Satan" which the coreferentiality theory cannot explain. It can, however, be explained by a difference in the order in which it is constructed by operations on a one-place predicable "— pities Peter". "Only Satan pities himself" is constructed from this by (i) removing "Peter" to form the two-place predicable "— pities . . . ", (ii) linking the two argument places of this together to produce the one-place predicable "— pities himself", (iii) operating on this with the predicable forming operator "Only —" to form the one-place predicable "Only — pities himself", (iv) attaching this predicable to "Satan". "Only Satan pities Satan" would be produced by performing two of these operations: first (iii), to produce "Only — pities Peter"; then (i), to produce "Only — pities . . . "; and finally filling each of the blanks in this two-place predicable with "Satan". Geach holds that we can turn "Only Satan pities Satan" without loss of force into "Satan is pitied only by himself"; but this latter proposition, in my view, would be obtained only by proceeding from operations (iii) and (i) to operations (ii) and (iv).

Now this is paralleled by the "Ethiopia" example. Starting with the one-place predicable "Abyssinia was once invaded by Mussolini and — is now at war with Somalia" we (i) remove "Abyssinia" to produce the two-place predicable (1B). Next (ii) we link together the two argument places of this predicable to form the one-place predicable represented by (6B)(=(6B^g)). We then (iii) operate on this with the predicable-forming operator "Mark believes that —" to produce the one-place predicable "Mark believes that — was once invaded by Mussolini and is now at war with Somalia". Finally (iv) we attach this predicable to "Ethiopia" to form (6A)(=(6A^g)). (2A^g), on the other hand, would have been produced by performing these operations in the order (iii), (i), (ii), (iv); and (2A) is the result of performing operations (iii) and (i) and filling each of the argument-places of the resulting two-place predicable with the name "Ethiopia".

Evans fails to appreciate the force of Geach's argument, because he does not notice that "Only Satan pities Satan" contains, not only the two-place predicable "— pities . . . ", but also the equally good two-place predicable "Only — pities . . .", equivalent to "— alone pities . . .". According to the coreferentiality principle,[12] if the first place in such a predicable is filled by a name and the second place by a pronoun the denotation of the pronoun must be the same as that of the name. According to this principle, "Only Satan pities himself" should be true iff only Satan pities Satan. Evans tries to avoid this by insisting that the antecedent of "himself" in this sentence is the whole phrase "Only Satan" which he treats as a quantifier. This analysis of the proposition is not, perhaps, impossible. "Only Satan" in "Only Satan pities himself" could be construed as a second-level predicable. The important point, however, is that the other analysis is possible also. "Satan," on this other analysis occurs as a logial subject in the proposition, as is still more evident in the equivalent "Satan alone pities himself". The example is, as Geach originally maintained, fatal to the coreferential theory.

10. Geach, however, would not be happy with the parallelism between the Satan case and the Ethiopia case. He holds that the rôle of a reflexive pronoun is different from that of a pronoun occurring in a complex predicable like that to which "Ethiopia" is attached in (6ᵉ). Both sorts of pronoun correspond to repeated bound variables in quantification theory, the reflexive one to the final variable in "For any x, $F(x, x)$" and the other to the final variable in "For any x, Hx and Gx". But Geach maintains that the repetition of bound variables is essentially different in the first case from what it is in the second.[13] His reason is that the latter sort of repetition can be avoided by joining predicables in a truth-functional way: instead of writing "For any x, Hx and Gx" we can write "For any x, $(H \& G)x$". This device will not, Geach points out, get rid of the repetition in

"For any x, $F(x, x)$". For this we need some device such as Geach's operator "(—; u, v,)" which will allow us to render "For any x, $F(x, x)$" as "For any x, $(x; u, v) F(u, v)$". What Geach seems here to ignore is that the operation thus symbolised is also implicit in the definition which allows us to substitute "$(H$ & $G)x$" for "Hx and Gx". What is shown by the repetition of the variable in the latter expression would be made explicit by using Geach's symbol and writing "$(x; u, v) Hu$ and Gv". Two logical operations are implicit in the abbreviatory expression "$(H$ & $G)x$", conjunction and identification. It was precisely this which we argued for in presenting (6B^g) as giving the form of (6B). This is apparent in the symbolism of Combinatory Logic: "Univ Ref J" could equally well express "For any x, $F(x, x)$" and "For any x, Hx and Gx", provided "J" in the first case represented the atomic two-place predicable "$F(—, \ldots)$" and in the second one the complex two-place predicable "H — and $G \ldots$". In this symbolism it is the combinator "Ref" which does the work done in the natural language by pronominal expressions like "it" or "the same object" as well as by the reflexive pronoun "himself". This is recognised by Geach himself in a later paper.[14] He should not find it difficult to reconcile himself to the generalisation of the rôle of the Geach operator suggested above.

11. Geach, in the paper just cited, has argued that the syntactic category of the combinator "Ref" is "$: :sn(: :snn)$", that is to say, it reduces a predicable of $n + 1$ places to a predicable of n places. The same may be said for the symbol "(—; u, v)", for the pronouns of natural language and for expressions of the form "the same A" when they function anaphorically. We may compare them with the combinator "Cnv" or "Inv" (crucial for Quine's elimination of variables, but also part of the symbolism of *Principia Mathematica*), which makes explicit as a separate operation what is shown implicitly by reversal of the order of names or variables in the argument places of a polyadic function. This operation, whether explicit or implicit, belongs to the syntactic category "$: : :snn(: :snn)$". In the same way, the identity operation is of the syntactic category "$: :sn(: :snn)$", whether it is made explicit by an operator or shown implicitly by repetition of names or variables. Wittgenstein's refusal to

G

employ a sign for identity is as unreasonable as would be a refusal to allow that "CnvRxy" was a viable alternative to "Ryx". His prejudice here is due, perhaps, to his failure to see that a sign for identity could, and indeed should, be of a syntactic category other than that of a two-place predicable of first level.

It would be absurd to make a distinction between what is shown by repetition of names or individual variables and what is shown by repetition of expressions of other syntactic categories. We may express the proposition that James's mother is the same as John's mother by "For some x, both x bore James and x bore John" or by "For some x, Ref both x bore James and bore John" (The rule for "Ref" requires the deletion of the final repeated variable from an open sentence to which it is prefixed). And just as it seems reasonable to express the proposition that something James believes is the same as something John believes by "For some p, both James believes that p and John believes that p", so it is an obvious extension of the use of "Ref" to allow the same proposition to be expressed by "For some p, Ref both James believes that p and John believes that", from which the second occurrence of the variable "p" has accordingly been deleted. I have argued elsewhere[15] that the supposed "relation" of correspondence involved in saying that what Andrew says corresponds with the facts is more perspicuously expressed by the repetition of the variable in "For some p, both Andrew says just that p and p". What is expressed by this repetition of "p" would, on the proposed extension of the sense of "Ref" be expressible also by this combinator. We should regard "Ref" as the canonical expression, not only of the concept of identity, but also of the concept of correspondence. Here, however, the combinator would not be an expression of the syntactic category " : :sn(: :snn)" but one of the category " : :ss(: :sss)", one which reduces a sentence-forming operator on $n + 1$ sentences to a sentence-forming operator on n sentences. This should not worry us. The quantifiers, once they are allowed to bind variables of other categories than that of name-variables,[16] have to be recognised as forming expressions of different categories: "For some x, . . . x . . . " is of the category " :s :sn", but "For some p, . . . p . . . " is of the category " :s :ss". Existence is thus shown to transcend the categories, as the Aristotelians always held that it did. What is true of existence is true also of identity. But that identity should be numbered amongst the *transcendentalia* will surprise no one who has a feeling for Metaphysics.

NOTES

1 I must here record my debt to Roger White. Not only have I found his remarks in this paper (*PAS*, 1977–78, pp. 157–174) deeply illuminating, but I have been helped greatly by his comments in the preparation of my own paper.

2 A full treatment of identity would, of course, have to provide an account of difference. Suffice it to say that neither on Russell's analysis of propositions like "John's father is the same person as Mary's boss", nor on Wittgenstein's, nor on the one presented in this paper, is that the contradictory of "John's father is a different person from Mary's boss". My feeling is that, while Wittgenstein's account of identity requires modification, his account of difference is all right as it stands.

3 Propositions with "A" in their labels all begin with the words "Mark believes that".

4 Expressions with "B" in their labels are all predicables. In this paper I use the word "predicable" in the sense explained by P. T. Geach in *Reference and Generality* (Ithaca: Cornell University Press, 1962), §18, to describe an expression which could be used as a predicate, even if, in the proposition under consideration, it is not being so used.

5 A. N. Prior, "Is the Concept of Referential Opacity Really Necessary", in *Acta Philosophica Fennica*, vol 16, 1963, p.192.

6 *Op. cit.*, §82, 83.

7 *Cf.* W. V. Quine, "Variables Explained Away", in *Selected Logic Papers*, New York: Random House, 1966, pp. 227–235.

8 See Prior, *ibid.*, for the distinction between such cases in respect of Leibniz's Law.

9 Andrew Woodfield has pointed out to me that the same method may be used to block the move from "Ralph believes of Ortcutt that he is a spy and Ralph believes of Ortcutt that he is not a spy" to "Ralph believes of Ortcutt that he both is and is not a spy". The latter will be true only if, per impossibile, Ralph believes that a predicable of the form "(—; u,v) F(u) & ∼F(v)" is satisfied by someone. (*Cf* W. V. Quine, "Quantifiers and Propositional Attitudes" in *Reference and Modality*, ed L. Linsky, Oxford: Oxford University Press, 1971, p.106.)

10 *Cf.* "Pronouns, Quantifiers and Relative Clauses", in the *Canadian Journal of Philosophy*, VII, 1977, pp. 467–537, 777–797.

11 *Op. cit.* §§80, 83.

12 Formally set out in (F) on p. 479 of Evans's article.

13 *Op. cit.* §84.

14 *Cf.* P. T. Geach, "A Program for Syntax", section V, in D. Davidson and G. Harman, edd., *Semantics for Natural Language*, second edition, Dordrecht: D. Reidel, 1972, pp. 483–497.

15 *What is Truth?*, Cambridge: Cambridge University Press, 1976, chapter 5.

16 And even before. Without going outside classical first-order predicate calculus, we have to recognise the possibility of using the quantifiers in an infinite number of expressions of different syntactical categories: "($\exists x$) . . . x . . ." is of the category ": s : sn", "($\exists x$) . . . x . . . x . . ." of the category ": s : : snn", ($\exists x$) . . . x . . . x . . . x . . ." of the category ": s : : : snnn", etc. The "embarrassment" to which Prior confessed (*Objects of Thought*, Ch.III, §7) in allowing the syntactical category of quantifiers to vary with the category of the variables they bind was, therefore, needless.

VII*—DESCRIPTIONS AND REASONS

by Julius Kovesi

It might seem unfair to take as my point of departure an isolated argument from Professor Perry's *Moral Reasoning and Truth*, but although I make some critical comments on that passage I make them in order to continue the struggle with the difficult problems Professor Perry there presents rather than to show imperfections in it. In fact Professor Perry does mention in a footnote that my comparison of judging an object to be a table and an action to be a murder is similar to the one he presents there, so my critical comments are intended more as a further contribution to the clarification of a problem that interests us both.[1]

Professor Perry points out, I think rightly ,that the appropriate analogy of a moral judgement in the world of objects is not with contingent generalisations, explanations or predictions, but with empirical classifications. "More concretely, statements like 'That action of Jones (of which we are otherwise fully informed) is wrong' should be compared with statements like 'That object before us is a table' or 'That other object before us is a person', and not with statements like 'That table will still be in this room tomorrow' or 'that person will never marry' . . ." He wants to use this analogy to cast light on the question whether a particular action, say a particular sadistic killing, would still *be* what we now call wrong even if practically everyone who considered it from a moral point of view would say it is *not* wrong. And to do this, he first considers this imaginary case : suppose that practically everyone who is in a position to observe and use English normally, no longer calls even paradigmatic tables, "tables". Would they still *be* tables?

If the object we pointed to had the same *uses* as what we now call table, then whatever other word we used in place of our present word, it would have the same meaning as our present word "table", "for it is the uses of a thing which determine

* Meeting of the Aristotelian Society held at 5/7 Tavistock Place, W.C.1 on Monday, February 4, 1980 at 6.30 p.m.

the meaning of the words we use to refer to it". But if the object did not have the same uses then it would be a "useless object, or perhaps a device for warding off evil spirits, or just some curiously arranged wood we can build a fire with".

It is in the application of this theory to moral judgements that I find some ambiguity in Perry's argument. Coming to the question whether the sadistic killing of a human would still *be* wrong even if practically everyone who might consider it from the moral point of view would say that it is not wrong, this is how Perry formulates his answer: "Yes, it would still be what we now call wrong if the people who take the moral point of view towards things continued to have the same 'uses' for it: that is, if they continued to have the same evaluative response to the sadistic killing of humans." Although the "it" refers to the sadistic killing of a human, we do not hear of its "uses" at all but instead we are asked to envisage a different moral judgement of it. This is far from what Perry intends to say, rather it is almost the opposite of what the whole machinery of the comparison was meant to show; nevertheless something went wrong, for this is what he goes on to say: "But if they would not so characterise it with a synonym of 'wrong', but would use some value term of an entirely different meaning—one expressing mild approval, for example—then under this more radical supposition it *wouldn't* still be wrong, just as this table I am now writing on wouldn't still be a table under the corresponding radical supposition."

I cannot blame Perry for some ambiguity here, for the problem he has attacked is very complex and subtle, and furthermore, our philosophical habits of thinking have hardly prepared us for handling it. I am not sure that I can clarify the problem, but I would like to attempt it for I think it is a very important one.

The main problem is, of course, what is parallel to what; what should be compared to what in judging physical objects and judging moral acts. But before we can map that, we should clarify an important point. The operative concept is not that of *using* something, but is a higher or more embracing concept, of which using is an instance in the case of tables and bicycles. We have to ask something like "what is the place of that something-or-other in our lives", or "what is the point of having something-or-other in our lives", or even "what was the point of forming the idea of and then making and maintaining certain objects". It just so happens that the answer to such questions in the case of tables is in terms of their use.

It is strange to ask for the uses, even in a very broad sense of "uses", of a sadistic killing of a human. We should look for the appropriate comparison in terms of the point of selecting certain features of human actions for special recognition, which in the case of actions is not their "use".

Perry suggested that to continue to have the same "uses" for it is to continue to have the same evaluative response to the sadistic killing of humans, and to change its use is to have a different response to it, perhaps one expressing mild approval. My further objection now is not only that this should not be discussed in terms of "uses", nor that its "use" in a broad sense of it is perhaps different from what Perry suggests. The whole logic of the problem and the whole point of drawing the parallel are distorted here. As Perry presents the case it looks as if the very same action, the sadistic killing of a human, could be right or wrong, *everything else remaining the same.* I am sure this is not what he would have liked to say, but by presenting the *judging* of the action to be right or wrong as the parallel to the *use* of the table, he has destroyed his parallel, with drastic consequences. To reverse the parallel: it is as if the use of tables consisted of judging them to be tables.

Now in the case of actions (though less so than in the case of making and doing) one must bring about some observable movements or interfere with the world in some way, but those movements or interferences are not the equivalents of observable objects that we have in the case of tables. In the case of actions we have only descriptions, or if this offends anyone, we have only specifications. So the parallel to the use of tables should be something like the reasons for selecting certain features of our lives, actions and situations for special recognition.

The elusive nature of our problem is such that it is very easy, or natural, to make two mistaken and diametrically opposite assumptions at the same time. This can happen because the comparable levels or elements of the parallel are shifted but at the same time there *is* a parallel, so the two mistakes are due to a sort of distorted double vision. Incidentally, I believe that it is at the heart of so much of the cross-purpose arguments about "description" and "evaluation", and this is why I said that our philosophical habits of thinking have hardly prepared us for handling this problem.

Since in the case of actions there is no observable object such as we have in the case of tables, we easily fall into the assumption that a wrong act continuing to play the rôle that wrong acts play is to be continued to be judged wrong, and *at the same time* to asume that since in the case of objects there is something observable even when its use and its rôle in our life have changed, so in the case of actions there must be as it were some residue of the action which remains the same. In the process the most important element in the comparison, the very element which the comparison was meant to bring out and spotlight, was conjured away: namely that there is something in our moral life comparable to the rôles which objects play in our lives. What the parallel intended to show was that in the same way as we cannot succeed in judging a table other than a table as long as it continues to play the rôle tables play in our lives, so we cannot succeed in judging a wrong act other than wrong as long as that act continues to play the rôle wrong acts play in our lives.

The philosopher who came nearest to seeing what is happening is Locke in his analysis of mixed Modes. Moral notions for Locke are mixed Modes, and mixed Modes are made by the understanding. They are not copies of real existing things in the world but "are the creatures of the understanding, where they have a being as subservient to all the ends of real truth and knowledge as when they really exist".[2] The names of mixed Modes always signify the real essence of their species. "For, these abstract *Ideas* being the Workmanship of the Mind and not referred to the real Existence of Things, there is no supposition of anything more signified by that Name, but barely that complex *Idea,* the Mind itself has formed . . ."[3] In mixed Modes the real and nominal essence is the same. The examples of mixed Modes are moral notions, and he does call them notions. There is a reason for forming these notions. "But though these complex *Ideas,* or *Essences of mixed Modes,* depend on the Mind, or are made by it with great liberty; yet they *are not made at random*."[4] Now of course the reason why we select certain features of our lives, actions and situations into one notion and describe them by one term is because certain such configurations have moral significance. Taking away that reason is like taking away a kingpin, and the whole configuration will fall apart and the bits and pieces will take their place in other, not necessarily moral, configurations, or just remain as scattered pointless pieces. And those features of our lives that are features because of their moral significance will cease to be features at all. Here is the equivalent to tables turning into useless objects or perhaps devices for warding off evil spirits.

We see now another reason why Perry made that slight mistake in his analogy, but we can also see now a further consequence of that mistake. If their wrongness is the point of bringing together certain configurations into one notion, then it is easy to mistake this rôle of these notions in our lives for *judging* them wrong. But by conflating the two—their rôles and judging them—Perry has let slip from our attention the point that the *reason* for judging a notion wrong is the rôle it plays in our lives.

Locke's views on mixed Modes are hardly made use of in moral philosophy. Such views as these are put down to his rationalist side and his analogy with "Mathematicks" makes him a bit of a curiosity in the history of moral philosophy. It even seems incredible that anyone could compare the practical affair of morals with such theoretical study.

Before we go further I just want to mention one of Locke's examples, an example I look on as one looks on past battles or skirmishes, the different outcome of which could have changed our whole subsequent history. Here is one of Locke's examples with which he illustrates how mixed Modes have no natural articulations corresponding to them in nature from which they could be derived. "What Union is there in Nature," asks Locke, "between the *Idea* of the Relation of a Father, with Killing, than that of a Son, or Neighbour; that those are combined into one complex *Idea* and thereby made the Essence of the distinct Species *Parricide*, whilst the other make no distinct Species at all?"[5] This is indeed the question Hume asked later, and as we know, Hume's answer was not that it is our mind and understanding that creates such mixed Modes and creates them for good reasons. He looked for the answer in his breast and we know what consequences it had for moral philosophy, while Locke himself went on to make the unfortunate analogy with mathematics. A few chapters later he says " . . . I am bold to think that *Morality is capable of Demonstration*, as well as Mathematicks: Since the precise real Essence of the Things moral Words stand for may be perfectly known, and so the Congruity or Incongruity of the Things themselves, be certainly discovered, in which consists perfect Knowledge".[6] No wonder Hume treated Locke's question on parricide in the same chapter in which he argued against Wollaston.

There is an interesting philosophical tradition where we find the constant recurrence of the partly helpful but also rather misleading analogy of our knowledge of what we have made with our knowledge of mathematics and geometry. The analogy is usually invoked to show the superiority and completeness of the maker's knowledge. Vico, for instance, claims that God knows the world as we know mathematics, not because the world is mathematical, but because God made the world as we made mathematics, and concluded that since we made history, we should have a divine knowledge of history and adds that the historian should have divine pleasure in contemplating history. Hobbes also draws the same analogy: "Geometry therefore is demonstrable, for the lines and figures from which we reason are drawn and described by ourselves; and civil philosophy is demonstrable, because we make the commonwealth ourselves".[7] Earlier still, Maimonides made use of the idea in order to show the difference between God's complete knowledge of the universe and our incomplete understanding of it. He makes use of the example of a water clock which is known by its producer according to the principles by which he made it but which others know only by observing it as an object. This is how he contrasts God's perfect knowledge of the world with our poor understanding of it.[8]

Interestingly we find the same idea in Lukacs' interpretation of Marx: throughout history we make the object of our knowledge, nature and society, more and more intelligible by transforming them. Finally in the proletariat this social reality becomes completely rational and knowable, and at the same time this subject matter is the knower, so in the proletariat the knower and the known become one, as God is described in some theories.

Locke, in his theory of mixed Modes, gives, I think, without mystification and without megalomania, a very helpful account of what is involved here. In our knowledge of substances like gold or cabbages, the nominal essences never really exhaust, do not really coincide with, the real essences. However much we know them there is always a residue beyond what we know or what is knowable. But, as I said, in mixed Modes the real and the nominal essences coincide.

The claim that maker's knowledge is divine knowledge is of course an admission that we haven't got that knowledge; and the mathematical analogy is a very misleading attempt to indicate something which is true about our moral and social life, namely that in studying it we have to chart out and explore intricate structures of conceptual relationships. But knowing this is not like knowledge of our intentions and in fact it is even more difficult to know than the physical world. The embodiments of our intentional endeavours in our language and culture are not the making of an individual agent, and yet only individuals can know, so however much that world is in a sense our creation, the maker and the knower are not the same. This is what is partly behind the prescriptivist's objections that on the descriptivists' account our moral decisions are, at least in part, made for us by others. But of course it is not our *decisions* which are made for us by others, but what we make our decisions about, the world in which we make our decisions, the world which includes the reasons why we have to make decisions at all. As others cannot know for us, our decisions cannot be made by others, only what we know about or make decisions about can be made by others. But as some Husserlian phenomenologists fear that our knowledge is falsified as soon as an intentional object is described, some prescriptivists have similar fears about the embodiments and expressions of our decisions in moral terms. Such terms can only be a descriptive corpse without a vital element. We can see also in the views of the prescriptivists another way in which the tradition of maker's knowledge went wrong. We meet here again the promethean temptation of a world where I *make* my own values, and values not made by

me confront me like *objects* made by others : they appear to me
as *descriptions*.

We are further handicapped in our knowledge by the moral
world's differing from that other branch of the subject matter
of maker's knowledge, from the world of artefacts. As Locke
so clearly argues the mixed Modes of our moral notions, unlike
complex ideas of substances, do not have references to substances
existing in the world; they come to exist only when by our
actions we instantiate them.

We just have not got the models and the vocabulary to chart
properly this world of conceptual structures, their multiple inter-
relationships and the patterns of structural and other changes
within it. I am not referring to problems of methodology
developed and argued over by philosophers and social scientists.
Our handicap is inherited from our pre-academic development
and perhaps from our pre-intellectual development, from the
time when we developed primarily as visual observers.

Even Wollaston who came very near to saying that by our
actions we instantiate concepts and propositions which are appropriate or inappropriate in relation to other instantiated concepts,
retained a correspondence theory of truth, appropriate to propositions we use in talking about the physical world. For this
Hume rightly criticised him by arguing that in all his arguments
"there is an evident reasoning in circle". To make a false statement by my action presupposes a moral world *about* which my
action makes the false statement. It is very difficult to express
the idea that my action is not a statement *about* a moral world
but in a sense constitutes it.

Others who borrow from the models of the visual world to
express the fact that they are not talking about the visual
world postulate non-natural qualities or other invisible entities.
What should strike us about these is not the implausibility of
such qualities or entities but that in trying to talk about our
moral life they only extend the furniture of the physical world.

But the most prevalent way in which we borrow models from
our dealings with the physical world is when, in order to draw
the distinction between talking about the physical world and
talking about our moral life we first draw it *within* the ways in
which we talk about the physical world and then transfer that
model to our moral life, without the objects, in connection

with which we made the distinction. We are all familiar with those introductions to moral reasoning which begin by saying that there are two sorts of things we can say about strawberries or tables : one sort is to say that they are sweet or round, the other sort is that they are good. Then, in order to have a reason to choose we have to add that I like strawberries. I have argued elsewhere that the difference between these two is not as great as that between both of these types of statements about objects, and our statements about our moral life.[9] We must not assume that out of the two ways—among many others—*in which we can talk about objects* one of them provides the pattern for talking about objects and the other provides the pattern for talking about our moral life.

I want to bring out by the help of an absurd sounding example the difference between the two worlds. The difference is *not* that in one case we say that this is a table, or that it is round, and in the other we say that it is a rather good table. To envisage our moral life we have to envisage *ourselves* as instantiating a table. If I want myself to be described as a table I have to be careful not to wobble, and whenever I see that the occasion demands it I would have to bend down sufficiently low so that the appropriate people could write on me or place objects on me.

Let us observe the completely different relationship between description and action on the pattern I am suggesting. On the model of choosing *objects* we are choosing from already existing objects and we choose the one which comes up in a sufficient degree to what the object is supposed to be under that particular description. On my pattern I am not choosing the best instance of different particulars for there are no particulars there to choose from. The connection between description and action is that I am *instantiating* by my behaviour the description. I choose, if I can, what description I want to instantiate, or choose actions falling under different descriptions. I choose an act not because it is the best instance of something under a certain description but because I want to instantiate that description—or I refrain from doing something because I do not want to instantiate that description.

Of course, on the slave market I might be chosen because I am a good instance among other slaves of a sturdy physical specimen. But I am being chosen as an object; the choice is not a moral choice. The moral choice is choosing to choose you under that description, and what is more, it involves *treating you* under that description. We can see that there is a connection not only between the description I instantiate and my behaviour but also between that and the behaviour of others: both I and the slave owner enter into a world of conceptual relationships. And now we can see that the absurd sounding example was not quite so absurd after all. The absurdity is only in our repulsion at thinking of a man as a table, to think of him and to treat him as what he is not. As Wollaston said: "To talk to a post, or otherwise treat it as if it was a man, would surely be reckoned an absurdity, if not distraction. Why? Because this is to treat it as being what it is not. And why should not the converse be reckoned as bad; that is, to treat a man as a post. . . ."[10]

We can work out, for instance, as a theoretical exercise, what is implied in the notion of a friend. In analysing the concept we work out what is entailed in being a friend, what behaviour we expect from friends, with what intentions they do what they do, and so on. And when I am a friend, I have to act out in my life the implications of the concept. When someone reproaches me by saying "I do not mind you doing that but do not call yourself a friend" he is pointing to the logical incompatibility of my action and describing myself as a friend.—Of course if I have reason to take on a different description I can cease to regard myself as a friend. But my description of myself needs justification just as much as the description of anything else. Moreover, changing it is itself an action, just as much as resigning, marrying or divorcing or joining the resistance movement are actions.

I am not giving in this paper an account of moral obligation, nevertheless I want to mention some reasons why we cannot lightly take on or abandon descriptions, reasons that are connected with my limited objective in this paper.

One is the interrelatedness of whole webs of connection in such a way that I have to consider a whole set of consequences —and I do not mean utilitarian but logical consequences—in renouncing or taking on a description. During the height of student revolutions some years ago a student handed in to me a sheet of paper at the time when essays were due. On the paper was a drawing of a steam engine with a flower in its funnel and with big bold letters the inscription : "I expressed my freedom but you academics do not care about it." With my limited artistic ability I drew a little pussycat in the corner of that paper, the sort children draw, with whiskers, and handed it back to the student next day. He came to me fuming that I had penalised him, that he was right to say that I did not care about his freedom to express himself. I did my best to look puzzled and asked him in what way he was penalised. "You did not give me a mark".—"I cannot mark your expression of freedom. If you expected a mark then perhaps what you submitted was an essay".—"You just want to treat me as a student, you don't treat me as a human being".—"In that case my giving you a mark is even more incomprehensible. I cannot mark you as a human being. But if I treated you as a human being I would certainly ask you not to intrude on me and not to take up my time. For as a human being you are disagreeable, and I don't want to talk to you. But in so far as you are a student I would have to give you a distinction if you produced good work. In this case it is not because I do not like you that I did not give you a mark but because I took your paper as an expression of freedom and not as an essay. So instead of a mark I just expressed my freedom and do not know why you are so upset about my expression of my freedom."

This was regarded as bourgeois formalism. I don't think that young man had worked out the implications of opting out of certain descriptions. Notions like relevance, fairness, corruption and a whole host of vital moral notions come to life and into prominence as relevant concepts logically connected even with such a simple case as this.

Another type of consideration that one might have for not wanting to get rid of a description is the recognition that the aspects of our life that it carves out and brings together into what Locke calls a mixed Mode, and other aspects that it leaves out and sharply distinguishes itself from are important and worthwhile distinctions. To use again my example of a student, we have to realise what conceptual transformations were needed to separate out and to create the notion of student in distinction to the notion of disciple. In marking the essay of a *disciple* it would be relevant to consider whether he is reproducing *my* thought and whether he is furthering the cause I am dedicated to. In considering the value of having such a description as being a student again we have to trace and chart a whole set of relationships with other concepts with which our concept is connected and of which it forms a part. But without such a description one might not be able to be a student at all.

This illustrates also the reverse relationship between description and action. Very often when people are told that moral distinctions are man made they are not only shocked but think that moral distinctions cannot be very important—if they are only man made. But this is all the more reason for their importance and we cannot take it for granted that they will exist by nature. If we value some concepts we have to exemplify them and instantiate them by our actions in order to keep them alive. I do not mean "exemplify them" in the sense that by our example like a living advertisement we shall propogate them. I mean that only by us being instances of it can the concept stay alive for this is its mode of existence.

I think, incidentally, that Locke could have dealt with the connection between the conceptual relationships of moral notions and our actions in a similar fashion. "If it be true in Speculation, *i.e.* in *Idea*, that *Murther deserves Death*, it will also be true in "Reality of any Action that exists conformable to that *Idea* of *Murther*."[11]

Someone might object that this shows how wrong Locke was, and say that most people would dispute that murder deserves death. The point is however, that we do work out "in Speculation" whether murder deserves death and if we come to the conclusion that there is no such implication then "it will be true in Reality of any Action that exists conformable to that Idea of Murther".

But the problem still remains, even supposing for the sake of argument that murder deserves death, why should I *do* anything about it. This would depend on my description, or on what idea I instantiate, and how I am related under the appropriate description to the rest of the situation which consists of a configuration of other appropriate descriptions. If it be true in speculation that judges should sentence criminals and I am the judge then I should be doing the sentencing. If I am the murderer then I should think of myself as deserving death. But however much murderers deserve death, if I am not the executioner and he has not yet been condemned, then if I killed him I would be described as someone who took the law into his own hands, and that has yet further implications. If however, there is no appropriate legal system in the land and I am the murdered person's brother, I could not be described as taking the law into my own hands, there being no laws that I could be supposed to take into my own hands. This last example also shows how an act of revenge could change its rôle, which would help to illustrate Professor Perry's discussion of actions which could play different rôles in our lives.

If, on the other hand, I am not in a situation, that is, if I am not related conceptually to the other concepts in question, all I might be expected to do is *merely to make a moral judgement.* Versions of the fact/value distinction which locate the distinction in the gap between describing something and doing something, suffer from a systematic confusion because we have not worked out the difference between moral judgements and moral decisions. Let me just say here that the occasions for making judgements, and along with them the reasons for making judgements are quite different from the occasions and reasons for making decisions. I am making a moral decision when I *have* to make one, and I have to make one when I am in a situation. I am in a situation when I lock in, under a certain description, to an interlocking conceptual field, *as one of the elements of that interlocking conceptual field.*

So the connection between a description and an action is not like the connection between describing something and judging it a good object of that sort; nor is it like the connection between describing it and choosing it, when the connection has to be supplied by our liking it or wanting it or making a decision about it. In a situation I have to choose because I *have* to choose, that is what puts me in a situation. And my reasons for choosing are in the descriptions under which the alternatives present themselves.[12]

H

NOTES

[1] Thomas D. Perry *Moral Reasoning and Truth* Clarendon Press 1976 pp. 132–134.

[2] *Essay,* III.Ch.V.§5.

[3] *Ibid* III.V.14.

[4] *Ibid* III.V.7.

[5] *Ibid* III.V.6.

[6] *Ibid* III.XI.16.

[7] English Works Vol. 7, p. 184.

[8] Maimonides: *Guide for the Perplexed* Part III. Ch.XXI, p. 295, Routledge.

[9] "Against the ritual of 'is' and 'ought'" *Midwest Studies in Philosophy* Vol. III 1978 pp. 10–16, and "Valuing and Evaluating' in *Jowett Papers* ed. by B. Y. Khanbhai, Blackwell 1970

[10] Raphael: *British Moralists*, Clarendon Press 1969, Vol. I, par. 283.

[11] *Essay* IV.Ch. 4.8.

[12] I worked on versions of this paper while I was Visiting Fellow at the Research School of the Australian National University. I would like to thank the University for its hospitality and especially Stanley Benn for his persistent helpful criticism.

VIII*—DUMMETT'S ARGUMENTS ABOUT THE NATURAL NUMBERS

by Geoffrey Hunter

The first arguments of Dummett's that I shall examine are contained in the two papers "The Philosophical Significance of Gödel's Theorem" (1963) and "Platonism" (1967), both in his *Truth and Other Enigmas* (1978). In the Preface to that book Dummett implies that he is not completely satisfied with either paper.

By 'the natural numbers' I mean 0, 1, 2, 3, etc. and by 'propositions of elementary arithmetic' I mean those propositions about the natural numbers that can be expressed using only '0', 'the successor of', '+', '.', '=' (where those terms have their usual arithmetical meanings), quantification over the natural numbers, and the standard propositional operators of logic ('~', '&', etc.).

By one form of Gödel's Theorem no formal system (1) that is adequate for the expression of the propositions of elementary arithmetic and (2) all of whose theorems are true on the intended arithmetical interpretation and (3) for which there is an effective method for telling whether or not something is a proof in the system can have as theorems *all* truths of elementary arithmetic (more exactly: all formulas of the system that are true on the intended arithmetical interpretation).

A common interpretation of this result is that we have a certain, quite definite, concept of the natural numbers, which we can never succeed in completely characterizing by means of any formal system. Dummett says that this common account will not do, for several reasons:

1) It is incompatible with the thesis that the meaning of an expression is to be explained in terms of its use.
2) The account operates with the notion of a model as if it were something that could be given to us independently of any description.

---

* Meeting of the Aristotelian Society held at 5/7 Tavistock Place, W.C.1 on Monday, February 18, 1980 at 6.30 p.m.

3) There is a circularity in trying to explain the concept of natural number in terms of the standard model, for that can only be given to us by means of some description involving the notion of natural number or some closely related notion.

4) The account would be tolerable only if we had some other means of communicating our concept. But the only alternative candidate is by means of a second-order induction principle mentioning *all* properties, and this is subject to non-standard interpretations, so we cannot know that others understand that notion as we do.

So Dummett rejects the standard interpretation and suggests the following alternative account:

The ordinary concept of 'natural number' is inherently vague, in the sense that it involves the validity of induction with respect to any well-defined property, and the concept of a well-defined property in turn exhibits a particular variety of inherent vagueness, namely indefinite extensibility. A concept is indefinitely extensible if, for any definite characterization of it, there is a natural extension of this characterization, which yields a more inclusive concept. (N.B. Dummett says that there is no vagueness as to the *extension* of 'natural number'. He distinguishes between the criterion for recognizing a term as standing for a natural number and the criterion for asserting something about all natural numbers, and says that the second is not fully determined by the first.)

So there is not a perfectly definite concept of 'natural number' incapable of a complete description. Rather, there is a not fully determinate concept capable of indefinite extensibility. The only way to explain the meanings of quantification over the natural numbers is to state the principles for recognizing as true a statement which involves it; Gödel's discovery amounted to the demonstration that the class of these principles cannot be specified exactly once for all, but must be acknowledged to be an indefinitely extensible class.

The reality we are trying to characterize is not *fully*

determinate (cf. Preface to *Truth and Other Enigmas*, p. xxix).

The first of Dummett's reasons for rejecting the common account is that it is incompatible with the thesis that the meaning of an expression is to be explained in terms of its use. No account of our—or any possible—use of the expression 'natural number' can exhaustively explain what it is for it to have the meaning that the standard account ascribes to it (cf. p. 187 in *Truth and Other Enigmas*).

I understand Dummett's line of thought to be this:—"The standard account takes the expression 'natural number' and other related expressions (such as 'zero', 'successor', 'sum', 'product') to have meanings such that whatever is true in elementary arithmetic is true in virtue of those meanings being what they are; hence a full account of the meanings of those expressions should be such that all truths of elementary arithmetic are consequences of it: so, if meaning is to be explained in terms of use, the same should be true of a full account of the use of those expressions; but no satisfactory formal system with an effective method for telling whether or not something is a proof can have as theorems all truths of elementary arithmetic; so no account of our use of the expression 'natural number' can exhaustively explain what it is for it to have the meaning the standard account ascribes to it; so on the standard account meaning cannot be identified with use."

There are two weak points in this argument. The first is that the penultimate step appeals to the dubious principle that if the use of an expression cannot be characterized in a formal system with an effective method for telling whether or not something is a proof in the system then no account of its use can exhaustively explain its meaning. Now it may well be that no account of the use of any expression can ever exhaustively explain its meaning (see the next paragraph below), but that does not make the principle true. For one thing, Gödel's work showed that for sufficiently rich systems the set of semantic consequences of the axioms always outruns the set of formulas that are formal consequences by the rules of the system (provided that the system is consistent). So one cannot now trust a formal system of an arbitrary set of propositions to yield as consequences all the propositions that really are consequences of the set. The failure, then, of a *formal* system to give us all the consequences of a certain set of propositions does not rule out the possibility of an "exhaustive" account that makes use of some unformalized notion of *consequence*. I think that the mediaevals were right in distinguishing consequences *ex vi terminorum* from formal consequences, and that in general it is very difficult to capture those consequences exhaustively and unambiguously, for a particular set of propositions, by means of a formal system. For example, I do not think it has been done for Euclid's geometry. So I am not convinced that there is as close a connection as the principle claims between being able to give an account of the use of an expression and being able to characterize that use in a formal system with an effective method for telling whether or not something is a proof in the system. After all, number theorists were able to learn their subject from their predecessors, and contribute to it, for centuries before Dedekind produced Peano's axioms or Frege invented the notion of a formal system.

The second weakness is in the last step of the argument. From the proposition that no account can be given of X that is an exhaustive explanation or account of Y it does not follow that X cannot be identified with Y: it may simply be that no exhaustive account can be given of either X or Y. If one cannot give an account of the use of a word that is a complete, non-circular, purely verbal account of the meaning of the word, that could be because one cannot give a complete, non-circular, purely verbal account of the *use* of the word, and not because the meaning is not identical with the use.

So this first argument of Dummett's is inconclusive. There is no compelling reason for thinking that the use of an expression must be capable of being exhaustively and unambiguously given by a formal system with an effective method for telling whether or not something is a proof, and so no compelling reason for thinking that if the meaning of an expression cannot be so given then we have to reject the thesis that meaning is use.

Dummett's second reason for rejecting the standard account is that it operates with the notion of a model as if it were something that could be given to us independently of any description, as a kind of intuitive conception which we can survey in its entirety in our mind's eye, even though we can find no description which determines it uniquely (cf. *Truth and Other Enigmas* p. 191).

My first comment on that reason is this. Dummett in his description of the standard account makes use of such expressions as "an intuitive faculty", "intuitive conception", "intuitive grasp", "intuitive apprehension of a model", "an ineffable faculty of intuition", "a faculty of intellectual intuition", "an intuitive apprehension", "an intuition which resists complete expression". Yet in fact a supporter of the standard account need not use the term "intuition" or any of its cognates to say what he wants. He has merely to say that some people do understand what is meant by the expression 'natural number', that natural numbers are not the sort of things that can be seen, touched, tasted, heard or smelt, that understanding of the meaning is gained by learning the use of numeral words in various contexts and in the normal ways that people do learn the meanings of the words: and that as a result of this training some people do understand what is meant by saying that certain propositions about natural numbers are true even when they do not know whether or not they are true (e.g. Goldbach's conjecture that every even number greater than 2 is the sum of two primes, or Fermat's claim that there are no positive integers x, y, z and n such that $x^n + y^n = z^n$ for n greater than 2, or the proposition that there is no greatest pair of twin primes). The realist does not have to claim anything about an ineffable faculty of intuition of an abstract structure when he interprets Gödel's theorem as showing limitations on the powers of characterization of formal systems. All he need say is that he understands what it is for something to be a natural number, and that the work of Skolem and Henkin, e.g., shows that any first-order formal system that can be interpreted in terms of the natural numbers can also be interpreted in terms of things that are *not* natural numbers.

My second comment is that it just does not appear to be true that the standard account operates with the notion of a model as if it were something that could be given to us independently of any description and that we can survey in its entirety in our mind's eye. I gave a brief description of the model in my second paragraph; I made no claim to be able to exhibit it to you without any description, and no claim to be able to survey it in its entirety in my mind's eye. You, if you understood my description, did so because you had learned the meanings of the words I used, and that did not involve surveying the natural number system in its entirety in your mind's eye either. It is not necessary for the upholder of the standard account to think otherwise.

So I believe that Dummett's second objection to the standard account is not right.

His third reason for rejecting the account arises in the context of a consideration of non-standard models of arithmetic. He says that there is a circularity in trying to explain the concept of a natural number in terms of the standard model, for that can only be given to us by means of some description involving the notion of natural number or some closely related notion (cf. *Truth and Other Enigmas* pp. 191–2).

I agree that that *is* viciously circular. But I do not see that the standard account involves that circularity. Its upholders are not trying to explain the concept of a natural number in terms of the standard model : in saying that whenever a formal system can be interpreted in terms of the natural numbers it can also be interpreted in terms of things that are not natural numbers, and that therefore no formal system unambiguously catches our notion of natural number, they are not trying to *explain* the notion of natural number at all, and so they are not involved in the circularity that Dummett describes.

Dummett's fourth argument against the standard account is this :– "To say that we cannot communicate our intuition of the natural numbers unequivocally by means of a formal system would be tolerable only if we had some other means to communicate it. The only candidate for this alternative method of communication is a second-order induction principle, where the predicate variables are interpreted platonistically as ranging over *all* properties. But this merely throws the problem back on to how *this* notion is communicated. Since, for any given formalisation of second-order logic, there will be a non-standard interpretation, we cannot know that other people understand the notion of all properties (of some set of individuals) as we do . . . But this would reduce the intuitive observation of abstract structures to something private and incommunicable" (*Truth and Other Enigmas* p. 210).

One objection to this is that it is not true that the *only* ways there are of communicating the notion of natural number are (1) by means of a formal system and (2) by means of a second-order principle of induction involving the notion of all properties. For generations people have been successfully communicating the notion to others without using either of those methods.

Nor does it follow from the fact that a given sentence could be interpreted in a way different from the way we intend it that we can never know that others understand it as we do or that what we are saying is private and incommunicable. The sentence 'Arthur's plot is well under way' could be interpreted as being about some sly plan of Arthur's, but when it occurs in the context that follows we can know that others understand it as we do, and what is being said is neither private nor incommunicable : —

8.45–7.15
Gardeners' World
Easter Special from Clacks Farm
with Arthur Billitt, Peter Seabrook
Easter is traditionally the start of the
gardening year for many families, particularly
with vegetable growing. Arthur's plot is
well under way and this evening he discusses
with Dr. Peter Salter, from the National
Vegetable Research Station, the results of the
latest experiments in crop growing . . .

I hesitate to suggest it, but is there in this argument of Dummett's a repetition of the mistake that Plato saddles his "Socrates" with, viz. that unless you can unambiguously define the words you use, you cannot know what you are talking about and nobody else can either?

The last argument I shall consider comes from a third paper of Dummett's, "The Philosophical Basis of Intuitionistic Logic" (1973), and can be found on pp. 224–5 of *Truth and Other Enigmas* : —

> On the theory of meaning which underlies platonism, an individual's grasp of the meaning of [a sentence whose truth-value we are not capable of effectively deciding] consists in his knowledge of what the condition is which has

to obtain for the sentence to be true, even though the condition is one which he cannot, in general, recognise as obtaining when it does obtain. This conception violates the principle that use exhaustively determines meaning; or, at least, if it does not, a strong case can be put up that it does . . . For, if the knowledge that constitutes a grasp of the meaning of a sentence has to be capable of being manifested in actual linguistic practice, it is quite obscure in what the knowledge of the condition under which a sentence is true can consist, when that condition is not one which is always capable of being recognised as obtaining . . . It is, in fact, plain that the knowledge which is being ascribed to one who is said to understand the sentence is knowledge which transcends the capacity to manifest that knowledge by the way in which the sentence is used. The platonistic theory of meaning cannot be a theory in which meaning is fully determined by use. (Cf. also Dummett's *Elements of Intuitionism* p. 376 *et circa*.)

I think something has gone wrong here. In the ordinary sense of the words, we know perfectly well how to test whether or not someone understands a mathematical sentence that is, in Dummett's sense, "effectively undecidable". Let me give Dummett a few aces by going to an area where anti-realist arguments are much more plausible than in the case of the theory of natural numbers, namely set theory. The Continuum Hypothesis is not known to be true and not known to be false and at present nobody knows how to go about settling its truth-value. A sentence expressing it would presumably be one "whose truth-value," in Dummett's words, "we are not capable of effectively deciding". According to Dummett, "it is plain that the knowledge which is being ascribed to one who is said to understand the sentence is knowledge which transcends the capacity to manifest that knowledge by the way in which the sentence is used". But is it? Teachers know how to tell from what a student does whether or not he understands the Continuum Hypothesis. One way, for example, would be to ask him to pick out from the following list just those sentences that expressed the Continuum Hypothesis or some proposition equivalent to it :

A. There are no atoms, properly so called.

B. There is no cardinal number greater than aleph nought and less than the cardinal number of the continuum.

C. There is no end to the series of transfinite cardinal numbers.

D. For each transfinite cardinal number n, there is no cardinal number greater than n and less than 2^n.

E. The cardinal number of the continuum is the cardinal number next greater than aleph nought.

F. Every set of real numbers is either countable or of the same cardinality as the whole set of real numbers.

G. None of those.

If a student picked out B and E and F, and only those, I should be fairly confident that he understood what the Continuum Hypothesis was. Of course, there are degrees of understanding, and further questions might reveal deficiencies in his understanding, but with particular people one might be absolutely confident that they understood it. Now what is wrong with that as an example of manifestation by behaviour of understanding of the meaning of a sentence that, in Dummett's terms, is "effectively undecidable"? His objection is (*Truth and Other Enigmas* p. 224) that what is manifested here is no more than an ability to express the content of the sentence in other words and that is evidence of a grasp of the meaning of the sentence on the presumption that the speaker understands the words in which he is stating its truth-condition; "but at some point it must be possible to break out of the circle : even if it were always possible to find an equivalent, understanding plainly cannot in general consist in the ability to find a synonymous expression." (Cf. *Elements of Intuitionism* p. 376. "The understanding of an expression cannot, in general, be taken to consist in the ability to give a verbal explanation of it".) Now we may agree that understanding an expression "cannot in general consist in the ability to find a synonymous expression" : in translating a passage from Latin I might come across the word 'cicer', whose meaning I did not know : on looking it up in a dictionary I find that the dictionary gives just the one synonym, 'chick-pea'; so I "have the ability to find a synonymous expression"; but since I do not know the meaning of 'chick-pea' I still do not understand the meaning of 'cicer' : I have not broken out of the circle of words.

(Another example: s.v. 'blind-shaft' the big Oxford dictionary has simply 'a winze'. Another: s.v. 'Schorl'—'Tourmaline, esp. the black variety'. Another: s.v. 'Sciaena'—'In the 18th c. a name of the MAIGRE'. Another: s.v. 'Epimeron'—'That part of the lateral wall of a somite of a crustacean which is situated between the articulation of the appendage and the pleuron.') But the behaviour of a mathematical student responding to a quiz about the Continuum Hypothesis is to be taken in conjunction with a web of behaviour that he manifests, has manifested, and might manifest, including, for example, his behaviour in using numeral words to count things. So the mere fact that in a quick quiz a man immediately manifests only the ability to find synonymous expressions does not mean that his *total* manifested relevant behaviour never breaks out of the circle of words.

"But the question is not about understanding the *words* that make up the sentence but about understanding the *sentence*. I understand each of the words in the sentence 'Jones has just discovered how to see what people look like in the dark', but it does not follow that I understand what that *sentence* means. How is the *sentence* 'There is no greatest pair of twin primes' to be understood when the condition which must obtain for it to be true is not one which we are capable of recognizing whenever it obtains?" (Although I use double inverted commas here, not everything in this paragraph is a quotation from or summary of Dummett. A similar *caveat* applies to my use of double inverted commas from now on.)

Well, in the case of 'discovering how to see what things look like in the dark' it is evident that the phrase does not carry its meaning on its face, that anyone who did happen to guess what the speaker meant *without having any further information to go on* would be just guessing. It is not like that with the twin primes: there, anyone who knows the mathematical meanings of the words used (including of course the meaning of the expression 'twin prime') is capable of knowing, *without guessing,* what the sentence means. The twin prime case differs significantly, therefore, from the case of 'seeing what things look like in the dark'.

"But the claim that you understand the meaning of 'all' in cases where it is applied to an infinite domain and you have no method for telling whether what is said is true or false, *because* you understand it in cases where you do have a method, is as dubious as the claim that you understand what it is to be ten o'clock on the sun because you understand what it is for it to be ten o'clock in Bangor." (Not from Dummett).

There is a significant difference between the two cases. In the time example I know that the conventions are such that, so far as the clock times of everyday life are concerned, the meaningfulness of 'it is ten o'clock in Bangor' does not imply the meaningfulness of 'it is ten o'clock on earth' (let alone 'on the sun'), and I do not at present remember enough about astronomers' time to know whether they have a meaning for 'ten o'clock on the sun' or not. Nothing corresponding to those two points applies in the case of the twin primes.

"But does not the move from finite sets to infinite sets affect the meaning of the word 'all'?"

I do not see that it does, any more than I see that the meaning of 'all' changes when it is attached first to 'mountains' and then to 'dreams'.

"How about the move from cases where you have a method for finding the answer to cases where you do not? Does not that affect the meaning?"

I do not see that either the meaning, or my understanding of the meaning, of (what can now be called) the Four Colour Theorem changed with the discovery of a proof of it.

"But is not the meaning of sentences to be identified with the methods of their verification or with their truth-conditions?"

No. In the first place to know the meaning of the sentence 'Please shut the door' is not to be identified with knowing either methods for verifying the sentence or its truth-conditions. In the second place, the sentences 'If anything is a cow it is a cow' and 'If anything is a cat it is a cat' have different meanings but the same truth-conditions, namely all conditions.

I think that by the perfectly ordinary criteria for testing understanding we can tell from manifested behaviour whether or not someone understands an (in Dummett's phrase) "effectively undecidable" mathematical sentence, and that the understanding ascribed to one who does understand does not transcend the capacity to manifest that knowledge by the way in which the sentence is used.

Frege wrote :—"Being true is different from being taken to be true, whether by one or many or everybody, and in no case is to be reduced to it. There is no contradiction in something's being true which everybody takes to be false. I understand by 'laws of logic' not psychological laws of takings-to-be-true, but laws of truth. If it is true that I am writing this in my chamber on the 13th of July, 1893, while the wind howls out-of-doors, then it remains true even if all men should subsequently take it to be false. If being true is thus independent of being acknowledged by somebody or other, then the laws of truth are not psychological laws : they are boundary stones set in an eternal foundation, which our thought can overflow, but never displace" (Frege, *Grundgesetze der Arithmetik,* Introduction pp. xv–xvi, translated by Montgomery Furth, under the title *The Basic Laws of Arithmetic,* University of California Press 1964, p. 13). I still do not know of any satisfactory argument against that general position, discounting the metaphors.

IX*—UNDERSTANDING AND THEORIES OF MEANING

by R. M. Sainsbury

The expression 'theory of meaning' can be used in at least these two distinct ways:

> A theory₁ of meaning relates to a single language, L, and purports to state, or in some other way to fix, the meaning of each L-sentence.

> A theory₂ of meaning relates to language in general, and attempts to analyze, elucidate, or determine the empirical content of, the concept of meaning in general.

The issues I wish to discuss lie within the hypothesis that a theory₂ of meaning should essentially involve consideration of theories₁ of meaning. But this terminology is cumbrous. I shall reserve 'theory of meaning' for theories₁ of meaning. Reformulated, the hypothesis is that a philosophical account of meaning should proceed by considering the nature of theories of meaning.

The hypothesis has initial plausibility, for it might seem that if theories of meaning specify meanings for particular languages, to reflect on the general nature of theories of meaning is generally to reflect on what each specifies, and is thus to reflect on the general character of meaning.

I do not seek to destroy this framework, but only to challenge certain contentions that have been made within it. I shall assume that, in the present discussion, our only ultimate philosophical goal is to attain a philosophical understanding of the nature of meaning in general. What I shall challenge is either the justification for or the correctness of certain constraints on theories of meaning that, it has been proposed, are required in the light of this ultimate aim. The constraints are these:

---

* Meeting of the Aristotelian Society at 5/7 Tavistock Place, W.C.1 on Monday, March 3, 1980 at 6.30 p.m.
I wish to thank the following for comments on drafts of this paper: Martin Davies, John Foster, Hans Kamp and David Wiggins.

(i) A theory of meaning for L should exhibit the semantic structure of L;

(ii) A theory of meaning for L should have a syntax no less extensional than the syntax of L;

(iii) A theory of meaning's pairing theorems should not use as filling the expression 'means that', or cognates like 'can be used to say that'.

[The 'pairing theorems' are those which are supposed to state, or in some other way to fix, the meanings of the object language sentences, and I shall assume that they have the syntactic form '*s* . . . *p*', where what replaces '*s*' designates a sentence, whose content is supposedly given by the sentence in use which replaces '*p*'; the 'filling' is what fills the dots.]

The following three sections take up these claims in turn. All three constraints are satisfied by identifying a theory of meaning with a truth theory of the kind that Donald Davidson has proposed.[1] Thus, much of what I argue for could be expressed: it is a mistake to think that truth theories, or philosophical reflection thereupon, can assist a philosophy of meaning in the way often supposed in the Davidsonian tradition.

1. Understanding and structure. If a theory of meaning for L exhibits the semantic structure of L it does so by identifying L's semantic elements and deriving the pairing theorems relating to L-sentences from axioms relating to (typically subsentential) L-elements. In this section I consider some, but not all, of the ways one might attempt to justify the requirement that theories of meaning should exhibit semantic structure. In particular, I shall consider how one might attempt to derive it from two claims about the nature of theories of meaning, claims which would link the theories with the philosophy of meaning:

(*a*) A theory of meaning for L is a theoretical representation of a practical ability possessed by anyone who understands L: that of recognizing the force and content of suitably presented L-utterances.[2]

(*b*) A theory of meaning for L states something knowledge of which is sufficient for understanding L.[3]

(Those who define 'theory of meaning' so as to exclude theories which do not exhibit semantic structure can regard the issue of this section as how to justify considering theories of meaning (in their sense) rather than other kinds of meaning-specifying theories.)

Bending our thoughts to (*a*), let us consider the nature of recognitional abilities in general. One who can under certain circumstances recognize objects of kind K as objects of kind K is one who can, under those circumstances, come to know of any such object, suitably related to the circumstances, that it is of kind K. Recognition relates to kinds or types, and is explicitly or implicitly relative to appropriate circumstances, typically those of sensory presentation. Thus one who can, just by looking, recognize *Amanita Phalloides* as *Amanita Phalloides* is one who can, when any mushroom of this kind is close enough within his visual range, come to know of it that it is an *Amanita Phalloides*. This exemplifies a shallow representation of the ability, since the very concepts which occur essentially in the knowledge which the recognitional ability is the ability to acquire also occur, accidentally, in the description preferred of the kind of objects recognized. A deeper representation will describe the input to the ability in terms closer to what we take to be its *raw* material. In the present case, one would most naturally think of visual properties, and the representation would consist of a pairing of these with species and genus.

To simplify the comparison with the linguistic case, let us partially abstract from force by pretending that all utterances are sayings. One who understands a language must be able, when suitably presented with any particular utterance, *u*, of type *U*, where particular *U*-type utterances are used to say that *p*, to come to know that the speaker who uttered *u* thereby said that *p*. He recognizes the force as *saying* and the content as *that p*. Setting aside force completely (though still only to simplify the formulation), the necessary recognitional ability is that of recognizing the content of utterances. A very shallow representation would take the form: if any L-speaker, S, sufficiently close within his auditory range, uses an L-utterance whose content is that *p*, one with the relevant ability in L is able to know that S uttered something whose content is that *p*. A deeper representation would associate L-utterances, described in non-

I

semantic terms, with their contents. In short, such a representation would be a theory of meaning, though we have as yet found no trace of the requirement that the theory should exhibit semantic structure.[4]

One might hope to derive this requirement from two further premises :

(P1) The semantic structure of a language is isomorphic with the causal structure of the competence of one who uses it.

(P2) A full representation of an ability must exhibit its causal structure, which in this case will be the very structure, mentioned in P1, which semantic structure must reflect.

If one can exhibit a causal structure without exhibiting it *as* causal, then the desired conclusion follows fairly straightforwardly. Something like P1 cannot, in my view, be denied, though one might well challenge the rather simple connection which P1 itself claims between semantic structure and the structure of competence.[5] However, P2 is certainly false. It rests on the mistaken view that the causal structure of a recognitional ability is essential to its identity. Unless this were assumed, there is no way in which the obligation to represent an ability can impose the obligation to represent that ability's structure.

Before arguing against this assumption, it is well to see just what the relevant causal structure is supposed to be. In English, it will consist in such facts as these : an English speaker's understanding of the sentence 'John runs' causally could not be impaired without thereby impairing his understanding of all such sentences as 'Harry runs', 'George runs', 'Mary runs' . . ., or else of all such sentences as 'John walks', John talks', 'John laughs'. . . . A speaker's understanding of 'John runs' is thus causally bound up with his understanding of other sentences containing 'John' and 'runs', and a language's semantic structure is rightly seen as dependent, directly or indirectly, on facts of this kind.[6]

I shall first try to show that it is not generally true that the causal structure of a recognitional ability is essential to it, and then I shall try to show this specifically for the case of the linguistic ability under discussion.

Let us suppose that there are chicken sexers who associate young birds with a number from 0 to 1, taken to represent the probability of that bird being male, and that they cannot articulate the features which cue their response. They might share a common ability: over a given range of inputs (these being visual or tactile properties), they assign the same number. One learnt slowly, requiring at least one lesson from an old hand for each type of input, and the sub-abilities which make up the overall ability are causally independent: it is causally possible that the ability to associate any one set of observable properties with a number fail, yet the other property-number associations remain untouched. Another sexer learnt quickly, and extrapolated to associating a number with hitherto unperceived combinations of properties along lines reflected in the theory of probability, and there are causal dependencies among the sub-abilities: there are pairs of sets of properties such that it is causally impossible, as things are with him, that his ability to associate one set of the pair with the appropriate number should disappear yet his ability to associate the other set of the pair with the appropriate number survive. Here we have a clear case in which the same ability is realized in distinct causal structures.

To transpose the analogy in the most immediate way to the case of linguistic ability one must consider a finite language (i.e. one with only finitely many sentences). One speaker has come to learn it on a sentence-by-sentence basis, and his sub-abilities are causally independent. Another has learnt the language on the basis of its structure and there are causal dependencies among his sub-abilities. Yet each might have this ability: suitably exposed to any utterance in the language he can recognize its content.

Extending the case to infinite languages is more controversial, but I can see no logical impossibility in a person's having the ability for an infinite language in a causally structureless way: God might make him know the content of utterances as wholes, yet keep the sub-abilities causally independent. God could, for example, make a person recognize the content of 'John runs' and 'Harry walks' and not recognize the content of 'John walks'. If there are logical impossibilities here they permeate the concept of an omnipotent and omniscient being. Fortunately, my case does not turn on such an extreme example as a structureless ability with an infinite language. To convince ourselves that, even in the infinite case, the ability is independent of its causal structure, we can imagine a language with a suffix '-ette' which, attached to any simple predicate 'F', forms a complex predicate with the meaning 'little F'. One speaker's recognition of the content of the (finitely many) '-ette' complexes might be based on a sensitivity to this fact of semantic structure, a sensitivity recorded by such counterfactuals as: if he were to come to fail to recognize the content of 'F-ette (this)', while still recognizing the content of 'F (this)', he would also, and thereby, come to fail to recognize the content of 'G-ette (this)', 'H-ette (this)', etc. Another speaker's recognition of the content of utterances containing '-ette' complexes might be insensitive to this aspect of semantic structure: he has had to learn the meaning of each '-ette' complex separately. The common ability of the two speakers extends over infinitely many sentences, but the causal structure of it is different in the two cases.

One who would insist that a theory of meaning exhibit semantic structure might, when faced with this difficulty, simply claim that an exhibition of a structure isomorphic with the structure of competence is of intrinsic interest. This move, however, would seem to sever, or at least make it hard to explain, the connection between theories of meaning and the philosophy of meaning. Let us, rather, consider whether the structural constraint can be derived from the requirement that a theory of meaning should state a condition knowledge of which would suffice for understanding. If understanding a semantically complex sentence required a sensitivity to its semantic structure the derivation would be made. But this dependence of understanding on sensitivity to structure is open to challenge.

Christopher Peacocke has argued for the dependence, deploying the following example.[7] If Brezhnev tells you (in English, for you do not speak Russian) that in the first sentence of his speech (call it 's') he will say that production doubled in 1973 you will know, as the speech begins, what Brezhnev says by uttering s, so you will recognize the content of the utterance, but, according to Peacocke, you will not understand it. The example would indeed establish the failure to understand if we build into it the feature that you cannot identify tokens of s as tokens of *s* on the basis of their auditory characteristics, so that, for example, you would be at a loss to say whether Brezhnev uttered *s* just once or more than once in the course of his speech. But if we build in this feature, then the case ceases to be one in which knowledge of what Brezhnev said by uttering *s* amounts to recognition of the content of the sentence- or utterance-*type, s*. For it ceases to be the case that *whenever* you are suitably confronted with a token of *s* you recognize the content of the linguistic act the speaker performed by making the utterance. (I do not need to assert that there could not be 'one-off' recognitional abilities, independent of the ability to re-identify (*'another* death cap', 'Margaret Thatcher *again*'). I need only assert that the linguistic ability I have discussed is not of this kind.)

What Peacocke could certainly show is that from the fact that you know what Brezhnev said by a token of *s* one cannot deduce that you understood *s*, but this could be established by an example which would make clear that the point does not in itself drive a wedge between a recognitional ability relating to an utterance type and understanding that type : for example, suppose you are told merely that in the first sentence of his speech yesterday (i.e. in uttering *s*) Brezhnev said that production doubled. You plainly could know this without having any access to the auditory or visual properties of *s*, and thus without having the beginnings of the recognitional ability relating to *s*, for this depends on being able to have the relevant knowledge of content on the basis of suitable auditory or visual presentations of *s*.

Suppose someone insists that you could recognize the content of every token of *s*, on the basis of its auditory or visual properties, yet not understand *s* if your recognition was not based on a sensitivity to the semantic structure of *s*. Then, I think, the issue will degenerate into a terminological one about how 'understand' is to be used. I have no particular objection to reserving the word for cases in which not only can a person recognize the content of an utterance, *U*, on the basis of its visual or auditory properties, his recognition is, in addition, based on sensitivity to the semantic structure of *U*, a sensitivity manifested by causal dependencies between the understander's grasp of *U* and his grasp of other utterances with semantic elements in common with U. In return, I would have it conceded that one who has the recognitional capacity for every utterance in a language, yet in whole or part lacks sensitivity to semantic structure, is none the less able to use that language for every communicative purpose for which language serves us.

My claim is that a structural constraint on theories of meaning does not follow satisfactorily from either of the theses (*a*) or (*b*)—not satisfactorily from (*b*) because the derivation would involve a somewhat *ad hoc* stipulation about understanding, not justified in terms of the essence of the function of language. But I leave open the possibility that the constraint be derived from elsewhere, for example from the plausible hypothesis that if we are engaged in the task of radical interpretation it is only by guessing at semantic structure that we can reduce the indeterminacy of interpretation to manageable proportions: to the extent that structure is discerned, evidence for an interpretation of an utterance-type U will flow not merely from data concerning uses of tokens of U, but also from uses of tokens of other utterance-types having elements in common with U.[8] The source of such a constraint will help determine its place in the philosophy of meaning. The source just mentioned would at first glance seem to lie within the epistemology of language rather than its metaphysics and, from a realist perspective on these matters, these two locations are distinct: if there could be a determinate language which *we* could never interpret (to a reasonable degree of determinacy), a constraint flowing merely from the possibility of interpretation will not pertain to the essence of language. I shall note, but not discuss, the delicate issue that now arises: if it is part of the essence of language to be usable for communication, then there can be no absolutely uninterpretable language, but this may perhaps leave logical space for the notion of a language, uninterpretable by us, but interpretable by other sorts of beings (e.g. infinite beings).

2. *Extensionality.* Should a theory of meaning for L avoid non-extensionality (save at most in so far as this is required by non-extensionality in L)?[9]

I stipulate that the extension of a name or singular description is its bearer or denotation, of a predicate the things of which it is true, and of a sentence its truth value. A language is extensional if its every sentence is, and a sentence is extensional if, for each of its parts covered by the stipulation, only the extension of these parts is relevant to the extension of the sentence as a whole.[10] The test is that the replacement of any such part by a coextensive one leaves the extension of the sentence as a whole unchanged. It is an immediate consequence of this definition that it is contradictory to hope that a theory of meaning for L should meet all of the following conditions:

(a) that it state the meaning of the L-sentences;
(b) that its pairing theorems have the overall logical form 's . . . p';
(c) that its pairing theorems be extensional.

The reason is that if a sentence 's . . . p' states the meaning of s, its truth value must be sensitive to the meaning of p, and not merely, as extensionality requires, to the truth value of p. One who would adhere to extensionality must either abandon the hope that his theory of meaning will state meanings, or else abandon the idea that its pairing theorems will have the logical form 's . . . p'.[11]

One reason that has been offered for adhering to extensionality is that mastery of non-extensional idiom 'requires an implicit grasp of the . . . concept of meaning' (Foster[12]). The reason would be good only on the assumption, to be challenged in the next section, that a theory of meaning would fail of its purpose if it contained the concept of meaning. But even if we accept this assumption, Foster's reason is still inadequate. For there exist non-extensional idioms, including one which Foster himself cites, namely 'It is necessary that . . .', mastery of which do not require implicit grasp of the concept of meaning. I can envisage only two ways in which such implicit grasp might seem to be required. On the one hand, it could be held that modal sentences are true wholly in virtue of meanings, and that grasping an idiom requires implicit grasp of what makes sentences containing the idiom true. The shortest way with this suggestion is to consider an idiom of causal modality, which will introduce non-extensionality, but concerning which it would be absurd to suggest that sentences containing it are true wholly in virtue of meanings. On the other hand, it might be held that an idiom requires implicit grasp of the concept of meaning if recognition of the validity of inferences involving the idiom requires sensitivity to difference or sameness of meaning. However, not this sensitivity, but rather sensitivity to the presence or absence of necessary coextensiveness, is required in the case of inferences involving modality. So non-extensionality does not, *per se,* introduce the unwanted concept of meaning.

One might rely on a converse claim to support the extrusion of non-extensional idiom from a theory of meaning : that extensionality at least ensures that the concept of meaning is absent. An initial response might be that this begs the issue of whether or not a reductive analysis of meaning is possible, for example, an analysis initially in terms of psychological concepts, these giving place to behavioural ones. In the face of this response, one might wish to distinguish the explicit occurrence of the concept, as when it is introduced by some particular short phrase or construction, and its implicit occurrence, as when, as a result of analysis, the concept is, so to speak, dispersed throughout a sentence or set of sentences and is not specifically associated with any short component. The suggestion may then be that all that is objectionable is the explicit occurrence of the concept of meaning, and that this is avoided if the syntax of the theory is extensional.

An *ad hominem* point against those who advance this suggestion yet accept Davidson's paratactic analysis of *saying that*[13] is that this style of analysis can translate away the non-extensionality of the idiom 'means that' without thereby translating away the explicit occurrence of the concept of meaning. Paratactically construed, '*s* means that *p*' will be seen as being (or as being translatable by) two sentences, '*s* means that' and '*p*', where, in the first, 'that' is a demonstrative pronoun referring to the subsequent utterance of '*p*'. Since the meaning idiom is confined to the first sentence, and since this sentence is extensional, the concept of meaning, on this construal, can occur explicitly yet not be responsible for the introduction of non-extensionality.

3. 'Means that' and theories of meaning. Both arguments in favour of the extensionality constraint assumed that a theory of meaning for L should make no use of the concept of meaning (except so far as is required by the occurrence of the concept in

L), and in particular that the theory's pairing theorems should not have the form 's means that p', or anything synonymous with this. Davidson speaks in 'Truth and Meaning' of the obscurity of 'means that' in the course of the discussion which leads to the advocacy of truth theory. Foster more explicitly claims that the occurrence of 'means that' would diminish the light we could expect a theory to throw on the notion of meaning.[14] The fear seems to be of circularity. In this section I argue that this fear springs from a faulty conception of what could be hoped for from a theory of meaning,[15] and that one ought to prefer a 'means that' theory if one hopes that a theory of meaning should state something, or at least contribute essentially to the statement of something, knowledge of which is sufficient for understanding.

If a theory of meaning for L stated the meaning of each L-sentence, for example by having pairing theorems of the form 's means that p', then, if true, it would certainly state something knowledge of which suffices for understanding L. But in the tradition which I am discussing it is generally assumed that the pairing sentences will be T-sentences, having the form 's is true $\leftrightarrow p$', and thus will not state the meanings of L-sentences. Rather, the idea is that by imposing certain constraints on the theory, in each pairing theorem the used sentence in p-position will have the same content as the mentioned sentence designated by the term in s-position. The T-sentences will thus 'fix' the meanings of the sentences they mention, without stating them.

Let us use 'D' to abbreviate the predicate expressing the constraints which, supposedly, ensure that all the pairing theorems fix meanings, or, as I shall say, that the theory is interpretative. Then one way in which a non-meaning-stating theory, θ, might contribute to a sufficient condition for understanding is as follows: one must know θ, and know that $D(\theta)$.

John Foster has pointed out a difficulty with this proposal. One might know θ, that is know the propositions that θ states, and know that $D(\theta)$, yet not realize that θ states these propositions (e.g. if θ is in a language one does not understand), and so not know enough for understanding.[16] I shall ignore this difficulty (though this will lead to some strictly nonsensical oscillations between sentences and propositions), assuming that it can somehow be overcome. Instead, I shall press two consequences of any proposal of this general form.

First, such a proposal can be adequate only if it is knowable *a priori* that for all θ if $D(\theta)$ then θ is interpretative. To know a theory (i.e. to know the propositions stated by a theory) is to know (the propositions stated by) its axioms, and to be able to come to know any (proposition stated by a) theorem, by a process wholly *a priori* relative to knowledge of the axioms. Likewise, a proposal of the present form must state conditions sufficient to enable one to extract the meaning of the L-sentences, by a process wholly *a priori* relative to knowledge of the stated conditions. Only in this way can the obligation to state a condition knowledge of which would suffice for understanding be discharged. Allowing that knowledge of θ will enable one, on confrontation with an arbitrary sentence s, to work out θ's pairing theorem for s, and that knowledge that $D(\theta)$ will enable one to work out that this is a pairing theorem of a D theory, one cannot proceed unless one knows that the pairing theorems of D theories fix meanings, and if this is not stated explicitly in the conditions for knowledge, it must be extractable from them *a priori* if the conditions are sufficient.

In effect, the whole burden of furthering our understanding of meaning in general is borne, in such an account, by whatever light 'D' sheds on 'interpretative'. But any such elucidation would be just as good an elucidation of what it is for a meaning-stating theory to be true as of what it is for a non-meaning-stating theory to be interpretative. This holds in virtue of the obvious *a priori* truth that '$s \ldots p$' is fit to be a pairing theorem of an interpretative theory iff 's means that p' is true. Hence a proposal of this kind would licence, rather than prohibit, the use of 'means that' as the filling of pairing theorems.

Secondly, not only is this permissible, it is mandatory if knowledge of a theory of meaning is going to be a necessary part of a minimal sufficient condition for understanding. For if we accept any proposal of the kind under discussion, knowledge of θ becomes otiose. So long as, in knowing that $D(\theta)$, one knows enough to identify θ-theorems as θ-theorems, one need not know the axioms or theorems of θ. The reason is that it is enough for understanding to know that, e.g., the proposition that 'snow is white' is true $\leftrightarrow$ snow is white is a theorem (or rather is expressed by a theorem) of a D theory. For then one already knows enough to know that this is a meaning-fixing proposition (true or false) and thus that the sentence 'snow is white' expresses the proposition that snow is white.

Davidson has to some extent accepted this etiolation of the rôle of a theory of meaning in providing a sufficient condition for understanding. In 'Radical Interpretation' he allows that knowing a theory does not enter into this condition. Rather, he claims, it is enough for understanding a sentence s that one know that s is true ↔ p 'is entailed by some true theory that meets the formal and empirical criteria' (326); in my terminology, that this is entailed by some true D theory. But the insistence on the truth of the theory is otiose. For suppose a *false* theory, e g. one with a theorem saying that 'snow is white' is false ↔ snow is white, satisfies 'D'. Then one who knows this can come to know that the sentence 'snow is white' expresses the proposition that snow is white.

'D' might itself contain the requirement of truth; or we might in any case decree it as a further condition. In the first case, 'D' would go beyond what an account of interpretativeness requires. In either case, the addition could not be motivated by the search for a sufficient condition of understanding.

An interpretative theory, even if false, can always be transformed into a theory with true pairing theorems, indeed into a theory with T-sentences as theorems. For if the original false, but meaning-fixing, theorem is '$s \ldots p$', it follows that 's means that p' is true, and so is 's is true ↔ p'.[17] But the fact remains that if only interpretativeness concerns us, given in terms of 'D' then the filling of meaning-fixing theorems is irrelevant. A D theory must yield pairing theorems, but neither their overall content nor their truth matters. This affects any non-meaning-stating theorem. So only if a theory is meaning-stating can its truth play a non-redundant rôle in the formulation of a sufficient condition for understanding. This is one answer to the question why one should hanker after a theory which states meanings.[18]

A corollary is that one for whom a truth theory plays the rôle characterized by the remark that 'truth is what a theory of sense is a theory of'[19] has, in virtue of this alone, no commitment to realism or to the rejection of bivalence. The reason, affording a more immediate route to the conclusion than the one which McDowell himself offers, is that even a verificationist, anti-realist or intuitionist can accept the inference from '*s* means that *p*' to '*s* is true ↔ *p*'. What he will perhaps reject is a realist or knowledge-transcendent interpretation of the latter.

There is still a positive though slender rôle for theories of meaning in the philosophy of meaning, as can be brought out by considering an oversimplified version of an account that McDowell has offered of, in effect, the predicate 'D':[20]

> (M) 'D(θ), relative to L-users' abbreviates 'No theory other than θ can be used, by treating its pairing theorems as fixing meanings, to give a better account of the behaviour of L-users in terms of their professional attitudes'.

Compare this with what would result if one tried to apply these ideas directly to the 'means that' scheme:

> (M') *s* means that *p* among L-users iff no other interpretation of *s* enables us to give a better account of the behaviour of L-users in terms of their propositional attitudes.

M' is obviously false, for it would permit adjustment of the interpretation of *s* (e.g. so that it no longer expresses a weird belief of L-users) without a thought for the interpretation of sentences other than *s* sharing some of its syntactic parts. But if M is false, its falsehood is not in this way obvious, at least for structured languages.

From the perspective of one who would advance an account along the lines of M of the enterprise of interpretation, the rôle of a theory of meaning consists wholly in ensuring that the enterprise relates to language as a structured whole and not to individual utterances considered apart from their structural interrelatedness. (And it will perhaps be said that if there are structureless languages, their interpretation is, for us, open to an indeterminacy no less radical than that alleged by Quine.) But this rôle could be adequately fulfilled by a theory whose pairing theorems have the form '*s* means that *p*'; and we have already seen that there is a positive reason for preferring a meaning-stating theory of this kind.

Postscript: on truth and 'truth conditions'. If 'truth conditions' is so defined that any truth of the form '*s* is true ↔ *p*' states the truth of the sentence designated, then no one has ever seriously supposed that a sentence's truth conditions come at all close to its meaning. If 'truth conditions' is so defined that only an interpretative theory yields truth conditions, it is trivial that what yields truth conditions fixes meanings.

These terminological points should not be allowed to obscure substantial issues, notably :

(i) According to the common usage of 'truth conditions', stating a sentence's truth conditions involves stating a genuinely necessary and sufficient condition for its truth, where such a statement involves modality, and is, perhaps, initially representable as the result of applying the operator 'necessarily' to a 'T'-sentence.[21] It is trivial that, thus understood, the truth conditions of sentences do not amount to their meanings (for all necessary truths have the same truth conditions). But it is a substantial and controversial contention that the way in which a sentence's truth conditions are fixed by its semantic structure determines its meaning.[22] The issue reduces to that of whether intensional isomorphism is necessarily coextensive with synonymy, which in turn involves the question whether there could be genuinely simple cointensive but non-synonymous expressions.

(ii) One sometimes hears the suggestion that, inextricably bound up with the claim that a Davidsonian truth theory can serve as a theory of meaning is the view that truth can thereby be made to illuminate meaning.[23] Davidson does not advance this view explicitly in 'Truth and Meaning', and the following suggests that he would reject it : 'It may be that the success of our venture depends not on the filling but on what it fills' (309).[24] McDowell explicitly rejects it : 'The concept of truth as such . . . need not figure in the certification of a theory as a theory of sense' ('Bivalence' 146; *cf* 'On the Sense and Reference of a Proper Name' 160). This rejection would also follow from the consideration I advanced in the last section, where it was argued that in a theory which failed to state meanings, the filling of the theory, and even its truth, would drop out as irrelevant. One who would try to use truth, within a theory of meaning, to illuminate meaning, would do best to

opt for the controversial contention of (i). The concept of
meaning would not figure explicitly in a genuine truth conditions
theory, yet it is plausible to argue, if the contention is accepted,
that knowledge of such a theory would suffice for understanding
the language. The contention thus promises an analysis of
meaning in terms of truth together with ancillary notions,
notably modal ones (which might in turn yield to further
analysis).[25]

It is just possible that by using phrases like 'truth conditional
semantics' to apply not only to theories of genuine truth conditions but also to Davidsonian truth theories one would slip into
the error of supposing that in the latter the concept of truth
might reasonably be hoped to illuminate the concept of
meaning.[26]

NOTES

[1] In 'Truth and Meaning', *Synthese vii*, 1967, and subsequent writings:
see in particular 'Radical Interpretation', *Dialectica xxvii*, 1973.

[2] Michael Dummett characterizes a theory of meaning as a theoretical
representation of the practical ability of knowing how to speak the language:
'What is a Theory of Meaning? (II)' 69, in Evans and McDowell, eds.,
Truth and Meaning, Oxford, 1975. John McDowell identifies understanding
a language with the recognitional ability I invoke: 'Understanding a
language consists in the ability to know, when speakers produce utterances
in it, what propositional acts, with what contents, they are performing'
('Truth Conditions, Bivalence and Verificationism', 45, in Evans and
McDowell, *op. cit.* McDowell imposes a structural constraint, but does not
attempt to derive it from the requirement that a theory represent the
recognitional ability.

[3] This claim is implicit in Davidson's 'Truth and Meaning' (317) and
explicit in his 'Radical Interpretation' (313). *Cf* also the editors' introduction to Evans and McDowell, *op. cit. ix,* and John McDowell, 'On
the Sense and Reference of a Proper Name', 159, *Mind lxxxvi*, 1977.

[4] I gloss over the point that my original definition of a theory of meaning
made its pairing theorems apply to sentences, whereas this already presupposes discerning structure in the raw data of utterances, any one of which
may contain many sentences.

[5] P1 would probably have the implausible consequence that something
that would normally be considered a single language would not have a
unique semantic structure.

[6] *Cf* Martin Davies, 'Meaning, Structure and Understanding', forthcoming.

[7] 'Truth Definitions and Actual Languages', 170, in Evans and McDowell,
op. cit.

[8] Gareth Evans, in 'Identity and Predication', *Journal of Philosophy
lxxii*, 1975, argues convincingly that consideration of the obligation to
uncover structure would require an interpreter to discern an ontology of

rabbits in a case in which, were the obligation neglected, full Quinean indeterminacy would reign.

⁹ Evans and McDowell, in their editorial introduction to *Truth and Meaning*, express a preference for an extensional theory, but do not attempt to justify it. John Foster's 'Meaning and Truth Theory', in Evans and McDowell, *op. cit.*, contains an argument for the preference which I discuss below. *Cf* Mark Platts, *Ways of Meaning*, Routledge and Kegan Paul, 1978 (53, 55). Davidson's preference for extensionality in 'Truth and Meaning' would appear to be founded more on (unstated) technical grounds than on grounds of increased insight. In this paper I do not consider technical justifications for extensionality, but I know of no good ones. For a non-extensional theory see, e.g. John Wallace, 'Logical form, Meaning, Translation', in Guenthner and Guenthner-Reutter, *Meaning and Translation*, Duckworth 1978.

¹⁰ This definition of extensionality is crude. For example, Frege's semantic theory can justly be called extensional, in virtue of its preservation of the principle that only the reference which, in that context, the referring parts of a sentence have, bears on the reference of the sentence as a whole. But no more refined notion is required for the present discussion.

¹¹ John McDowell takes the first option in his 'Truth Conditions, Bivalence and Verificationism' 45–7 and esp. n 14. John Foster takes the second option in his 'Meaning and Truth Theory'. A quite different version of the second option is available to one who accepts Davidson's paratactic analysis, as I point out shortly below.

¹² *Op. cit.* 6.

¹³ 'On Saying That', in Davidson and Hintikka, eds., *Words and Objections: Essays on the Work of W. V. Quine*, Hingham, Mass., 1969.

¹⁴ *Op. cit.* 6.

¹⁵ The conception is faulty only against the background assumption that either the philosophical account of meaning involves no reduction of that concept, or else the reduction occurs not in the theory of meaning but in the account of what it is for a theory of meaning to be correct. Foster's own position is best seen as one which rejects this assumption, and aims to reduce meaning to intensional structure, within a theory of meaning (*cf* Postscript below). This aim would of course be thwarted by the explicit occurrence of the concept of meaning in the theory of meaning.

¹⁶ *Op. cit.* 19.

¹⁷ In 'Truth Conditions, Bivalence and Verificationism' (46) John McDowell makes this last inference rest on the claim that ' "*p*" is true' says the same as '*p*'. But the claim is false, as can be seen from the fact that one could know that *p* without knowing that '*p*' is true, and know that '*p*' is true without knowing that *p*. Fortunately the inference does not require this falsehood, but only the truth that ' "*p*" is true (in L)' has the same truth value as '*p*' has (in L).

¹⁸ McDowell implies that the hankering is groundless: 'On the Sense and Reference of a Proper Name' 161.

¹⁹ McDowell, 'Truth Conditions, Bivalence and Verificationism' 47.

²⁰ McDowell, 'On the Sense and Reference of a Proper Name' 161.

²¹ *Cf* Foster, *op. cit.* 11.

²² Commitment to this contention can inhabit quite different formal semantic frameworks. Compare e.g. Foster, *op. cit.* sc IV; David Lewis, 'General Semantics', in Davidson and Harman, eds., *Semantics of Natural Languages*, Dordrecht 1972.

[23] It is not easy to understand Dummett's 'What is a Theory of Meaning? (II)' except as making this association, though of course he goes on to challenge the views he associates.

[24] This is in line with the position of 'Radical Interpretation', which is easily read as placing the whole weight of illumination on the constraints rather than the content of the theory. But it is out of line with the following: 'a theory of truth patterned after a Tarski-type truth definition tells us all we need to know about sense' ('Moods and Performances', in Avishai Margalit, ed., *Meaning and Use* Reidel 1979, 9).

[25] As Foster would hold: *op. cit.*, sc. IV.

[26] This error must be distinguished from the plausible claim that illumination of meaning by truth can be provided by informal accounts.

X*—MATHEMATICAL INTUITION

by Charles Parsons

In a much quoted passage, Gödel writes:

> But, despite their remoteness from sense-experience, we do
> have something like a perception of the objects of set theory,
> as is seen from the fact that the axioms force themselves
> upon us as being true. I don't see any reason why we should
> have less confidence in this kind of perception, i.e. in
> mathematical intuition, than in sense-perception.[1]

If we leave aside its specific reference to set theory, the passage
is a classic expression of what might be called the philosophical
conception of mathematical intuition. As I see it, the principal
mark of this conception is an analogy between sense-perception
as a cognitive relation to the physical world, and "something
like a perception" giving a similar relation to mathematical
objects, and perhaps other abstract entities. If it is to be central
to the philosophy of mathematics, it should play a role like
that of sense-perception in our knowledge of the everyday world
and of physics.

My aim in this paper is to begin a reasoned explication of
this conception. I shall argue that something answering to it
does in fact exist. However, this positive result is very limited
in scope, and we shall already see some limitations of the conception. Unlike Gödel, I shall not focus on set theory, where
the conception of intuition has special difficulties, which I have
discussed elsewhere.[2] One is more likely to make progress by
concentrating on the simplest case, such as elementary geometry
or arithmetic. I shall concentrate on the latter, but look at it
from a somewhat geometric point of view.

I

When Gödel speaks of something like a perception *of* the objects

* Meeting of the Aristotelian Society held at 5/7 Tavistock Place, WC1
on Monday, March 17, 1980 at 6.30 p.m.

K

of set theory, he expresses something central to the conception I am examining: mathematical intuition has a certain *de re* character; it involves a relation of a person to (presumably mathematical) *objects*. The vocabulary of sense-perception contains locutions expressing relations to physical objects or events: *a* sees *x*, *a* hears *x*, *a* smells *x*, *a* perceives *x*, etc. Just how literally this is to be carried over into the concept of mathematical intuition is one of the trickiest questions about it.

For some perceptual verbs, notably "see" and "perceive", we can contrast such object-relational uses with uses with sentence complements, which we can call propositional attitude uses. Which type of use is more fundamental has been controversial, but the *existence* of the object-relational uses is obvious. The matter is otherwise with mathematical intuition, and philosophers have not expressed themselves very clearly on the point. However, we can find both kinds of use in the philosophical literature.[3] To abbreviate reference to the object-relational or propositional attitude use of "intuit", I shall talk of intuition *of* and intuition *that*.

We find some unclarity already in the above-cited passage of Gödel: that there is "something like a perception of the objects of set theory" is, he says, "seen from the fact that the axioms force themselves on us as being true". Here he seems to conclude from the evident character of certain *statements,* which we might express as intuitions *that,* to the existence of intuitions *of*. The premiss may be disputed, but even if it is granted the *inference* seems to be a *non sequitur.* What Gödel says in the next paragraph by way of explanation (and probably qualification) is quite obscure.

Intuition *that* is of course a very traditional rationalistic theme. It might be taken to subsume almost any conception of the evidence or self-evidence of truths of reason, where this is taken not to be derived from habit, practice, or convention. Just for this reason, the analogy with perception does not enter the picture until it is used for an *account* of such rational evidence, or perhaps to mark clearly the distinction between a proposition's being genuinely evident and its merely seeming obviously true. At this point the analogy is likely to be developed in the direction of intuition *of,* simply because the presence of an object is so central to perception.

I suggest that we can find such a picture in Descartes, for whom *clear and distinct perception* is certainly mainly a propositional attitude.[4] Two important philosophers of the past who seem more directly committed to intuition *of* where the objects involved may be mathematical are Kant and Husserl. In Kant, intuition as a propositional attitude plays no explicit role. By definition, an intuition is a singular representation, that is a representation of a single object.[5] When Kant in the *Critique of Pure Reason* says that it is through intuition that knowledge has "immediate relation" to objects (A19 = B33), this immediacy seems to be a direct presence of the object to the mind, as in perception. At all events, intuition gives "immediate evidence" to propositions of, for example, geometry.[6] Thus intuition that seems to be present in Kant, although his official use of "intuition" is only for intuition of.

Husserl's discussions of "categorial intuition" in the *Logische Untersuchungen* and of "intuition of essences" in the *Ideen* represent a sustained and interesting attempt to develop a theory of rational evidence based on an analogy with perception, in which the feature of perception as being of an object is central. Husserl understands rational evidence in general as intuition and undertakes to give a unified account of intuition of and intuition that.

Both Kant's and Husserl's conceptions have had some influence on discussions of the foundations of mathematics in this century. Kant's influence is more visible and pervasive. Hilbert's conception of the intuitive character of finitary mathematics is explicitly based on a Kantian conception of pure intuition, though perhaps more on Kant's theory of geometry than on his theory of arithmetic. Intuitionism also owes much to Kant, particularly to the notion of time as the form of inner sense. Husserl's ideas have not had nearly so much influence, but he did have an impact on Weyl and Gödel.[7]

II

The idea of "something like a perception" of mathematical objects seems at first sight outrageous. If mathematical objects are given to us in a way similar to that in which physical objects are given to our senses, should it not be *obvious* that this is so?

But the history of philosophical discussion about mathematics shows that it is not. Whatever mysteries and philosophical puzzles there may be about perception, it works to a large extent as a straightforward empirical concept. We can make a lot of assured judgements about when we perceive something, and confidence about the description of our experience can often survive doubt about what it is an experience of. Thus the proposition that I now *see* before me a typewriter with paper in it is one that I expect that no other philosopher, were he in this room now, would dispute except on the basis of sceptical arguments, and many of these would not touch weaker statements such as that it *looks* to me as if I see these things. There is a phenomenological datum here that is as close to being undisputed as anything is in philosophy.

It is hard to maintain that the case is the same for mathematical objects. Is it *obvious* that there is an experience of intuiting the number 7, or a triangle, or at least of its "looking" as if I were intuiting 7 or a triangle? Are there any experiences we can appeal to here that are anywhere near as undisputed as my present experience of seeing my typewriter? If we don't know what to point to, isn't that already a serious disanalogy between sense-perception and whatever consciousness we have of mathematical objects?

This embarrassment is connected with an obvious disanalogy. In normal cases of perception, there is a physical action of the object perceived on our sense-organs. Our perception is as it were founded on this action, and there are serious philosophical reasons for holding that such a causal relation is a necessary condition for perceiving an object.[9] It would be implausible to suppose that in *mathematical* intuition there is a causal action of a mathematical object on us (presumably on the mind). Moreover, this is no part of the view of the upholders of mathematical intuition that I have mentioned, though it is sometimes included in popular conceptions of "Platonism".

At this point we find qualifications in accounts of mathematical intuition, which raise the question just how close an analogy with perception is intended. Gödel says that "mathematical intuition need not be conceived of as a faculty giving an *immediate* knowledge of the objects concerned.[9] Husserl is even prepared to call categorial intuition "perception" (*Wahr-*

nehmung),[10] but he contrasts sense-perception as *schlicht*, in which the object is "immediately given", with categorial intuition which is *founded* in other "acts" such as ordinary perceptions and imaginings.[11]

Kant expresses puzzlement about how intuition can be *a priori*. In the *Prolegomena*, after introducing the notion of pure intuition, he writes (§8):

> An intuition is such a representation as would immediately depend on the presence (*Gegenwart*) of the object. Hence it seems impossible to intuit spontaneously (*ursprünglich*) *a priori* because intuition would in that event have to take place without either a former or a present object to refer to, and in consequence could not be an intuition . . . But how can the intuition of an object precede the object itself?[12]

Here (and elsewhere) Kant does not explicitly express a view about intuition of *mathematical* objects. It is clear from the context that by "object" he means *real* object, in practice physical object. So the question is how it is possible for a priori intuition to be "of" physical objects that are not given a priori.

In §9 Kant claims that the puzzle is resolved by the fact that a priori intuition contains only the form of our sensibility. It is a nice question just what this does to the characterization of intuition that gives rise to the puzzle. Clearly, in the a priori case, the causal dependence of the intuition on the object has to go. Whether and how the *phenomenological* presence of an object is preserved is a further question, as is the question whether the object thus present is a physical or a purely mathematical object. The former is not ruled out by the a priori character of pure intuition, since the "presence" might be that characteristic of *imagination* rather than sense. In fact, a number of passages in Kant indicate that just that is his position.

We might find a difficulty for the idea of intuition of mathematical objects in what, following Leibniz, might be called their incompleteness. I do not need to go into this much, because it has been much discussed, not least by me.[13] The properties and relations of mathematical objects that play a role in mathematical reasoning are those determined by the basic relations of some system or structure to which all the objects involved belong, such as the natural numbers, Euclidean or some other space, a given group, field, or other such structure, or the universe of sets or some model thereof. It seems that the properties and relations of mathematical objects about which there is a "fact of the matter" are either in some way expressible in terms of the basic relations of this structure or else are "external relations" which are independent of the choice of a system of objects to realize the structure.

Consider for example the natural numbers, with o and the successor function S as giving the relevant structure (perhaps with other functions such as addition, if we give ourselves no second-order apparatus). Examples of the former type are number-theoretic properties such as being prime or being the sum of four squares. External relations include those arising in counting other objects, and such properties as being believed by me to be prime. Such relations will not in general be definable in the language of number theory, even higher-order, but they are in general definable in terms of the basic relations and others that do not depend on the choice of a system of objects and relations to realize the structure.

Now the question is, is, how can mathematical intuition place objects "before our minds" when these objects are not identifiable individually at all? For example, unless one is presupposing a structure including numbers and sets, it seems indeterminate whether the number 2 is identical to the one-element set $\{\{\Lambda\}\}$, the two-element set $\{\Lambda, \{\Lambda\}\}$, or neither.[14] How can this be if numbers and sets are objects of mathematical intuition? Can such intuition be a significant source of mathematical knowledge if it does not determine the answers to such simple questions?

One could press the matter further and urge the possibility of an interpretation of mathematics which dispenses with distinctively mathematical objects. One such possibility is a nominalistic reconstrual of such objects. Another, more promising as an approach to the whole of mathematics, is a modal interpretation of quantifiers in which, roughly, statements of the existence of a mathematical object satisfying some condition are rendered as statements of the *possible* existence of an object satisfying purely structural conditions.[15]

These difficulties are at bottom one. What is really essential to mathematical objects is the relations constituting the structure to which they belong. Accordingly, in the end there is no objective ground for preferring one realization over another as "the" intended domain of objects, in particular for rejecting concrete (nominalistic) realizations if they are available. Moreover, actual, as opposed to merely possible, realization of a structure adds nothing mathematically relevant. Both these points need *some* qualification, first because often actually given realizations of a structure presuppose some more comprehensive structure, such as the natural numbers or sets, and because in discussions of potential totalities, something like a distinction between actual and potential existence can be made. However, the exactly right way to put these points need not concern us here.

III

I propose to show that there is at least a limited application of the notion of mathematical intuition *of* which is able to meet these objections. First, let us review briefly the reasons why one might introduce the concept. Intuition *that* becomes a persuasive idea when one reflects on the obviousness of elementary truths of mathematics. Two alternative views have had influential advocates in this century: conventionalism, the view that at least some mathematical propositions are true by convention, and a form of empiricism according to which mathematics is continuous with science, and the axioms of mathematics have a status similar to that of high-level theoretical hypotheses. Both these views have unattractive features. Conventionalism has been much criticized, and I need not repeat the criticisms here.

The empiricist view, even in the subtle and complex form it takes in the work of Professor Quine, seems subject to the objection that it leaves unaccounted for precisely the *obviousness* of elementary mathematics (and perhaps also of logic). It seeks to meet the difficulties of early empiricist views of mathematics by assimilating mathematics to the theoretical part of science. But there are great differences: first, the "topic-neutrality" of logic, which receives considerable recognition in Quine's writings, although he insists that it depends on a specification of the logical constants that is at bottom arbitrary; second, the very close connection of mathematics and logic, where the potential field of application of mathematics is as wide as that of logic, in spite of the fact that the existence of mathematical objects makes mathematics not strictly topic-neutral; third, the existence of very general principles that are universally regarded as obvious, where on an empiricist view one would expect them to be bold hypotheses, about which a prudent scientist would maintain reserve, keeping in mind that experience might not bear them out; fourth, the fact that differences about logic and elementary mathematics, such as the issues raised by intuitionism, are naturally explained as differences about *meaning*. Quine recognizes this by the role that logic plays in his theory of translation, but the obviousness of logic is an unexamined premiss of that theory.

Some version of the pre-Quinean view of logic as true by virtue of meaning may be the most promising way of addressing the difficulties of the Quinean view of *logic*. There is no a priori reason why the conception of intuition we are examining should play a role in working out such a view. In the case of arithmetic, the situation is different because unlike logic, it has ontological commitments. That a structure such as the natural numbers should exist, or at least should be *possible* in some mathematically relevant way, is hard to make out as true by virtue of the meanings of arithmetical or other expressions.

Just at this point, the idea of intuition *of* suggests itself. We are taking as a gross fact about arithmetic, that a considerable body of arithmetical truths is known to us in some more direct way than is the case for the knowledge we acquire by empirical reasoning. And this knowledge takes the form of truths about certain objects—the natural numbers. What is more natural than the hypothesis that we have direct knowledge of these truths because the objects they are about are given to us in some direct way? The model we offer of this givenness is the manner in which a physical body is given to us in perception.

IV

As applied to the natural numbers, this picture is oversimplified. However, I propose to meet the difficulties by a strategy suggested by Kant's conception of pure intuition as giving the *form* of empirical intuition and by Husserl's thesis that categorial intuition is *founded* on sensible intuition. The quasi-perceptual manner in which mathematical objects can be given to us is in a certain way exemplified by situations of *ordinary* perception *or imagination* of realizations (sometimes partial) of the structures involved.

Elsewhere I presented an account of arithmetical intuition.[16] However, the presentation was tied to a modal interpretation of quantifiers, and the idea was intended to have greater generality. The following exposition is intended to make some other aspects of the earlier account more explicit.

It is well to follow Hilbert and to begin by considering the "syntax" of a "language" with a single basic symbol "|" (stroke), whose well-formed expressions are just arbitrary strings containing just this symbol, i.e. |, ||, |||, . . . This sequence of strings is isomorphic to the natural numbers, if one takes "|" as 0 and the operation of adding one more "|" on the right as the successor operation. This yields an interpretation of arithmetic as a kind of geometry of strings of strokes. At first sight the interpretation leaves out the concept of *number,* that is the role of natural numbers as cardinals and ordinals.

Ordinary perception of a string of strokes would have to be perception of a *token,* but we naturally think of such symbols as types. Beginning with the notion of a token being *a* stroke, we can recast the explanation of the stroke-language in such a way that types are not presupposed as objects. Two strings are "of the same type" if they *can* be placed side by side so that strokes correspond one-to-one.[17] The use of "can" in the criterion for sameness of type may be nonessential; someone, such as an actualist nominalist, could argue that some other type of empirical test is sufficient, or he might appeal to an inductive definition : two strings are of the same type if they are both single strokes, or if the strings consisting of all but the rightmost stroke in each are of the same type. However, shortly we shall face a much stronger temptation to use modality.

That one can go this far (and indeed much farther) in doing syntax nominalistically is not news. What is less widely appreciated is that we have here the basis of an explanation of types, which first of all makes them no more mysterious than other objects, in spite of their "abstractness", and secondly makes it quite reasonable to say that they are *given* in a way analogous to that in which middle-sized physical objects are given. Indeed ordinary language recognizes this, in that we speak of hearing or seeing *words* and s*entences,* where what is clearly meant are types.

Of course a perception of a string of stroke-tokens is not by itself an "intuition" of a stroke-string type. One has to approach it with the *concept* of a type, first of all to have the capacity to recognize other tokens as of the same type or not. Something more than the mere capacity is involved, which might be described as seeing something *as* the type. But this much is present in ordinary perception as well. One can of course see an object without recognizing it as this or that, but when it does occur such recognition is part of normal perception, and when one sees an object one at least recognizes it under *some* description that permits reidentification.

One might object that in the case of ordinary perception, the *Auffassung* as an object, even of a particular kind, is entirely spontaneous and natural, whereas what I want to call "intuiting" a symbol-type is a conscious exercise of a conceptual apparatus which may be quite artificial. I agree that this may be true in this case and is certainly true in some. However, in some cases, taking what is given as a type is quite spontaneous and natural. The most obvious is the understanding of natural language : the hearer is without reflection ready to reidentify the type (in the linguistic, not the acoustic sense). Typically, the hearer of an utterance has a more explicit conception of *what was uttered* (e.g. what words) than he has of an objective identification of the *event* of the utterance.[18] I believe that the same is true of some other kinds of universals, such as sense-qualities and shapes.[19] Indeed, in all these cases it seems not to violate ordinary language to talk of perception of the universal *as an object,* where an instance of it is present. This is not just an overblown way of talking of perceiving an instance *as* an instance (e.g. seeing something red *as* being red), because the identification of the universal can be firmer and more explicit than the identification of the object that is an instance of it.

These observations should begin to dispel the widespread

impression that mathematical intuition is a "special" faculty, which perhaps comes into play only in doing pure mathematics. At least one type of essentially mathematical intuition, of symbol- and expression-types, is perfectly ordinary and recognized as such by ordinary language. If a positive account of mathematical intuition is to get anywhere, it has to make clear, as its advocates intended, that mathematical intuition is not an isolated epistemological concept, to be applied only to pure mathematics, but must be so closely related to the concepts by which we describe perception and our knowledge of the physical world that the "faculty" involved will be seen to be at work when one is not consciously doing mathematics.

V

The preceding discussion indicates that we should be careful in talking, with Husserl, of "intuition" of a type as founded on perception of a token. In ordinary cases there will be perception in the full sense, which requires physical presence and action on the senses. Ordinary talk of hearing *words* normally carries this implication. In many cases the token will be pushed into the background by the type, but that does not make the former not an object of perception. However, even in normal cases the background and further experience that are necessary to the perception's being of something physically *real* are irrelevant to its being of the *form* given by the type. In most cases, physical reality is important not for taking in the type, but for further considerations: what is likely to be of interest about the words is that they were spoken by a speaker at a certain time, or stand written in a certain book.

Perceptions and imaginings, as founding such intuitions, play a paradigmatic role. It is through this that intuition of a type can give rise to propositional knowledge about the type, i.e. intuition *that*. A simple case is singular propositions about types, such as that ||| is the successor of ||. We see this to be true on the basis of a single intuition, but of course in its implications for tokens it is a general proposition. Let a be the token of ||| above; let b be the token of || above; the statement implies that if c and d are respectively of the same type as a and $b,$ then c consists of a part of the same type as b, and one additional stroke on the right. We can of course buttress the statement that $|||$ is the successor of $||$ by considering arbitrary tokens of the relevant types and verifying the above consequence. But we have to verify it in the same way, by instances that we take as paradigmatic. This situation is not peculiar to our artificial framework. The same is true of calculations done on paper and of formal proofs, such as the deductions done in elementary logic courses.

A more problematic situation arises when we consider general propositions about *types*, which have in their scope indefinitely many *different* types. It is this which prompts us to follow Husserl in saying that sometimes *imagination* of the token can found intuition of the type. Consider for example the assertion that each string of strokes *can* be extended by one more. This is the weakest expression of the idea that our "language" is potentially infinite. But we cannot convince ourselves of it by perception or by the kind of mathematical intuition we have talked about so far, founded on actual perception. But if we imagine any string of strokes, it is immediately apparent that a new stroke can be added. One might imagine the string as a *Gestalt*, present all at once : then since it is a figure with a surrounding ground, there is space for an additional stroke. However, this may not be the right way to look at the matter, since the imagination of an *arbitrary* string in this way will have to leave inexplicit its articulation into single strokes. Alternatively, we can think of the string as constructed step by step, so that the essential element is now succession in *time*, and what is then evident is that at any stage one can take another step.

Either way, one has to imagine *an arbitrary string of strokes*. We have a problem akin to that of Locke's general triangle. If one imagines a string in a specific way, one will imagine a string with a specific number of strokes, and therefore not a perfectly arbitrary string. There seems to be a choice between imagining *vaguely*, that is imagining a string of strokes without imagining its internal structure clearly enough so that one is imagining a string of n strokes for some particular n, or taking as paradigm a string (which now might be perceived rather than imagined) of a particular number of strokes, in which case one must be able to see the irrelevance of this internal structure, so that in fact it plays the same role as the vague imagining.

We naturally think of perception as at least sometimes uncorrupted by thinking, in that without conscious thinking one can take in some aspect of the environment and respond to it, and one can take a stance toward one's perceptions that is largely noncommittal with respect to the judgements we would ordinarily be prepared to make. However that may be, it is clear that the kind of *Gedankenexperimente* I have been describing can be taken as intuitive verifications of such statements as that any string of strokes can be extended only if one carries them out on the basis of specific concepts, such as that of a string of strokes. If that were not so, they would not confer any generality.

Brouwer may have been trying to meet this difficulty, in a special case of this sort, with his concept of two-one-ness, according to which the activity of consciousness brings about "the falling apart of a life-moment into two qualitatively distinct things", of which the moment then present retains the structure of the original, so that the resulting "temporal two-ity" can be taken as a term of a new two-ity, giving rise to temporal three-ity.[20] Thus the process can always give rise to a new moment, which for Brouwer is the foundation for the infinity of the natural numbers. One has something similar in the figure-ground structure of perception, which was appealed to above. However, in all versions we think of whatever step it is as one that *can be iterated indefinitely*. In a sense this is given by the fact that after the step of "adding one more" one has essentially the same structure. But a concept such as that of a *string* of strokes involves the notion of such iteration. To spell that out, we are led into the circle of ideas surrounding mathematical induction. Although the view has been attributed to Brouwer that "iteration" is the fundamental intuition of mathematics, my view is that the particular concept of intuition I am explicating runs out at this point, and it is only in a weaker and less clear sense that mathematical induction is a deliverance of intuition.

Although the concept of a string of strokes involves iteration, the proposition that every such string can be extended is not an inductive conclusion. A proof of it by induction would be

158CHARLES PARSONS

circular. Such a proof would be called for only if we really
needed the fact that every string of strokes can be obtained by
iterated application of the operation of adding one more. In
fact, I think the matter is thus: we have a structure of perception, a "form of intuition" if you will, which has the essential
feature of Brouwer's two-one-ness, that however the idea of
"adding one more" is interpreted, we still have an instance
of the same structure. But to see the *possibility* of adding one
more, it is only the general structure that we use, and not the
specific fact that what we have before us was obtained by
iterated additions of one more. This is shown by the fact that
in the same sense in which a new stroke can be added to any
string of strokes, it can be added to any bounded geometric
configuration.

VI

It should be clear that we do not acquire in this way any
reason to believe it *physically possible* to extend any string of
strokes. At most the structure of space and time is at stake here,
and physical possibility requires something more, whatever
makes the difference between the space of pure geometry and
the physical universe, consisting at least of space containing
matter. Actually we require less than the space of pure geometry,
since even if we do hold to the spatiality of the strokes (which
perhaps we can avoid), only very crude properties of space are
appealed to, in particular not its metric properties.

We can call the possibility in question *mathematical possibility;* this expresses the fact that we are not thinking of the
capabilities of the human organism, and it may even be extra-
neous to think of this "construction" as an act of the *mind*.
The latter construal agrees with the viewpoint of Kant and
Brouwer. It is very tempting if we want to say that any string
of strokes is *perceptible* or *imaginable*. (It is preferable to reserve
these words for tokens, but then one can speak of the *intuit-
ability* of the type.) The idea is that no matter how many times
the operation of constructing one more stroke in imagination
has been repeated, "we" can still construct one more. However,
I think there is really a hidden assumption that there is no
constraint on what "we" can perceive beyond the open tem-

porality of these experiences, and some very gross aspects of spatial structure. Kant and Brouwer thought these were contributions of our minds to the way we experience the world. Kant of course thought that we could not know these things *a priori* unless our minds had contributed them. I am not persuaded by this, and in any case I do not want my argument to rest on the notion of *a priori* knowledge. If we express the *content* of the proposition in a way as independent as possible of the description of the insight, then it is just that for an arbitrary string of strokes, it is possible that there should be one that extends it by one stroke.

The nominalist seems to demand both more and less than we do. He may try to get on without even the potential infinity of a sequence like that of stroke-string-types, but then he will have to do without the infinity of the natural numbers. His position is really the embarrassing one that Russell found himself in about the axiom of infinity. He can treat it as an hypothesis to whose truth he is not committed, but then mathematics allows the possibility that where we have proved by ordinary mathematical means a proposition B, we are not entitled to reject its negation, since, where A is the relevant axiom of infinity, if A is false both $A \rightarrow B$ and $A \rightarrow \sim B$ are true.

Alternatively, he may accept as an empirical hypothesis some proposition entailing the existence in space and time of a ω-sequence such as a sequence of tokens of stroke-strings, each one extending the previous one.[21] Since he is talking about physical existence, he is making a stronger claim than we do, which mathematics does not need. (He could be a traditional empiricist and discern such a sequence in some phenomenal field, but on empiricist grounds this seems very questionable, and it has the same mathematically irrelevant strength.) Such an hypothesis clearly has a theoretical character, and it might even be rejected if physics were to evolve in such a way that space-time came to be understood as both finite and discrete. Any reason we have for believing it depends on the historically given physics, constructed in tandem with an arithmetic with an infinity of numbers.

A third position which might be called nominalistic is one alluded to above : one continues to hold that in strict usage one should talk only of tokens; the relation *same type* is available but is understood as just a useful equivalence relation, not the foundation of identity of types; and one meets the problem of the potential infinity of types by a modal interpretation of quantifiers.[22] Earlier I gave some reasons for denying this view the title of nominalist,[23] but although I still hold to them I would now say that the question whether it *is* nominalist is in the end terminological. So long as we stay short of set theory and other impredicative mathematics, and the modality involved is mathematical possibility, the position is not importantly different from my own. However, the latter qualification is important. If the modal theory of tokens is understood as a theory of physical tokens, and the modality is physical, then I think the view faces the same difficulties as the actualist forms of nominalism.

VII

I now turn to the question whether our conception of an intuition of types faces serious objections because of the timelessness, acausality, or incompleteness of types as abstract entities. Stroke-string-types and other such expressions are minimally abstract, since they are types of tokens which are concrete. Our intuitions of them are founded on sense-experience or on imaginings which imagine their objects as in space and time, even if not at any particular location. The timelessness of types is simply universality: since they can be instantiated anywhere, they are understood as located nowhere. Because the existence of a type depends on the possibility of a token, they cannot be understood as mereological sums. The *problem* about the timelessness of types is really epistemological: how can we know truths about types by a certain kind of perception of tokens, which are then valid for *any* tokens of the types involved. In my remarks above, I have done little more than try to make clear that we *do* have such knowledge. More explanation should be given, though some experience tends to show that explanations of such matters are always in the end question-begging. Observe, however, that the problem is not created by an ontology of types. On the nominalistic views I have mentioned, there is also a question about knowledge of the general truths about tokens that are the nominalistic versions of the truths about types.

It might be questioned whether types are acausal after all; for example, I might say, "His words made me furious." Suppose he said, "You have no right to call yourself a philosopher." But in fact we do not think of the *sentence* as making me furious (and not just because of the indexicality of this particular example). Nor do we attribute the effect to the proposition expressed, although that might be more plausible in this case. It is much more natural to attribute the effect to the event of his saying the words, or his expressing that proposition, on the occasion on which he did. This preserves the acausality of the sentence, but its relation to causality is like its relation to space and time. Its tokens are caught up in the causal nexus, and indeed affect our senses. Once we see the relation between intuition of types and ordinary perception, I think this difficulty rather dissolves. However, an objector may be thinking of Benacerraf's dilemma (note 12). To deal with this requires a longer story than I can tell now.

About incompleteness, one might first think that the closeness to the concrete of such abstract objects as strings of strokes would make them *not* incomplete. For example, it would be simply false that $|||$ is identical with an object given in some other way, say the number 3. $|||$ has some properties 3 lacks, such as that it is composed of strokes. Another problem is cognitive relations, including *de re* propositional attitudes; if I see on a blackboard the formula "$\forall x\, (x \neq 0 \to \exists y\, (x = Sy))$", I do not see the number that corresponds to it under some arithmetization of the syntax of first-order arithmetic.

I suggest the following explanation. What is basic to the concept of type gives identity and difference relations only to other types in the same system of symbols. (Two inscriptions may be of the same type with respect to one symbolism and not with respect to another.) Since this is a distinctive feature of what types *are,* common sense tends to treat the types of a given symbolism as *sui generis,* so that none is identical with anything given in some other way. In one sense this resolves the incompleteness, since it determines all predicates (at least from the point of view of classical logic), but in a negative way: all atomic predicates except those from the structure and those expressing the basic facts about its instantiation, are

L

false. But this inclination of common sense does not correspond to a feature of the nature of things, at least not to one that cannot be overridden when it comes to the regimentation of language.

However, this kind of consideration does show a significant disanalogy between this kind of mathematical intuition and ordinary perception. *What is intuited* depends on the concept brought to the situation by the subject. In some cases, such as natural language, the concepts involved may be innate or develop more or less spontaneously and unreflectively. In the more characteristically mathematical cases of geometric figures and the sort of artificial symbolism we have been discussing, this is not so. Therefore we do not have the scope that we have with ordinary perception for identifying the object of intuition independently of the subject's conceptual resources. If someone feels heat, and heat is the motion of molecules, then he feels something that is the motion of molecules. If we are using "feel" in an object-relational way, he feels the motion of those molecules, even if he has no conception of molecules. But no one could intuit a stroke-string-type unless he saw it *as* a type constructed from strokes, and this requires that he have the concept of stroke. If, in regimenting our theory, we identify ||| with the number 3, then perhaps we can say that he is intuiting 3, although he may have no idea that that is what he is doing. But we can only say that because he has *some* identifying concept. There is probably an ordinary concept of perception for which this holds as well, but it does not obviously hold for the most ordinary object-relational uses of "see", "hear", and perhaps "feel".[24]

VIII

Our investigation so far has reached a significant positive result. It is quite permissible to say that types of perceptible tokens are objects of intuition, where the concept of intuition involved is strongly analogous to that of perception. Moreover, we can represent some propositions about these objects as known intuitively.

This result is of very limited scope. Even though they form a model of arithmetic, from a mathematical point of view strings of strokes are rather special objects. The perception-like character of what we call intuition of types may be thought to be due to the closeness to perception of the objects involved. Perhaps our concept of mathematical intuition will not carry us beyond elementary syntax and maybe traditional geometry. Are we prepared to say, for example, that the *natural numbers* are objects of intuition?

I have to deal with this question more briefly than I would like. Our discussion so far suggests a moderate position: intuition gives objects which form a model of arithmetic, and this model is as good as any both for the foundations of arithmetic and for applications. But it may not be right to say that *the* natural numbers are objects of intuition, since intuition does not give a unique sequence to be "the" natural numbers, and the concept of number does not rule out as the "intended model" objects that are not objects of intuition.

However, we should try to come to terms with the higher-order aspects of the concepts of cardinal and ordinal number. I shall restrict myself to cardinal number. The formulation of a statement of number requires an operation on predicates, either a numerical quantifier like "there are n x's such that Fx" or a term-forming operation like "the number of x's such that Fx". This point, however, imposes no constraint at all on what kind of objects the natural numbers are. We should resist the temptation to identify the numbers with the numerical quantifiers themselves (as "second-level concepts" or the like) as well as the subtler temptation, to which Frege succumbed, to try to find an object that represents the numerical quantifier in an especially intrinsic way.

A more serious matter is that apparently the truth-conditions for statements of number must incorporate the Fregean criterion for sameness of number: the number of F's is the same as the number of G's if and only if *there is a one-to-one correspondence of the F's and the G's.*

We might seek to accommodate this in a way which makes numbers objects of intuition by understanding numbers as a kind of generalized types, in which the tokens are numeral-tokens serving as counters.[25] The relation playing the role of sameness of type is that of "representing the same number". Since what is involved in this relation is what is involved in *counting,* observe that verifying by counting that there are *n* *x*'s such that *Fx* involves exhibiting a one-to-one correspondence between the F's and a sequence of *n* "counters"—standardly numerals. If the predicate "*F*" is simple enough and the objects are objects of perception, "there are *n* *F*'s" can be verified by perception. We do not have to take it as *saying* that there *is* such a correspondence between the *F*'s and the counters. But it does in some way imply it, and in order to establish the elements of number we do have to reason about such correspondences.

For arithmetic, however, the correspondences we need are finite. I will assume that *finite sets* of objects of intuition are themselves objects of intuition. Space does not permit defending that assumption here. What I want to observe is that from it follows what is needed to justify the claim that the natural numbers, considered as "numbering" objects of intuition, are objects of intuition. Two numerals *a* and *b*, perhaps from different notation systems, represent the same number if there is a one-one correspondence of the numerals up to *a* and those up to *b*. Our assumption implies that this does not involve reference except to objects of intuition.

However, this approach would suggest that arithmetic, as applied to objects *in general,* belongs to set theory. We could still say in this context that finite numbers are objects of intuition, on the ground that for the constitution of numbers as objects this full generality is not needed. However, the general principles of cardinal and ordinal number, applied to arbitrary sets, even arbitrary (possibly not hereditarily) finite sets, will not be intuitive knowledge unless sets in general are objects of intuition. I have not tried to argue that they are.

Before we end this paper, we must say something about mathematical induction, which arises already for strings of strokes. I have not said much about our understanding of what an arbitrary string of strokes, or an arbitrary natural number, is. However this understanding should surely yield the relevant induction principle. What bearing does this have on our remarks on intuition?

Let us concentrate on the more intuitive case of strings of strokes. In such a case, the conclusion of an inference by induction is a general statement about objects of intuition. It does not follow that it is therefore intuitive knowledge. There is a temptation to call our understanding of the general notion of a string of strokes an intuition, because it is clear and seems to make inductive inferences evident.[26] However, this would have to be a different, and in this context potentially confusing, sense of "intuition", since what is involved is the understanding of a general term; this does not give any *object*.[27]

Because of the essential way in which this understanding is used, I am inclined to deny that even very simple inductive conclusions are intuitive knowledge. Gödel, however, in discussing a distinction between intuitive and abstract evidence, uses another criterion.[28] His line is drawn where one begins to refer to what he calls "abstract objects", by which he means statements and proofs.[29] I do not deny that this is also an important distinction. Moreover, I do not claim to have shown that his terminology is inappropriate. More needs to be said about the epistemological aspects of the concept of intuition, even the very limited concept that I have developed, than I have said in this paper.

NOTES

The author is a Fellow of the National Endowment for the Humanities and a Visiting Fellow of All Souls College, Oxford. He wishes to record his gratitude to both these institutions.

1 "What is Cantor's continuum problem?" in Paul Benacerraf and Hilary Putnam (eds.), *Philosophy of Mathematics: Selected Readings,* Prentice-Hall, Englewood Cliffs, N. J., 1964, p. 271. This passage and others cited below are from a supplement added to this edition of the paper, which first appeared in 1947.

2 "What is the iterative conception of set?" in R. E. Butts and Jaakko Hintikka (eds.), *Logic, Foundations of Mathematics, and Computability Theory,* Reidel, Dordrecht, 1977, at pp. 339–45.

3 The relevance of the distinction to mathematical intuition is pointed out by Mark Steiner in *Mathematical Knowledge,* Cornell, Ithaca, 1975, p. 131. Steiner maintains that no one would defend object-relational mathematical intuition. That seems to me clearly false.

4 Descartes seems to rely on perception of in his explanations, for example the explanation of clarity in *Principles,* I, 40.

5 *Logic,* §1 (Academy edition, IX, 91).

6 My interpretation of the immediacy of intuition in relation to *objects* is controversial. See my "Kant's philosophy of arithmetic," in S. Morgenbesser, P. Suppes, and M. White (eds.), *Philosophy, Science, and Method: Essays in honor of Ernest Nagel,* St. Martin's Press, New York, 1969, esp. pp. 569–71, and Jaakko Hintikka, "Kantian intuitions," *Inquiry* 15 (1972),

341–345. However, I do not see how there could be controversy about the fact that according to Kant intuition (in particular *a priori* intuition) confers *evidence* that is immediate. *This* immediacy can surely not be reduced to singularity, as Hintikka proposes for the other dimension of immediacy.

[7] Concerning Hilbert, Gödel writes, "What Hilbert means by 'Anschauung' is substantially Kant's space-time intuition confined, however, to configurations of a finite number of discrete objects." From note (h) added to "On an extension of finitary mathematics which has not yet been used," unpublished English translation, emended by the author with some additional notes, of "Ueber eine noch nicht benützte Erweiterung des finiten Standpunktes," *Dialectica* 12 (1958), 280–287. As if to stress the difference with the notion of intuition in "What is Cantor's continuum problem?" the term "Anschauung" is translated as "concrete intuition".

The aspect of intuitionism which was most original and may have proved most fruitful, seeing the meaning of a mathematical statement as constituted by what would be a proof of it, does not seem to owe its inspiration to Kant. In recent discussions of the foundations of intuitionism, the very concept of intuition seems to drop out.

[8] In attempting to develop an analogy between perception and knowledge of abstract objects, Husserl is helped by his phenomenological perspective. The causal foundation of perception is not part of the subject matter of phenomenology, even in the form it takes in the *Logische Untersuchungen* (hereafter LU). Husserl does undertake to show that in categorial intuition there is something analogous to sensations in sense-perception. In my view, he lapses into obscurity in explaining this (LU, VI, §56). I am not sure to what extent this can be cleared up.

[9] "What is Cantor's continuum problem?" p. 271.

[10] LU VI, §45.

[11] *Ibid.*, §46.

[12] Kant's puzzle is related to the dilemma about mathematical truth posed by Paul Benacerraf in "Mathematical truth," *The Journal of Philosophy* 70 (1973), 661–679: according to Benacerraf, our best theory of mathematical *truth* (Tarski's) involves postulating mathematical objects, while our best account of *knowledge* requires causal relations of the objects of knowledge to us; but mathematical objects are acausal.

One can present Kant's problem as a similar dilemma: Mathematical truth requires applicability to the physical world. But our best account of mathematical knowledge makes it rest on intuition, which requires the prior presence of the object. But this contradicts the *a priori* character of mathematics.

This is of interest because it is a form of the dilemma that does not require that the semantics of mathematics involve mathematical objects (which it seems one might avoid by a modal interpretation of quantifiers). But of course it depends on other assumptions, in particular that mathematics is *a priori*.

[13] "Frege's theory of number," in Max Black (ed.), *Philosophy in America*, Allen and Unwin, London, 1965; "Ontology and mathematics," *Philosophical Review* 80 (1971), 151–176, at pp. 154–7; "Quine on the philosophy of mathematics," in P. A. Schilpp (ed.), *The Philosophy of W. V. Quine*, to appear. Among others see esp. Paul Bernays, "Mathematische Existenz und Widerspruchsfreiheit" (1950), in *Abhandlungen zur Philosophie der Mathematik*, Wissenschaftliche Buchgesellschaft, Darmstadt, 1976; and Paul

Benacerraf, "What numbers could not be," *Philosophical Review 74* (1965), 47–73.

14 The first follows from Zermelo's proposal for a set-theoretic construal of numbers, the second from von Neumann's, the third if set theory takes the natural numbers as individuals.

15 Hilary Putnam, "Mathematics without foundations," *The Journal of Philosophy* 84 (1967), 5–22; my "Ontology and mathematics," pp. 158–64; Charles Chihara, *Ontology and the Vicious Circle Principle*, Cornell, Ithaca, 1973, p. 191.

Applied to arithmetic and other more elementary parts of mathematics, the modal interpretation of quantifiers may serve to defuse scruples about abstract objects. In "Quine on the philosophy of mathematics," I argue that this it not the case for higher set theory.

16 "Ontology and mathematics," section III.

17 *Ibid.*, pp. 159–60, to which I refer the reader for details.

18 Of course when we talk of what was uttered, and even more of what was *said,* this is often best understood in a way that invites regimentation in terms of *propositions.* One might then offer a similar argument for the claim that propositions are objects of intuition. However, such considerations cannot get us past the well-known doubts about the objectivity of propositions. A response to an auditory stimulus can count as intuition of a *sentence* because we can attribute to the hearer a reasonably sharp concept of *same sentence.*

19 Such a view is not necessarily incompatible with all versions of nominalism. The British empiricists sometimes understood sense-qualities as universals, but admitted them as "simple ideas" rather than "abstract ideas". Similarly the *qualia* admitted by Nelson Goodman in *The Structure of Appearance* (Harvard, Cambridge, Mass., 1951) are universals. Neither on the empiricist's view, nor Goodman's, nor on the view I suggest should sense-qualities be understood as a kind of *attribute* in the sense of something denoted by a nominalized predicate.

20 L. E. J. Brouwer, *Collected Works*, vol. I, ed. A. Heyting, North Holland, Amsterdam, 1975, p. 417 (from 1929). Cf. p. 17 (from 1907), p. 480 (1948), and p. 510 (1952).

21 This is, for example, entailed by the position of Hartry Field's interesting *Science without Numbers*, Blackwell, Oxford, forthcoming. His main project is to interpret physics in an extension of synthetic geometry, in which the variables range over points and regions of space-time, which he asserts to be physical. A model of arithmetic can certainly be constructed in his theory.

22 Chihara (see note 15), p. 191; "Ontology and mathematics," pp. 160–2. In the latter, the last two lines of p. 160 are ambiguous. One way of taking it would be to say that "∃xFx", where the variable "ranges over natural numbers", is *true if and only if* we can construct a perceptible inscription which can be put into the empty place of an inscription of "*Fa*" so that a truth results. Properly, this should be recast as a necessary statement about inscriptions. This truth-condition has a substitutional character, and then the resulting interpretation as a language of arithmetic is substitutional; inscriptions and construction thereof are talked of only in the metalanguage.

Other readings are possible that make the quantifier range over inscriptions.

23 *Ibid.*, pp. 162–4.

[24] In the case of natural language, we classify types according to the language, and not according to the conceptual apparatus of the perceiver. If I say to someone who has never heard English, "Where is the American Embassy?" he hears that sentence of English, even though he does not recognize it as such and is not able to recognize an utterance of the same sentence by someone with a different accent. This case is analogous to the role of natural kinds in the description of what someone sees.

[25] "Frege's theory of number," p. 201. Cf. "Ontology and mathematics," p. 160.

[26] For the natural numbers, Dummett makes such a suggestion, in order to criticize it, in "Platonism," in *Truth and other Enigmas*, Duckworth, London, 1978.

[27] Of course there are strings of strokes which as a practical matter can never be intuited, and it is only by means of the general notion of a string of strokes that we conceive such objects. But the thought of 10^{100} strokes, however clear, is not an intuition of them.

[28] "Ueber eine noch nicht benützte Erweiterung des finiten Standpunktes," pp. 280–2. In the translation referred to in note 7 above, "anschauliche Erkenntnis" (p. 281) is translated "immediate concrete knowledge".

[29] In my view, what is really essential is semantic reflection. See "Ontology and mathematics," pp. 165–7.

XI*—KNOWING AND BELIEVING
by J J. MacIntosh

In this paper I shall try to try to persuade you of the correctness
of Plato's conclusion that knowledge should not be analysed in
terms of belief, largely for the *kinds* of reasons that Vendler
offers in *Res Cogitans,*[1] though I approach the problem from a
slightly different angle. I shall, I say, try to persuade you : for
I do not think that there are conclusive arguments on either
side of this debate, and whichever side we find more congenial,
we may be sure we shall find ourselves with difficult questions
left unanswered. I think the problems are *greater* for the anti-
Vendlerians (or perhaps anti-Platonists) than they are for those
who accept Vendler's conclusions, but in this, of course, I may
be wrong. Moreover, I am not arguing for *all* of the claims that
Vendler brings to the debate. I shall argue merely for the
central point : that knowing is not any kind of believing. On
some other, associated points, I think Vendler is mistaken; and
on still other points, I think it is possible to find interpretations
which suggest that both he and his apparent opponents are correct.

I have divided this attempted persuasion into three parts.
In the first I point out some difficulties that arise for what is
often called the traditional view. In the second, starting anew,
I look at some reasons that might tempt the uncommitted
toward a Vendlerian view of knowledge. In the third, armed
with this new perspective, I look briefly at some arguments
that have been put forward in favour of the traditional view.
Throughout I shall be concerned only with the question, "Should
knowledge be analyzed in terms of justified true belief ?" and
not with associated questions concerning the ontological status
of facts or propositions, nor with questions concerning the subjective or objective nature of knowledge and belief. These are
interesting and relevant matters, but the present discussion can
proceed independently of their resolution.

---

* Meeting of the Aristotelian Society held at 5/7 Tavistock Place, WC1,
on Wednesday, 7th May, 1980 at 6.30 p.m.

1. The traditional view. I call it the traditional view, as do others, but it's worth noting in passing that it's a short tradition. This view is not a view espoused by the idealist or semi-idealist philosophers of the earliest part of this century, and it sets itself a little too far apart from science to be of any great concern to pre-second world war non-idealist epistemologists. Further, it is at once too precise, and too narrow, to be attributed to any philosopher before the twentieth century, despite Plato's flirtatious rejection of a verbally similar account. It is, in fact, a two to three generations old tradition. So, really, the sanctity which renders age immune from attack has not yet been bestowed upon it.

There are variations of opinion on the correct way to phrase this view, but these are comparatively minor differences, and what I have to say will, if it tells at all, tell equally against all of them. Briefly, then, the traditional view is that we can, without significantly being misled, concentrate on "know" as it appears in "knows that" constructions, and that in such contexts, knowledge may be analyzed as justified true belief, with or without suitable rephrasings or additional qualifications. It is with the most basic part of this claim that I want to disagree: that knowing is, no matter for the moment *what* kind, but anyway some kind of believing. John Bacon, for example, in his interesting and helpful "Belief as Relative Knowledge", begins:[2]

> The one obvious logical characteristic of belief, as opposed to mere belief, is that it follows from knowledge. Every knowing is a believing: knowledge is belief of some special kind.

Of course, these are really two separate claims: belief might follow from knowledge without it being the case that "every knowing is a believing", but, typically, they are conflated, and typically too, they are asserted, not argued for.

Still, it's not that there are no arguments. For example, one of the most obvious differences between "believe" and "know" seems initially at least, to support the conviction that there is a strong link between them. Suppose that I claim to know something, as, for example, that mediaeval logicians were unaware of De Morgan's laws, and you, subsequently, convince me that this is (as it is) a mistaken claim. I will then retract my claim (which may well have been, and typically would have been, an *implicit* one) to *know* that mediaeval logicians were unaware of De Morgan's laws. And the reason for this is that while beliefs may be true or false, correct or incorrect, what we know must be so. And, we notice, when we take back our claim to know in this or similar cases, what we replace it with is not a claim that we used to know (though we now no longer do) but rather a claim that we used to *believe,* though we now no longer do. However, our mental state was what it was, and not another thing, all along : and if we are now correct in speaking of ourselves as having a *belief,* then a belief it also was when we were making our initial knowledge claim. But if this belief, which need not in itself have been any different, had been both true and (say) justified, then I would have known and not merely believed that the mediaevals were logically unsophisticated in the suggested way. What we can see from this, the argument goes, is that knowing involves, at least, believing truly : whatever I know, I also truly believe; indeed, *since* I know, I *thereby* truly believe. As Ayer says,[3] "what is known . . . must be true". Of course, the converse—that what is both believed and true must be known—does not hold, and, for familiar reasons, we must add the notion of justification to our account of what it is to know that something or other is the case.

It goes without saying that there are still problems : we still have to say what truth is, what belief is, and what will count as justification. But at least, given this analysis, the question of what knowledge is, is not something in addition to these, and these are questions that should be tackled on their own account anyway. Moreover, this picture allows us to see why we have or appear to have two notions here. For, on this account, we are splitting beliefs up along two dimensions : a true/false dimension, and a justified/unjustified dimension. And clearly for dealing with the world the quadrant that interests us will be the justified, true quadrant : the one containing those beliefs that are not only true but reliable, and these beliefs will be important enough to us to make a special way of referring to them desirable : and so we say of the possessor of these particular beliefs that he *knows* them.

At this point it might be worthwhile to notice the *weakness* of one objection that is standardly brought against the traditional view : that it involves us in an infinite regress. For, the argument goes, suppose we ask about the grounds that justify some knower, A, in believing some proposition, *p*, in having the right to be sure that *p* : must A, who knows that *p*, recognize *as* grounds, the grounds for *p*, and know, in addition, that they are *good* grounds? The difficulty is that if A *doesn't* know that these (good) grounds exist, then, it seems, from A's point of view, there *are* no grounds, but if, on the other hand, A must *know* that these grounds are available, then A must know an infinite number of propositions in order to know one, and this is clearly not the case.

If this argument is correct, there is no need to look further : the traditional view has received its death-blow. There are, however, two things wrong with this objection. The first, about which I shall say nothing further, is that, even allowing the supposed dichotomy (which is surely suspect), there is no reason to accept the first half of the objection as correct. Here, though, I want to look instead at the second part of the argument, to see just what the infinite regress in question looks like, at least in its initial stages. Suppose we consider an actual case.

If I claimed to know, at the time I was writing this paper, that there was one but only one typewriter in the room with me, what "grounds" might I offer in support? Well, (1) from where I was sitting, there were few places where a typewriter might escape my attention : the four drawers of a filing cabinet, the space under a desk, the large drawer of a typing table, and the tops of various bookshelves. (2) I looked in all these places and there was no typewriter in any of them. (3) There was, however, a typewriter on the table in front of me, the very one which I was intermittently using. I could see, touch, hear, and, if I cared to, taste and smell it. (4) Therefore there was one but only one typewriter in the room at the time.

But now, when we start looking into *these,* we find a different situation : we are making certain *very* general assumptions, as, for example, that our senses are reliable and can be known to be so; that the universe is not changing radically as we switch our attention from part to part of it, that memory is in general reliable, as are standard deductive procedures. That is, simply in investigating the value of the grounds for a simple knowledge claim, we come, immediately, hard up against *standard* philosophical problems: the external world, induction, memory, etc. So much for our infinite regress: there is just no space for it, because these brick walls get in the way. This does not *show* that the kind of justification required for belief in our senses and in the regularity of nature can not be the kind of justification required for our knowledge claims of simple empirical facts. And if it were, then there would be an infinite regress. However, once these underlying problems are exposed we in fact cease to expect the same sort of justification: we see that, or at least act as if, we need not fear an infinite regress because the sort of answer that is called for will be of a different type. At worst, we may say, the traditional view doesn't run up against *additional* problems in this area. At least, not on this account.

There are, however, a number of difficulties with it on other accounts. One of the most important, about which I shall say next to nothing, in view of the fact that only the most dedicated non-reader of philosophical periodicals could be ignorant of it (and who am I to end such innocence?), is Gettier's point that true propositions can be validly deduced from justified false ones, thereby leaving the deducer, in the case where he was the one who held the original justified false belief, with a justified true belief. One of the more interesting side-effects of the Gettier counter-examples has been the investigation of the question: "*Is* justification deductively transmissible?" but that need not detain us here.

The most plausible direct response to the Gettier counter-examples has probably been the causal theory of knowledge in which a qualification is introduced to the effect that there must, somewhere along the line, be a lawlike connection (typically a causal one) between a belief and the state of affairs that makes it true. All these theories have, however, generated more problems than they have solved, as again, a glance at the literature will reveal. (And, in passing, this should give us pause: it is not only in theology that theories can die Flew's death of a thousand qualifications.) There are, moreover, difficulties that are common to *all* such analyses, as we shall see, for all such analyses involve analyzing knowing as a suitably qualified kind of believing: "A knows that *p*" is to be interpreted as "A believes justifiably and correctly that p", or as "A believes, as a result of a causal (or what have you) connection with the state of affairs that makes p true, that p", etc. All such *adverbial belief* theories share common difficulties, which will be discussed in the next section, but one preliminary point may be noted straightaway.

The "know" of "knows that" is also the "know" of "knows who", "knows when", "knows if", etc. If you know that Coleridge wrote *Kubla Khan* in 1797, then you also and indeed thereby know *who* wrote *Kubla Khan, when* it was written, and *whether* or *if* Coleridge was the author of *Kubla Khan*. Consequently, a difficulty that any analysis of *knows* in terms of *believes* must face is the fact that *know* will, and *believe* will not, go with these *wh*-constructions. Thus we can know what won the Derby, how to get to Ulcinj, who kidnapped the butler, and when the film begins. But if to know is, for some ϕ, to believe ϕ-ly, we should be able to believe (ϕ-ly) what won the Derby, etc. And we can't. So, *prima facie,* knowing isn't any kind of believing. A recent critic of Vendler's, O. R. Jones,[4] has responded to this point by remarking that "It is already granted that *believe* cannot take *wh*-nominals." But admitting a point is not answering it.

There are other, independent, difficulties. For example, there is the apparently anomalous fact that we have no count noun corresponding to "know" as "belief" corresponds to "believe" : someone who knows three distinct facts about me does not thereby have three distinct knowledges, nor does the person who knows those three facts, believe them : facts may be known but not believed. This is a more important point than might initially appear, I think. Our language, not surprisingly in view of the nature of the world, and of our evolutionary origins in that world, allows us to be fairly precise about whether or not things actually happened, about whether or not, and to what extent, our claims are reliable, about whether we saw or merely imagined, and so on. Now, if knowing really is a kind of believing, believing ϕ-ly, say, it is odd, to say the least of it, that the principles of linguistic economy that operate elsewhere so signally fail to operate here, so that while we can talk about beliefs, and about ϕ-*beliefs,* we have no single term to render the (usually clumsy) term ϕ-*beliefs* more concisely. Stranger still is the fact that, if we were to invent one, we would find no use for it, "as anyone", in Locke's phrase, "may experiment for himself". Interesting, too, is the fact that even philosophers, paradigmatic hypostatizers, reifiers and neologists though they be, never *have* invented such a term. The analogous point concerning mass nouns is in certain ways even more suggestive, but I shall not discuss it here.

The two notions seem far apart in other areas as well. "Believe in" is clearly closely tied to "believe that" (though only a most injudicious selection of examples would lead us to believe that either can be analyzed in terms of the other, without remainder), but though "believe in" is closely tied to "believe that" it is not at all closely tied to "know". I may believe in your ability, or your courage, and my belief may be both justified and reliable : but I can never know in your ability or your courage.

Yet again, belief seems—though of course these things are relative—a more obscure notion than knowledge, and there are many truths about our beliefs and belief systems that are not recognized by most of us.[5] Explaining *knowing* in terms of *believing* is explaining the not quite transparent in terms of the semi-opaque, the dim in terms of the murky. This feature of the case has led John Bacon[6] to attempt to "turn the . . . problem around" and look for an account of belief in terms of (relative) knowledge. (Bacon believes that, having achieved this, the solution can itself be turned around, or at any rate inverted, to fit the original problem, but a discussion of his solution would take me too far from the central theme of this paper.)

Again, we ask (two further points of Vendler's) : *why* do you believe, but : *how* do you know? If the difference between knowing and believing is merely that knowing is believing plus certain qualifications this is strange, even when one of the adverbial modifiers is "justifiably". And : if A *no longer* knows that Lima is due south of Ottawa, then, typically, A has forgotten this fact, but if A no longer believes that Lima is due south of Ottawa, then, typically, he need have forgotten nothing : only A's attitude need have changed. Belief, in fact, consists in accepting something : knowledge in being aware of something; and there is no particular reason to think that what we accept, and what we are aware of, are members of the same logical category. Indeed there are reasons for thinking that they are not. But with this, as novelists no longer say, we anticipate.

Notice, as a further part of our catalogue, the very great difference between knowing what someone said and believing what someone said, one of the few cases in which we allow *believe* to be followed by a *wh*-nominal. If I believe what she said, then I believe that that which she said is true. But my knowing what she said does not consist in my knowing that that which she said is true. On the contrary, I may very well know both what she said, and know that what she said is false, with no trace of inconsistency.

What is coming out of all these contrasts? First of all, there are too many of them, and they are too consistent in pattern, to be written off merely as accidental anomalies of English usage. Many points are suggested by these contrasts, but it will suffice for our present purposes if they suggest that we should take a fresh look at the facts, *without* seeing them through a preconception that what is known must be true, that if A knows that *p*, then A believes that *p*, and so on.

2. *A naive look at knowing and believing.* Here are a number of ways of making what is essentially the same point.

(a) There is a difference between a description and what it describes, a claim and what it claims to be the case, an account and that of which it is an account.

(b) "The cat is on the mat" is true iff the cat is on the mat.

(c) Consider the following conversation:

A : "Do you know what's happening in the next room?"
B : "No, but I'll look and see."

*   *   *   *

A : "Well, what did you see?"
B : "The cat is on the mat."

We can say, of our second conversationalist, B, that he saw (noticed, observed) that the cat was on the mat. It may also be the case that, as a direct result of what B saw he formed the *belief* that the cat was on the mat. But what B saw, and what B believed are not one and the same thing. If this is not immediately obvious, a simple application of Leibniz's Law should make it so: for what was seen was neither true nor false, but what was believed *was* either true or false. For obvious reasons, however, the clause that follows "saw that" and the clause that follows "believed that" can consist of the same words. It should not need saying that the identity of the words in the "that . . ." clauses does not show that what is seen (noticed, observed, etc.) and what is believed are one and the same thing.

(d) If we are setting up a logic of action, or a logic of commands, we will find ourselves using variables that range over what von Wright has called "features" of the world, i.e., states of affairs, i.e., facts. None of these terms is satisfactory, incidentally, but what *is* clear (and what is important) is that the variables do *not* represent propositions, or statements, or sentences. If, in the rather clumsy contruction that allows us to give such logics a treatment analogous to our propositional logics, I say : "Bring it about that p", "p" is not a *propositional* variable. Of course *if* you bring it about that p, there will be—especially in the case where I've been able to give such an order *explicitly*— usually be a proposition such that that proposition is true in virtue of the fact that you have brought it about that p. Not surprisingly, your *description* of the state of affairs you have brought about will usually be done in terms which will also be the terms you would use if you were uttering the proposition that becomes true. If we label the state of affairs that you are to bring about π, and the (or a) proposition accurately describing that state of affairs p, then, when you bring it about that π you thereby bring it about that p is true. But π is not true, and p has not been brought about.[7] The same point holds for deontic logic.

Notice, in passing, that very often—deontic logic provides a good case—our non-truth-functional operators will, *inter alia,* form propositions when combined with our non-propositional variables. But they do this, in this case, because the variables are *not* propositional variables. This distinction is obvious, once seen, and, once seen, it is obvious why the words mask it.

(e) Still the same point. It is tempting to render a remark such as "If the cow has not been milked, then John ought to milk the cow" by $\sim p \rightarrow Q_j p$, but this is a distortion. In wanting John to bring it about that the cow is milked, we don't want him to bring about a certain proposition, and in saying that he *ought* to bring about this state of affairs, we are not

M

saying that he ought to bring about a proposition. A better, though of course less simple, rendering is $\sim p \rightarrow Q_j\pi$, where, as before, p reports that π is the case.

Throughout the above, I am not wedded to the notion that there are, e.g., abstract entities called *propositions,* or abstract entities called *facts* or *states of affairs.* The foregoing is, or at least is meant to be, ontologically neutral. All that is necessary is that we see the distinction between claims and what is claimed, between descriptions and what is described, between what is seen and an account of what is seen. And we might notice, too, that what is described is neither true nor false, correct or incorrect, accurate or inaccurate, though its description may be. "Description", incidentally, is not a particularly felicitous word in this context. I use it for want of a better. When I say, of the cat, "the cat is on the mat" what I am describing is, among other things, the cat, and I describe it by saying *of* it that it is on the mat. But of course my remark is true simply *in virtue of* the cat's being on the mat. We don't eliminate *this* by a reductionist analysis of "facts", and at any rate, the slogan of that analysis: "facts are what statements, when true, state" no more eliminates facts than "bullets are what six-shooters, when loaded, shoot" eliminates bullets.

(f) Our language contains two non-synonymous phrases: "it is the case that", and "it is true that". When you bring it about for some π that π you thereby, typically, make a certain proposition (or, more accurately, group of propositions) true, the proposition, namely, that says that just this state of affairs obtains. Of course, if the *claim* that π has been brought about is formulable, then there will usually be a proposition p which will be true. Someone says to me: "Put the cat on the mat", and I do. Then what I have done is, in a small way, to change the world: the world is now richer to the tune of one on-the-mat cat. When, and only when, it is the case that the cat is on the mat, then and only then will it be true that the cat is on the mat. Yes, but the important thing to notice here is that we *misrepresent* what is going on if we try to formalize this as:

It is the case that p iff it is true that p.

For if p ranges over propositions the left side of the equivalence is not well formed, and if p ranges over states of affairs the right side is not well formed. This point, needless to say, is not limited to first order claims. That certain propositions are true is also one of the features of the world, and whenever it is true that p (because p says that it is the case that π, and it *is* the case that π), then here will be a π' that is the case (namely, that it is true that p), and there will be a p' that is correspondingly true, and so on, until boredom sets in.

The application of these points to *know* and *believe* will, I expect, be obvious. If we do not come to the problem convinced in advance that the variable p in "$K_a p$" is of the same type as the variable p in "$B_a p$", we will find it unlikely that it *is* the same. This is perhaps not a very exciting point, but bearing it in mind will introduce a bit of clarity into the discussion. We might notice, too, that there is a special problem for epistemic logics, formal or informal, that does not arise for other, formally similar, logics. In modal or deontic logic the ambiguity over the variables either does not arise or is rendered harmless by syntactic considerations. In modal logic, for example, the variables are simply our normal propositional variables. In deontic logic, on the other hand, it is common enough to be offered a mixture as in our previous example: $\sim p \rightarrow O_j p$ but the result is, though ill-formed, harmlessly so, since we *treat* a variable letter standing alone as a propositional variable, and the states-of-affairs variables are always operated on by a term such as 'O' or 'P' which yields, as a result, a proposition. And since there is an entailment relation between a given proposition's being true, and a certain (related) state of affairs being the case, this syntactic point allows the system to operate smoothly.

We might note here that though, when a given proposition is true, some particular and knowable feature of the world must obtain, the converse seems not to hold in at least two cases: (i) we often know that certain things are the case without having the vocabulary available to *say* what it is that is the case. What we know is, unsurprisingly, more extensive and more precise than our ability to comment upon what we know. Our language lets us say with *generality, roughly*, what is the case, our survival often requires a more precise awareness of the situation. (Tacit knowledge provides a good example.) (ii) There are possible and, since they are uncomplicated, presumably knowable, states of affairs that certain reportings render false. A familiar example of Buridan's is:

There are no negative propositions.

The state of affairs reported by the proposition is clearly possible, but the proposition could not be truly uttered, even though its equivalent:

All propositions are affirmative.

clearly could be. (Remembering throughout that propositions for Buridan are always tokens, never types.)

3. *The arguments for the traditional view.* Since the traditional view encounters a number of difficulties, and since an unbiased look at the problems involved suggests that knowing may *not* involve either truth or belief, it is appropriate at this point to look at the kind of arguments that have been advanced in favour of the claim that what is known must be true, and that what is known must be believed. Such an unbiased look reveals, interestingly enough, that the required arguments are either non-existent or atrocious, the former, if I may be allowed a Meinongian perspective, outnumbering the latter. Still, the latter are not uncommon, and I think the reason they are *so* bad is that their proponents are convinced in advance that they are unnecessary. I shan't look extensively at the literature, though such a look is rewarding, but I would like to look at a brief selection in the remaining space. I shall in fact look at four.

(a) The first argument I shall consider is the one I advanced in the first section of this paper, the argument from the fact that we retreat to a belief claim when a knowledge claim is successfully challenged. And so we see, the argument went on, since the mental state is the same when the knowledge claim can be successfully challenged and when it cannot, knowing is a kind of, or involves, believing. Unfortunately, by the same argument we can show that seeing is a kind of, or involves, hallucinating; that being awake is a kind of, or involves, dreaming, and so on. In short, this is a thoroughly bad argument, and is not made any better by being, in a different guise, a favourite of sense data theorists.

(b) People sometimes, indeed often, say that what is known

must be true because it cannot be false, but as Prichard saw long ago, that will hardly do. As he says,[8]

> Though obviously knowledge is not false, and though obviously, when we know we are not mistaken, knowledge is not *true*. It is neither true nor false, just as a colour is neither heavy nor light. On the other hand, beliefs are either true or false.

Admittedly, Prichard's *argument* for this conclusion is unconvincing, but the insight remains a valuable one.

(c) I turn now to specific philosophers, singling out two who offer on this topic arguments which are surprisingly weak. "Surprisingly", not because others offer strong arguments in this area—they don't—but because these philosophers offer strong arguments in neighbouring areas where they don't expect their readers to be convinced in advance. Here is Keith Lehrer being uncharacteristically careless on knowledge and truth :[9]

> Another way to put the matter is to say that if I know that the sentence "The atom has been spilt" is true, then the sentence "The atom has been split" is true. I cannot possibly know that any sentence is true unless that sentence is true. Hence truth is a condition of knowledge.

By parallel reasoning, falsehood is a condition of knowledge. Indeed, by exactly parallel reasoning, we can allow in pretty well anything we like. For just as I cannot know that any sentence is true unless that sentence *is* true, so I cannot, for example, possibly know that any rose is red unless that rose *is* red. Hence redness is a condition of knowledge. And so on. This is, in fact, as it stands, a truly terrible argument. Could Lehrer patch it up? Possibly. Or he could simply drop it. But what is important to notice is that he was willing to offer us such an argument in its patched-up form, whereas we can be reasonably confident that if he did not think that his readers would automatically agree with this particular conclusion, he would not have put the matter in just this way.

(d) The final case I shall consider in this brief survey is provided by O. R. Jones.[10] I shall not deal in detail with Jones's paper, for two reasons. The first, and most important, is that, though he attacks Vendler on many points (often, I confess, seeming to me to miss, rather than actually attack Vendler's position, but the literature suggests that this is a minority opinion), he seems *not* to be claiming that the traditional analysis is acceptable, for he seems, at times at least,[11] to suggest *not* that knowing is a kind of believing, but rather that "every substitution instance of 'If someone knows that *p*, then he believes that *p*' is true and analytic." We might compare

> If someone intentionally brought it about that *p* then he knows that *p*.

to see both the mildness of Jones's claim and the possibility, at least, of its being ill-formed.

Secondly, much of Jones's attack depends on semantic intuitions which I simply don't share. Jones thinks, for example,[12] that "we find it quite natural to say . . . that someone's prediction became a fact," and I don't find this at all natural. Neither

> Thales' prediction became a fact.

nor

> Thales' prediction that there would be an eclipse became a fact.

strikes me as natural. Anything but. Of course, I can't use this fact to rebut Jones, but it does allow me not to be particularly swayed by arguments depending on the claim that such locutions are natural. It may well be that conflicting intuitions cannot refute arguments, but by the same token, they cannot be allowed to establish results, either.

Although Jones spends most of his time attacking Vendler's arguments, he does, as I understand him, offer two arguments of his own in favour of the traditional view. Here is the first:[13]

> Vendler's conclusion runs counter to our intuitions. One is not, and should not be, easily convinced that what I know and what you believe are different when, for example, what I know is that I have lost your book and what you believe is that I have lost your book. If a third person is asked what I believe and what you know, then he can, it would appear, give the same answer to each question.

Leaving aside the dubious appeal to "our intuitions", this

argument (which, to be fair, is clearly meant to be persuasive merely, and not conclusive) is based, it seems, simply on the fact that we use the same words in reporting what we know and what we believe. But as we saw this is also true with what we see or notice or observe, or do or ought to bring about. By a similar argument, then, we could show that what is seen or brought about and what is believed are one and the same thing. But they are not, and so this argument, too, fails.

Jones's second argument, which seems to be meant to be more than persuasive, is quite a bit worse. Concerning himself solely with the relative merits of the traditional view and that of Vendler, Jones writes:[14]

> Let us put the two views, Vendler's view and the traditional one, to the test for their power to explain a point. On Vendler's view what one knows is a fact, what one believes is a proposition, and believing is in no way a part of knowing. On such a view there appears to be no way of showing that if, for example, John knows that it is raining he may not, at the same time, believe that it is not raining; and similarly for everything anybody knows. In other words, there seems to be no way of showing that the move from something of the form K_ap to $\sim(B_a\sim p)$ is a valid inference. According to the traditional view, however, K_ap *will contain* B_ap as part of its analysis, and it is then no problem to explain how $\sim(B_a\sim p)$ is an entailment.

As a first comment, we might notice that, even in this (polemical) context, "everything" (in the phrase "similarly for everything anybody knows") seems unjustified: Vendler *might* be committed to "anything", but the move from *any* to *every* is clearly fallacious in modal contexts. Let us, however, leave that, for there are greater difficulties here. In the first place, the traditional view does not commit us to such claims, and Jones's "no problem" is in fact an insurmountable one. Or, perhaps better, it *is* "no problem", but not quite in the sense he means. It is "no problem" just in the sense that it is "no problem" to show how "I have four apples" follows from "$2 + 2 = 4$". It is no problem because it doesn't follow, and so showing *how* it follows is no problem. The confusion is like that displayed when people suppose, like Plato, that one and the same person cannot both want *s* and want not-*s*. Suppose though, just for a moment, that Jones was right, and it was the case that the traditional view showed that the inference from K_ap to $\sim B_a \sim p$ *was* valid, and Vendler's view didn't allow for this possibility. Then, since the inference is invalid, this can hardly be a good reason for accepting the traditional view. With advantages like this, the traditional view can do without disadvantages.

(Needless to say, I am not suggesting that it is impossible to set up a *formal* system in which we have

$$K_ap \vdash \sim B_a \sim p$$

But if we try to interpret such a system in terms of knowledge and belief we will find ourselves committed to claims which, though the world might be a better and would certainly be a more reasonable place were they true, will demonstrably be empirically false.)

So far, then, I have been arguing for the following unprovocative triad: (i) there are difficulties, to put it no higher, with the "traditional" analysis of knowledge in terms of belief; (ii) independently of (i), there are a number of reasons for doubting that knowing *is* a kind of believing; (iii) since intellectual history is littered with "self-evident truths" that turned out to be false, it would be nice to see *a* strong argument for the traditional view: but such arguments are conspicuous by their absence.

Is there nothing to be said on the other side? Of course there is, and as soon as one begins to expand on the kind of bare bones account I have given (no talk of *facts*, of *propositions,* or *objects* of belief and knowledge, etc.) difficulties proliferate. To finish this paper, I mention one which seems straightforward, and which, I think, casts some doubt on what I have been saying. Part, at least, of my strategy has been to suggest that "know" might go as easily with "observes" or "ought to be the case" as with "believe". But it is strikingly the case that, apart from "know", these *other* terms are clearly signalled in the language. For example,

A commanded (implored, suggested, advised, urged) that the cat *be put* on the mat.

And "see" and "bring it about" have clearly acceptable non-propositional paraphrases:

He saw the cat on the mat.
He put the cat on the mat.

So we need an explanation of the fact that "know" does *not* have such a paraphrase, but requires a "that . . ." clause.

If we don't find such an explanation—and I have none to offer—this will serve, not to strengthen (some version of) the traditional view, but at least to weaken the force of the kind of considerations that I have brought against it. (But that's all right: truth is more important than success in debate.)

NOTES

1 And in subsequent papers. See especially "Escaping From the Cave, A Reply to Dunn and Suter", *Canadian Journal of Philosophy, 8,* 1978, pp. 79–87.
2 John Bacon, "Belief as Relative Knowledge", in *The Logical Enterprise,* edd. Alan Ross Anderson, Ruth Barcan Marcus, and R. M. Martin, p. 189.
3 A. J. Ayer, *The Problem of Knowledge* (Penguin ed.), p. 9.
4 O. R. Jones, "Can One Believe What One Knows?", *Philosophical Review, 84,* 1975, p. 225.
5 See, e.g., A. N. Prior, *Objects of Thought,* ch. 6.
6 In "Belief as Relative Knowledge".
7 After writing this paper I discovered that Philip L. Peterson had made this point in a slightly different version independently and considerably earlier. See, e.g., his "How to Infer Belief From Knowledge", *Philosophical Studies, 32,* 1977, pp. 203–209.
8 H. A. Prichard, "Knowing and Believing", reprinted from his *Knowledge and Belief,* in A. Phillips Griffiths, *Knowledge and Belief,* p. 63.
9 Keith Lehrer, *Knowledge,* p. 24.
10 In "Can One Believe What One Knows?"
11 p. 232 provides an example.
12 p. 224.
13 p. 222.
14 p. 234.

XII*—ARISTOTELIAN INFINITY

by Jonathan Lear

Philosophers have traditionally concerned themselves with two quite disparate tasks : they have, on the one hand, tried to give an account of the origin and structure of the world and, on the other hand, they have tried to provide a critique of thought. With the concept of the infinite, both tasks are united. Since the time of Anaximander the *apeiron* has been invoked as a basic cosmological principle.[1] And the conceptual change that occurs as the *apeiron* of the Presocratics is refined and criticized by Plato and Aristotle, to the development of Cantor's theory of the transfinite and its critique by Brouwer, is one of the great histories of a critique of pure reason. For whether or not the world is infinitely extended in space or time would, for all we know, make no difference to the quality of our local experience of the world. Nor, for all we know, are we able to distinguish on the basis of how our movement seems to us whether we are moving through a continuous or a discrete world. "The infinite", says Aristotle, "first manifests itself in the continuous",[2] for instance, in motion, time and magnitude. But he does not rely on our experience of a continuous world to establish the world's continuity. In *Physics* VI. 1, 2, he offers a series of theoretical arguments to show that a magnitude must be infinitely divisible and that if a magnitude is continuous so too must be motion and time. To provide a critique of the infinite, Aristotle had to provide a critique of thought concerning the infinite; yet the result of such a critique was supposed to provide insight into the nature and structure of the world in which we live.

The infinite needs to be invoked, according to Aristotle, to explain three distinct phenomena : the infinite divisibility of magnitudes, the infinity of numbers and the infinity of time (*Physics* 206a9–12). Yet an understanding of Aristotle's account of magnitude, number and time is hindered by the fact that his

* Meeting of the Aristotelian Society held at 5/7 Tavistock Place, W.C.1 on Monday, May 19, 1980 at 6.30 p.m,

theory of the infinite poses a serious problem of interpretation. It is often said that, for Aristotle, the infinite could exist only potentially and not actually. But it is not at all clear what such a doctrine amounts to. Normally when we say something is potentially Φ we imply that it is possible that it should be actually Φ;[3] yet it is commonly thought that Aristotle denies this in the case of the infinite.

A similar problem about the relation between possibility and actuality confronts intuitionist mathematicians in their treatment of the infinite. Intuitionists criticize classical mathematicians for supposing that they understand quantification over infinite domains.[4] They argue that we do not have a conception of what it is for a mathematical statement to be true that transcends our understanding of how it would be *possible* to determine that it is true. Thus they do not accept the unrestricted validity of the Law of Excluded Middle '(Ex)F(x) v ⌐ (Ex)F(x)', even with F a decidable predicate, when the quantifiers range over e.g. the infinite totality of natural numbers, since for some F there may be no way we can *even in principle* decide which, if any, disjunct is true. In such cases, they argue, we cannot claim that we know that one of the disjuncts must be true even though we do not know which. The intuitionists will, however, allow the validity of '(Ex)F(x) v ⌐ (Ex)F(x)' when the quantifiers range over any finite subdomain of natural numbers, for they argue it is *possible* that we should decide which disjunct is true.

Yet consider the sentence, 'There is some even number less than 10^{100} that is not the sum of two prime numbers'. Intuitionists consider the disjunction of this sentence and its negation valid because they assert that the sentence is *in principle decidable*. But in what sense is such a sentence decidable? In the philosophy of mathematics this question has been asked by strict finitists,[5] but it could equally well be asked by a militant realist; and Dummett is correct to stress how important it is that the intuitionist should be able to answer this question.[6] The first answer the intuitionist offers—that there is a mechanical procedure by which we could in principle check each even number less than 10^{100} and determine whether or not it was the sum of two primes—is inadequate. For there may well not be enough ink, paper, computer time etc. to decide the question before the heat death of the universe. But then (to use a familiar phrase) what can the intuitionists' assertion that the sentence is in principle decidable consist in? If the intuitionists cannot show that their claims of possibility are well founded, then they are faced with one of two equally grave consequences. Either they must content themselves with a small fragment of finite mathematics; i.e. their position collapses into some variant of strict finitism. Or they must concede to the realists that they too have an epistemically transcendent notion of truth and that the disagreement with the realists is one of degree, not of kind.

Aristotle was able to offer at least a partial solution to his 'problem of potentiality' but, unfortunately for the intuitionists, his solution is not one of which they can take advantage. To see this we must first recognize that a commonly accepted interpretation of Aristotle is unacceptable.

I

Hintikka has argued that, for Aristotle, every genuine possibility is at some time actualized.[7] Aristotle's theory of the infinite seems to provide a counterexample, since it appears that the infinite has merely potential existence and is never actualized. However, according to Hintikka, the alleged counterexample is only apparent; he resolves the tension as follows.[8] Though the claim that 'the infinite is potential' may appear odd, Aristotle denies that 'potential' is being used in a deviant way: he says, rather, that 'to be' has many senses (206a16–27). A lump of bronze may at one time potentially be a statue and at a later time actually be a statue, because the process of sculpting it is one that can be completed. The result of the sculpting process is an individual statue, a *tode ti*. By contrast, the infinite is in the same sense in which a day is or a contest is (206a21–25). The point is that there is no moment at which the day exists as an individual entity (*tode ti*). Rather, one moment of the day occurs after another. Similarly with the infinite: if one begins dividing a line, there is no moment at which the infinite exists as a completed entity. One can continue the process of division without end. But Aristotle allowed that when a process is occurring, whether it be the passing of a day, the Olympic Games or the division of a line, we may say that it is actually

coming to be (206a21–25, 206b13–14). Aristotle is aware, says
Hintikka, that "the distinction between actuality and potentiality
applies also to the kind of existence that is enjoyed *inter alia*
by the infinite, by a day, and by the Olympic Games . . .
Although there is perhaps a rather loose sense in which the
infinite may be said to exist only potentially, *in the exact and
proper sense in which it exists potentially, it also exists actually.*"[9] (My emphasis). Thus, in Hintikka's interpretation, the
infinite does not constitute a counterexample to the principle
that every possibility is at some time actualized.

Though some variant of Hintikka's interpretation is commonly accepted, I do not think that it can be correct. Aristotle
is trying to account for three distinct phenomena—the infinite
divisibility of magnitudes, the infinity of numbers and of time—
and an adequate interpretation must see him as providing three
distinct, if related, solutions. For instance, there are at least
two important asymmetries between the case of a day or
contest on the one hand and the case of an infinite division
on the other. First, the successive divisions of a given magnitude
are discrete acts that occur one after another. The flow of time
during the course of a day is, by contrast, continuous. Second,
though there is no moment at which either the day or the
division will result in a completed entity, there at least comes
a time in the passage of the day when we can say that the
day is over. By contrast, there is no process which could correctly be considered the actualization of an infinite division
of a line. For any such process will terminate after finitely
many divisions. To see this more clearly, consider what sort
of process might be considered the actualization of an infinite
division. It could not be a physical process of actually cutting
a finite physical magnitude, for, obviously, any physical cut
we make in such a magnitude will have finite size and thus
the magnitude will be completely destroyed after only finitely
many cuts. Nor could it be a process of *theoretical division* :[10]
i.e. a mental operation which distinguishes parts of the magnitude. For no mortal could carry out more than a finite number
of theoretical divisions.[11] And even if, like Aristotle, we believed
in the permanence of the species, there is no way in which a
theoretical divider of the present generation could pass on his
work to a divider of the next generation.

However, this is a problem for Hintikka, not for Aristotle. Having compared the way a day or contest is with the way the infinite is, Aristotle continues:

> For generally the infinite is as follows: there is *always* another and another to be taken. And the thing taken will aways be finite, but always different (206a27–29).[12]

In general, the infinite *is* in the sense that there is *always* another *to be taken.* (206a27–28). The essence of Aristotle's interpretation of the way in which the infinite is said to exist is that there will *always* be possibilities that remain unactualized. Hintikka says that Aristotle's claim that the infinite exists potentially and not actually (206a16–19) "is a very misleading way of speaking . . . because it muddles an important distinction."[13] Aristotle is not muddled: he is making an important distinction to which Hintikka is insensitive. A magnitude is infinite by division (*apeiron diairesei*) and, in virtue of this, it is possible to begin actually dividing it. Of course, any such actual process will terminate after only finitely many divisions. But that does not mean that the actual process does not bear witness to the magnitude being infinite by division. Whether it does or not depends on whether, after the termination of that or any other process, there remain other divisions *which could have been made.* For whatever reason the actual division terminates, as terminate it must, the reason will not be that all possible divisions have been exhausted. Hintikka has failed to distinguish between an actual process bearing witness to the existence of the potential infinite and an actual process being a witness to the existence of the actual infinite. No actual process of division could bear witness to a length being actually infinite by division. However, an actual process of division which terminates after finitely many divisions, having failed to carry out all possible divisions, is all that a witness to the existence of the potential infinite could consist in. While such a process is occurring one can say that the infinite is actually coming to be, one division occurring after another. (The contrast is with a process that might be occurring but is not). (206a23–25, 206b13–14). But even as he says this, Aristotle can insist that the infinite by division is potential and not actual (206a16–18,

206b12–16) because the actual process can only reveal the
length to be potentially infinite.

Hintikka cites a passage from *Metaphysics* VIII. 6 which he
thinks supports his interpretation.

> The infinite does not exist potentially in the sense that it
> will ever exist actually and separately; it exists only in
> thinking. The potential existence of this activity ensures
> that the process of division never comes to an end, but
> not that the infinite exists separately. (1048b14–17, Hin-
> tikka's translation)

The central claim of this passage is that the infinite does not
exist as a separate, individual entity. The problem for Hintikka
is to explain how the potential existence of a mental activity
could guarantee that the process of division never comes to an
end. Hintikka's response is to invoke the so-called principle of
plenitude : that, for Aristotle, no potentiality goes forever unactualized. Thus, Hintikka concludes, not only does Aristotle's
theory of the infinite not constitute a counterexample to the
principle of plenitude, the principle is in fact required in the
exposition of the theory. This conclusion is, I think, unjustified.
Whether or not Aristotle subscribed to the principle of plenitude
is extremely contentious. That does not mean one should never
invoke the principle. Indeed its invocation might lend the principle support if it helped significantly to harmonize the data,
preserve the appearances. But Hintikka invokes the principle
in an instance where it is incredible that it should hold. Are
we really supposed to believe that the potential existence of a
mental activity ensures that the process of division never comes
to an end because, in the fullness of time, there will be an actual
mental activity that will ensure that the activity never comes
to an end? Hintikka acknowledges that the translation of the
second sentence quoted is disputed. The Greek sentence is :
*to gar mē hypoleipein tēn diairesin apodidōsi to einai dunamei
tautēn tēn energeian, to de chōrizesthai ou.* (1048b14–17) Hintikka
has had to take *to einai dunamei tautēn tēn energeian* as the subject, while I would agree with Ross that it is more natural to take
to gar mē hypoleipein tēn diairesin as the subject.[14] The sentence
would then be translated :

The division not being exhausted ensures that this activity (of dividing) is potentially, but not that the infinite exists separately.

On this reading, it is precisely because there are possible divisions that will remain unactualized that the line is potentially infinite.

II

Now it is easy to be misled into thinking that, for Aristotle, a length is said to be potentially infinite because there could be a process of division that continued without end. Then it is natural to be confused as to why such a process would not also show the line to be actually infinite by division. However, it would be more accurate to say that, for Aristotle, it is *because* the length is potentially infinite that there could be such a process. More accurate, but still not true, strictly speaking. Strictly speaking there could not be such a process, but the reason why there could not be is independent of the structure of the magnitude: however earnest a divider I may be, I am also mortal. But even at that sad moment when the process of division does terminate, there will remain divisions which could have been made. The length is potentially infinite not because of the existence of any process, but because of the structure of the magnitude.

This interpretation is borne out by Aristotle's first positive remarks on the nature of the infinite:

> To be is said on the one hand potentially and, on the other hand, actually; and the infinite is on the one hand by addition and on the other hand by division. On the one hand it is not possible that the magnitude be actually infinite, as has been said, but, on the other hand it is possible that the magnitude be infinite by division, for it is not difficult to refute [those who argue in favour of] the atomic 'lines'. Therefore what remains is the infinite that exists potentially. (206a14–17)

This is a curious passage. There are three *men . . . de . . .* clauses, and they establish an odd set of contrasts. *To be* is said on the one hand potentially and on the other hand actually;

N

the infinite exists on the one hand by addition and on the
other hand by division. The third contrast is:

> On the one hand it is not possible that a magnitude be
> actually infinite, as has been said, but on the other hand
> it is possible that the magnitude be infinite by division.

One would expect Aristotle to contrast the impossibility of a
magnitude being actually infinite with the possibility of its
being potentially infinite. This, I submit, *is* what is being
contrasted. For what is meant by the claim that a magnitude
cannot be *actually infinite*? It is merely the claim that there
cannot be an infinitely extended magnitude. Aristotle says that
'it has been said' that there cannot be an actually infinite
length—and what has been said, in *Physics* III. 5, is that
there cannot be an actual magnitude (or body) of infinite
extension. So it seems that Aristotle is, on the one hand, equating
a magnitude's being actually infinite with its being infinitely
extended and, on the other hand, equating a magnitude's
being potentially infinite with its being infinite by division.
Evidence for this interpretation is provided by Aristotle's conclusion:

> Therefore what remains is the infinite that exists poten-
> tially. (206a17)

Having eliminated the actual infinite and allowed only the
infinite by division, Aristotle concludes that what remains is
the potential infinite. The point he is making is that the structure of the magnitude is such that any division will have to be
only a partial realization of its infinite divisibility: there will
have to be possible divisions that remain unactualized.

Aristotle's treatment of the infinite by addition further con-
firms this interpretation (206b3–33, 207a33–b15). One might
reasonably think that the infinite by addition would be described
by a process which took some given unit length and repeatedly
added it. However, Aristotle categorically denies that such a
process could be a witness to the infinite by addition. The reason
Aristotle gives is that there is no actual infinitely extended body
(206b20–27). Thus we cannot think of such a process as showing that the infinite by addition exists even potentially. For
such a process could not (even if we were immortal) go on with-

out end. And given any such actual process of repeatedly adding a given unit length, when it terminates after finitely many additions we cannot be guaranteed that we can say that more additions could have been made. Thus no actual process of repeatedly adding a uniform finite length can bear witness even to the potential existence of the infinite by addition. The *only* way such a finite process could be considered a witness to the potential existence of the infinite by addition is if there were an actually existing infinite body.

With characteristic understatement Aristotle shows how the problem of the infinite by addition can be reduced to the problem of the infinite by division. "The infinite by addition" he says "is in one way (*pōs*) the same as the infinite by division" (206b3–4). The point is that given a successive division of a finite length AB, as prescribed in Zeno's Dichotomy 1/2AB, 1/4AB, 1/8 AB . . . one can use this division to form a process of addition 1/2AB + 1/4AB + 1/8AB + . . . Such a process could be a witness to the infinite by addition, though the addition of the lengths will never exceed the finite length AB. In no other way can the infinite by addition be said to exist, even potentially(206b12–13). But in so far as the infinite by addition does exist potentially, we say it exists in the same fashion as the infinite by division exists : i.e. there is always something outside of what has been taken (206b16–18). Again we have evidence for equating the potential infinite with the infinite by division and seeing both as existing in virtue of the continuous structure of a magnitude and not in virtue of the existence of any process.

One of the puzzles Aristotle hopes to solve is how numbers could be infinite (206a10–12). Numbers, for Aristotle, are not among the basic constituents of reality, but are the result of abstraction from physical objects (*Met.* M3). If we are to speak of an infinity of numbers, their existence must somehow be guaranteed. His solution is a direct consequence of his analysis of the infinite by addition (207b1–15). *Physics* III. 7 opens with an admission that, on his account, the most natural conception of the infinite by addition—that it is possible to exceed any given length—is impossible (207a33–35). Thus one cannot assign a numerical unit (1) to a standard unit length and hope that an infinity of numbers will be guaranteed by the fact that this length can be repeatedly added without end. Nevertheless, Aristotle concludes, it is always possible to think of a larger number *because* the divisions of a length are infinite (207b10–11). What he has in mind is that the infinity of numbers is guaranteed in much the same way as is the infinite by addition. Given a finite length AB we can assign numbers to the successive divisions:

$$1/2AB, \quad 1/4AB, \quad 1/8AB, \quad 1/16AB \ldots$$
$$\quad 1 \qquad\quad 2 \qquad\quad 3 \qquad\quad 4$$

Thus, though Aristotle thinks that number is not separable from things it numbers (207b13) he nevertheless sees the numbering as dependent upon the concept under which the things numbered fall.[15] In this case the number cannot be thought of as the number of *unit lengths,* but rather as the number of *divisions.*

The motivation for Aristotle's analysis of the infinity of numbers is clearly stated:

> It is always possible to think of a greater number, for the divisions of a magnitude are infinite. So it is potentially infinite, but not actually infinite; but the thing taken always exceeds any definite number (206a10–13).

By reducing the problem of the infinity of numbers to that of the infinite divisibility of a magnitude, Aristotle is able to reaffirm the potentiality of the infinite and deny its actuality. And the key to the potentiality of the infinite is that given any number a greater number could be found; for given any division of the line, another *could* be made.

But we must be clear about what possibility Aristotle is claiming if we are to understand how his treatment differs from the intuitionists' treatment. For the intuitionists do, in a way that Aristotle does not, make a fundamental appeal to actual human abilities to justify their claims about the infinite. Both Aristotle and the intuitionists agree that a magnitude is infinitely divisible and both will interpret this as a claim that no matter how many divisions of a magnitude have been made another *could* be made. But in fact each is claiming a very different possibility. Aristotle is claiming that the magnitude *is* such that if there *were* a divider who *could* continue to divide the length (i.e. a

Creative Mathematician, unhampered by human physical and mental limitations) then no matter how many divisions he made, he *could* always make another. Only the last 'could' is fundamental to Aristotle's claim that the magnitude is infinitely divisible, for it is a claim about the structure of the magnitude, not the existence of a process. On the question of whether there could be someone capable of carrying out the divisions, Aristotle is silent.[16] (Similarly with numbers: Aristotle is only claiming that if there were someone capable of continually abstracting numbers, then he *could* always abstract another number.) The intuitionists' possibility-claim is, by contrast, inextricably tied to an ability to carry out a certain procedure. But if we take this as a genuine claim that a certain procedure is possible, then either the claim is too weak to generate the potentially infinite totality that the intuitionist wants or the claim is false. If the claim is that a man may actually start by making a theoretical division and given any number of divisions he has made, he could make another, then such a claim will not provide the intuitionist with more than a vaguely determined totality. For example, even though it is absurd to suppose that there was a last heartbeat of my childhood, that only shows that 'the number of heartbeats in my childhood' determines a vague, not an infinite, totality. For there are finite numbers e.g. 10^{100} larger than the number of heartbeats in my childhood. Similarly, 'the number of theoretical divisions I could actually carry out' specifies only a vague totality: it is absurd to suppose that some particular division is the last division I could make, yet there are finite numbers, e.g. 10^{100}, larger than the number of divisions I could actually carry out. If, however, the claim is strengthened, it also becomes false: there is no process of physical or theoretical division which could make 10^{100} divisions. Unfortunately, the intuitionists cannot follow Aristotle's example and reinterpret their possibility-claim in such a way as to avoid recourse to our ability to divide. For the core of the intuitionist critique of the realist is that the realist's conception of truth for a sentence transcends his ability to determine whether or not a sentence is true. Thus the intuitionist must maintain that it is in principle possible to decide e.g. whether there are two prime numbers x and y such that 10^{100} divisions of a line are equal to x + y divisions. Nor can the intuitionist legitimately invoke a Creative

Mathematician for, according to him, our conception of truth is derived from our *own* ability to determine whether a sentence is true. Yet to decide such a question, the intuitionist must embark on a process of construction that it does not appear possible to complete. The intuitionist is thus in a radically unstable position, and he cannot adopt an Aristotelian approach to the potential infinite without sacrificing his own critique of the classical mathematician.

III

So far I have argued that for Aristotle it is because a length is infinite by division that certain processes are possible and not vice versa. A problem for this interpretation might be thought to arise with Aristotle's considered response to Zeno (*Physics* VIII. 8, 263a4–b9). While we may think that there exist infinitely many points on a line and that such existence is not dependent upon any process, Aristotle seems to deny this. He distinguishes between the potential and actual existence of a point: a point does not actually exist until it has been actualized (*cf.* 262a12–263a3). A point on a line may be actualized if one stops at it, or reverses one's direction at it, or divides the line at it. According to Aristotle a runner (call him Achilles) would indeed be unable to traverse the finite length AB if in the course of his journey he had to traverse infinitely many actually existing points. However, continuous motion along a length is not sufficient to actualize any point along the length. Thus Aristotle would be among those who think that while it may be possible for Achilles to traverse AB in one minute by moving continuously across it, it would be impossible for him to traverse it in two minutes if in the first thirty seconds he went to the midpoint (1/2AB) and then rested thirty seconds, in the next fifteen seconds to the three quarter point (3/4AB) then rested 15 seconds and so on. For such a 'staccato run' to be successful, Achilles would have had (by the end of two minutes) to actualize infinitely many points on the length AB and this Aristotle held to be impossible. I do not here wish to assess the adequacy of Aristotle's response to Zeno:[17] what is important for the present discussion is that Aristotle appears to make the existence of infinitely many points on a line dependent upon the existence of a process.

Aristotle does deny the actual existence of infinitely many points on a line and he does this because he takes certain kinds of processes—e.g. a staccato run—to be impossible. But he does not deny the potential existence of infinitely many points and he does not make this potential existence dependent upon the existence of any type of process. It is precisely because infinitely many points do exist potentially that an actual staccato run will be a witness to the infinite divisibility of the length AB, even though Achilles' nimbleness will give out after he has actualized only finitely many points.

Although Aristotle denies the actual existence of infinitely many points on a line, this is not as odd as it might first appear. For he denies that a line is made up out of points. A line is continuous and nothing continuous can be made up of unextended points or of indivisible magnitudes (cf. e.g. 231a20–b6, 227a10–12). So since we need not, in fact should not, think of a length as composed of points, we need not, in fact should not, think of the points as actually existing.

Michael Dummett has tried to envisage a 'reality not already in existence but as it were coming into being as we probe. Our investigations bring into existence what was not there before but what they bring into existence is not of our own making.'[18] According to Aristotle, points do not actually exist independently of our 'probing' for them, yet they are not of our own making. A point, for Aristotle, exists only in a derivative sense : it is, so to speak, a permanent possibility of division.[19] But these are possibilities which cannot all be actualized. In *De Generatione et Corruptione,* Aristotle considers the problems that arise from supposing that an infinitely divisible magnitude had actually been divided "through and through" (316a15–317a18). The situation Aristotle is envisaging is that all possible divisions of a magnitude had actually been made. What then will remain? No magnitudes can remain, for magnitudes are divisible and this would contradict the assumption that the division had been carried out through and through.[20] Nor could there be points without magnitude remaining. A division divides a whole into its constituents, yet one cannot without absurdity think of points without magnitude as constituents of a length.

Aristotle offers a paradigmatically Aristotelian solution. He distinguishes two senses in which a line may be said to be divisible 'through and through' (317a3ff). A length is divisible through and through in the sense that it could be divided *anywhere* along the length. But it is not divisible through and through in the sense that it could (even potentially) be divided *everywhere* along the length. One can thus actualize *any* point but one cannot actualize *every* point; for any process of division, there must be divisions which could have been made which in fact were not made.

IV

Aristotle is attempting a revolution in philosophical perspective. This is a revolution which cannot be appreciated if one thinks that, for him, every possibility must be actualized. Aristotle wants to remove the infinite from its position of majesty. The infinite traditionally derived its dignity from being thought of as a whole in which everything is contained (207a15–21). But the view that the infinite contains everything arises, Aristotle argues, from a conceptual confusion.

> The infinite turns out to be the opposite of what they say. The infinite is not that of which *nothing* is outside, but that of which there is *always something* outside . . . That of which nothing is outside is complete and whole, for we define the whole as that of which nothing is absent, for example, a whole man or a wooden box. . . . By contrast, that of which something, whatever it might be, is absent is not everlasting. *Whole* and *complete* are either altogether the same or of a similar nature. Nothing is complete (*teleion*) which has no end (*telos*), and the end is a limit (*peras*)" (206b33–207a15).

Aristotle here presents an argument to show that the infinite is imperfect and incomplete : 1. The infinite is that from which it is always possible to take something from outside (207a1–2). 2. That of which nothing is outside is said to be complete and whole (207a8–9). The examples Aristotle gives are paradigms of finite self-contained objects; they are individual entities, substance or artifact. 3. The whole = the complete (a13–14). But 4. Every complete thing has an end (a14). And 5. An end is a limit (a14–15). The reader is left to draw the conclusion from (3)–(5) that 6. The whole has a limit. Thus it would be absurd to equate the whole and the infinite, for that would be to say that the *apeiron* had a *peras*. Of course, we need not be persuaded by this argument to recognize its genius. This is an excellent example of how one can formulate an *a priori* argument which nevertheless fails to establish its conclusion because the concepts it employs—in this case the concept of a limit—are not sufficiently refined.[21] The claim that the *apeiron* must lack a *peras* would appear to Aristotle to be an analytic truth.

Having dethroned the infinite, Aristotle can argue that:
[The infinite] qua infinite does not contain, but is contained. Therefore [the infinite] qua infinite is unknowable, for matter does not have form (207a24–25).

Aristotle often draws an analogy between the infinite and matter. (*Cf. e.g.* 206b14–15, 207a21–25, 207a26, 207a35–b1, 207b34–208a3.) It is this assimilation of the infinite (*apeiron*) to matter which lies at the heart of the conceptual revolution he is trying to achieve.[22] For Anaximander, the *apeiron* served at least four functions. First it was a great unlimited mass enveloping the world. Second, it was the temporal *archē* of the world. Third, it provided a permanent, unchanging principle which governed the change and transition observed in the natural world. Finally it is that out of which things are formed. It is only this last function for which Aristotle had any use. For Aristotle, the world is finite and unenveloped, eternal and ungenerated; the natural processes could be explained without the governance of a transcendent principle. What Aristotle did need, however, was an underlying stuff from which things are formed: thus the *apeiron* was, if with rough justice, impressed into service as the material principle.[23]

The infinite, for Aristotle, is immanent in nature, not a transcendent principle; thus he can say that we first encounter the infinite in the continuous (200b17ff). The infinite, like matter, does not contain the world, but is contained; that which contains is form (207a35–b1). Most importantly, matter as such is merely a potentiality: the only way it can exist actually is as *informed* matter. (*Cf. Met.* 1050a15, 1049b13, *deАn* 430a10.

Cf. also *Met.* M3 1078a30–1). The infinite exists only potentially as matter does (206b14ff). Due at least in part to its
potentiality, the infinite, like matter, is unknowable. (*Cf.*
207a24—26, a30–32). Matter *qua* matter is unknowable
because it lacks a form and it is form that is knowable. The
infinite is unknowable both because that which is indeterminate
is unknowable and because that which the mind cannot traverse
is unknowable.

Here we encounter a thread that runs to the core of Aristotle's
philosophy. Were the chain of causes of a given thing infinite
we would not be able to know the explanation of that thing,
because the mind cannot traverse an infinite series, i.e. a series
that has no *peras*. But we *can* know the causes of a thing;
therefore they must be finite (*Met.*A.2). If those properties
which make a substance what it is were infinite in number, then
the substance would be unknowable. But we *can* know what
a substance is, therefore there are only finitely many properties
in its definition (*An.Pst.* 1.22). Throughout Aristotle's work this
theme recurs : the possibility of philosophy—of man's ability
to comprehend the world—depends on the fact that the world
is a finite place containing objects that are themselves finite.
And the possibility of philosophy is one possibility that Aristotle
spent his life actualizing.

V

Time, for Aristotle, is also supposed to be potentially infinite.
But the claim that time is potentially infinite is fundamentally
different from the claim that magnitude is potentially infinite,
for although a stretch of time is continuous and in virtue of
this infinitely divisible, and although the continuity of time
depends ultimately on the continuity of magnitudes (232a23ff),
it is not to the infinite divisibility of time that Aristotle wishes
to draw our attention when he says that time is infinite. Rather,
in the case of time, he does for once seem to emphasize the
idea of a process : time flows on and on.

However, when one tries to combine Aristotle's belief in the
infinity of time with his belief that magnitudes can be of only
finite size, his natural philosophy seems to verge towards inco-
herence. First, time is supposed to be a measure of change

(kinēsis) (220b32–221a7, 219b1–2).[24] One measures a given change by picking out a motion *(phora)*[25] which is uniform and letting that be a standard against which the time of a given change is measured. The paradigmatic measure of change is regular circular motion and he took the motion of the heavenly bodies to be eternal (223b12–21, *cf Physics* VIII.8,9). But, secondly, a body in motion traverses a spatial magnitude *(cf. e.g.* 231b18ff). So if time is infinite (206b9–12) and time is measured by motion, why does not the infinity of time bear witness to the existence of an infinitely extended magnitude?

The obvious response is that the only motion which Aristotle thought could be regular, continuous and eternal was circular motion *(Physics* VIII. 8–9). And circular motion is not truly infinitary (206b33–207a8). While traversing the circumference of a circle, one can always continue one's motion, but one cannot properly call the *circle* "infinite". For the circle to be infinite, it would be necessary that each part traversed be different from any part that had been traversed or could be traversed again. And this necessary condition is not fulfilled. So although the heavens have always moved and always will move in a regular circular motion and thus provide a measure against which the time of other changes can be measured, they do not themselves traverse an infinitely extended magnitude.

This response, as it stands, is inadequate, for although the sphere of the heavens may be finite, the *path* the heavens describe through all time must be infinite. Aristotle himself admits that if time is infinitely extended then length must be infinitely extended (233a17–20). To avoid the problem one must somehow sever the tie between the passage of time and the path described by a moving body. And this is precisely what Aristotle did.

But he did not do it by as simple a sleight of tense as Simplicius ascribes to him.[26] Simplicius draws our attention to 206a25–b3 at which Aristotle contrasts the passage of time with the successive divisions of a length: while the parts of a line that are divided remain in existence, in the case of time the moments cease to exist; past time has perished. Though the contrast is genuine, it does not of itself embody a solution to the problem. For Aristotle clearly says that a moving body moves across a spatial magnitude, and thus there is a magnitude that is traversed by a moving body, even though at any one moment the moving body is in only one place. That the time at which a body moved has 'perished' does not imply that the magnitude or path it traversed has perished. Thus one is still faced with the problem of why the path traversed by the heavens through all past time is not infinitely extended.

I would like briefly to suggest that Aristotle developed an anti-realist account of time, which enabled him both to show how time could be potentially and not actually infinite and to avoid 'spatializing' time.

To claim that Aristotle was an anti-realist with respect to time is not say that he succumbed to the sceptical *aporiai* of *Physics* IV.10 and concluded that time did not exist. It is only to say that, in company with McTaggart and Dummett, Aristotle did not believe one could give an observer-independent description of time.[27] Time seemed to Aristotle essentially to involve change (218b2ff), and it is to this aspect of time that a static, observer-independent description of the sequence of events cannot do justice. The claim that Aristotle thought time unreal amounts to no more than that he thought an adequate description of time must include a consciousness that is existing through time aware of the distinction between present, past and future. In a famous passage which, because it comes at the conclusion of his extended discussion of time, I take to contain his mature thoughts on the nature of time, Aristotle says:

> It is worth investigating how time is related to the soul and why time seems to be in everything both in earth, in sea and in heaven . . . Someone might well ask whether time would exist or not if there were no soul. If it is impossible for there to be someone who counts, then it is impossible that something be countable, so it is evident that neither is there number, for number is either the thing counted or the countable. If there is nothing capable of counting, either soul or the mind of soul, it is impossible that time should exist, with the soul not existing, but only the substratum of time [sc. change], *if* it is possible for change to exist without soul. (*Physics* IV.14, 223a16–28, my emphasis)

Time is above all a measure and, as such, could not exist were there no soul or mind of soul which could measure. This does not mean that the measurement is subjective or that any measurement a soul makes is correct : it only means that we cannot give an adequate account of time without including in the account a soul which is measuring the change.

Time exists, but in a derivative sense, dependent for its existence on a soul that is measuring changes. For an event to occur *at some time* it is necessary that that event stand in a determinate relation to the present (222a24–29). From, say, the fall of Troy until now the heavens have revolved continuously a finite number of times. A soul can measure the time that has elapsed and the path described by the heavens from the fall of Troy until now will only be finitely long. In so far as we are tempted to conceive of there being a stretch of time from that event to the present, that stretch will be finite.

But what if one should consider the entire previous history of the world? For Aristotle the world is uncreated and eternal. So if one were able to measure a stretch of time encompassing all events in the history of the world, that stretch would have to be infinitely extended. But Aristotle denies that such a measurement is possible. His theory is, so to speak, omega-inconsistent : *each event* is in time (*en chronō*), but *all events* are not in time (221a1–222a9). An event is *in time* only if it is encompassed by time; i.e. if there were events that occurred before and after it. So although each event in the history of the world is in time—and one can thus measure the time elapsed from that event until now—one cannot treat all events in the previous history of the world as being in time : one *cannot measure* the time elapsed in the entire previous history of the world.

This solution may appear unsatisfying. In order to appreciate it, one must confront another problem. How can Aristotle even *say* that the world is eternal? For the world to be eternal, it must have existed at all times, always. What, for Aristotle, can such a claim consist in? To say that the world must always have existed is to say that there is no time at which the world did not exist. But since time is the measure of change, and the motion of the heavens provides the standard measure, were there no world and thus no change, neither would there be any time. Thus the claim that the world is eternal seems in danger of collapsing from its vaunted position as a metaphysical claim about the nature of the world into a trivial analytic truth. *Of course* there was no time at which the world was not, for if the world were not there would be no time and *a fortiori* no time at which it was not. It does not help to claim that "there always was change and always will be change throughout all time" (266a6ff). For to claim that there always was change is to claim that there is no previous time at which there was no change; but that is trivially true. For were there no change there would be no time, since time is the measure of change. Similarly, the claim that there always will be change seems no longer to be a metaphysical discovery about the future, but an analytic triviality. Nor will it help to claim that time is a measure of rest as well as of change (221b7–14), for all rest is in time (b8–9) and thus time must extend in both directions beyond any given rest. One can say, for example, that a given animal rests because there is a finite interval in which the animal has temporarily ceased its motion, but during this interval, as during the entire period of the animal's life, the heavens continue to revolve, providing a measure against which the animal's change and rest can be measured. One cannot thus think of a stationary heaven as resting and so as being in time. Nor will it help to claim that the world is ungenerated. (*Cf. de Caelo* I.10–12.) For to claim that the world is ungenerated is to claim that there is no previous time at which it came into being and this may be trivially true.

However, Aristotle does provide us with an argument which enables us to break out of this circle of triviality. In *Physics* VIII.1 he argues that the supposition that there was a first change leads to absurdity.

> We say that change [*kinēsis*] is the actuality of the changeable thing in so far as it is changeable. It is necessary therefore that for each change there are things capable of being changed . . . Further these things necessarily either come to be (at some time they do not exist) or they are eternal. If therefore each of the changeable things came to be, before that change another change [*metabolēn kai kinēsin*] must have come to be, according to which the thing capable of being changed or changing came to be.

The supposition that these things existed always but un-changed appears unreasonable immediately, but even more unreasonable if one goes on to investigate the consequences. For if, among the things that are changeable and capable of producing change, there will at some time be something first producing change and something changing, while at another time there is nothing but something resting, then this thing must have previously been changing. For there was some cause of rest: rest being a privation of change. Therefore before this first change there will be a previous change. (251a9–28)

Aristotle is arguing that given any purported first change, there must have been a change which existed before it. Thus we can understand his claim that there has always been change as being more than an analytic truth, if we interpret him as claiming that it is absurd for there to have been a first change. Similarly, Aristotle's claim that the world is eternal should not be inter-preted in terms of an infinitely extended length of time, but only as a claim that no moment could be the first (or last) moment of the world's existence.

However, this claim does not establish that the temporal history of the world consists in more than a *vaguely* determined totality. (It is, for example, absurd to suppose that any given heartbeat was the first (or the last) of my adolescence, yet that only shows that the heartbeats of my adolescence constitute a vaguely determined totality). I am not sure how disappointed Aristotle would be with this result. Time, he admits, depends for its very existence on the existence of a soul or mind that is measuring change; the 'infinity' of time consists in the fact that no measurement could be a measurement of a first change. We seem to have been led from the introduction into a theory of time of an observer of change, via considerations of vagueness, to the conclusion that the 'observer' is not a mere observer of a phenomenon totally independent of him: for if the soul measuring change had an analogous relation to time as, say, a lepidopterist has to his butterflies, it is difficult to envisage how we could conceive of time as constituting a vaguely deter-mined totality.

If Aristotle's theory of time is coherent—and the answer to

that question waits upon a detailed study of *the now*—it slips through the net of Kant's so called First Antinomy.[28] Kant thought that reason could construct two equally valid arguments, one to the conclusion that the world had no beginning in time, the other to the conclusion that the world had a beginning in time. The proof that the world had no beginning is similar in structure to Aristotle's. To prove that the world did have a beginning, Kant supposes that the world had no beginning and then infers that an [actually] infinite extension of time must have passed before the present moment, which he takes to be impossible. Aristotle would accept both that the world had no beginning *and* that it is impossible that an actual infinity of time should have elapsed, but he would reject the inference and thus the argument as invalid. From the fact that the world had no beginning, all that follows is that there can be no measurement of a first change; and it is to the importance of so understanding our temporal claims that Aristotle is drawing our attention when he says that time is potentially infinite.

NOTES

* I would like to thank: M. F. Burnyeat, C. Farrar, T. J. Smiley, and R. R. K. Sorabji for offering valuable criticisms of an earlier draft; the President, Deans and Librarian of The Rockefeller University for their hospitality during the summer, 1979, when this paper was written; Ian Spence, who at age five asked me a question to which this paper is a partial response.

1 Cf. C. H. Kahn, *Anaximander and the Origins of Greek Cosmology*, New York, Columbia University Press, 1960; P. Seligman, *The Apeiron of Anaximander*, London, The Athelone Press, 1962.

2 *Physics*, III.1, 200b17.

3 D. Bostock, 'Aristotle, Zeno and the Potential Infinite', *Proceedings of the Aristotelian Society*, 73, 1972–3. Cf. W. D. Hart, 'The Potential Infinite', *Proceedings of the Aristotelian Society*, 76, 1975–6; J. Thomson, 'Infinity in Mathematics and Logic', *Encyclopedia of Philosophy*, New York, The Macmillan Company, 1967.

4 Cf. e.g. Michael Dummett, *Elements of Intuitionism*, Oxford, Clarendon Press, 1977; 'The Philosophical Basis of Intuitionist Logic', 'Platonism', 'Realism', in *Truth and Other Enigmas*, London, Duckworth, 1978.

5 Cf. A. S. Yesinin-Volpin, 'The Ultra-intuitionistic Criticism and the Antitraditional Program for the Foundations of Mathematics', in A. Kino, J. Myhill, R. Vesley (eds.), *Intuitionism and Proof Theory*, Amsterdam, North Holland, 1970.

6 Michael Dummett, 'Wang's Paradox', *Truth and Other Enigmas*, *op. cit*. Cf. Crispin Wright, 'Language Mastery and the Sorites Paradox,'

in G. Evans and J. McDowell, *Truth and Meaning*, Oxford, Clarendon Press, 1976.

[7] Jaakko Hintikka, *Time and Necessity*, Oxford, Clarendon Press, 1973.

[8] *Cf.* 'Aristotelian Infinity', in *Time and Necessity*, *op. cit.*

[9] *Ibid.* 116.

[10] David Furley, *Two Studies in the Greek Atomists*, Study I. 'Indivisible Magnitudes', Princeton, Princeton University Press, 1967.

[11] I deliberately ignore those who are able to perform Benacerrafian supertasks. See P. Benacerraf, 'Tasks, Supertasks and the Modern Eleatics', *Journal of Philosophy*, 59, 1962; J. Thomson, 'Comments on Professor Benacerraf's Paper', W. C. Salmon (ed.), *Zeno's Paradoxes*, Indianapolis, Bobbs Merrill, 1970.

[12] I have relied on the Oxford Classical Text of Aristotle's *Physics* (W. D. Ross, ed., 1973), the translations unless otherwise noted are my own.

[13] Hintikka (1973) *op. cit.*, 116. *Cf.* G. E. L. Owen, 'Aristotle on the Snares of Ontology', *New Essays on Plato and Aristotle*, R. Bambrough (ed.), London, Routledge and Kegan Paul, 1965.

[14] W. D. Ross, *Aristotle's Metaphysics*, v. II, Oxford, Clarendon Press, 1975; 252–3. *Cf. Physics* 203b23–25.

[15] *Cf. e.g. Physics* IV.14, 224a2ff.

[16] This I disagree with the emphasis Weiland places on the relation of infinite divisibility and motion. Weiland correctly relates infinite divisibility to the possibility of certain processes occurring, but I do not think he has accurately seen what this possibility consists in. *Cf.* W. Weiland, *Die aristotelische Physik*, Gottingen, Vandenhoeck & Ruprecht, 1962, 293–316. Compare his interpretation of *Met.* VIII.6, 1048b14ff (294) with the one I have offered above. And *cf. Physics* 208a14ff.

[17] *Cf. e.g.* D. Bostock (1972–3) *op. cit.;* G. E. L. Owen, 'Zeno and the Mathematicians', *Proceedings of the Aristotelian Society*, 58, 1957–8; J. Barnes, *The Presocratic Philosophers*, v.I, London, Routledge and Kegan Paul, 248ff.

[18] Michael Dummett, *Truth and Other Enigmas*, *op. cit.*, 18.

[19] Ross has said, 'and when it does not rest but moves continuously, the pre-existence of the points on its course is equally presupposed by its passage through them'. W. D. Ross, *Aristotle's Physics*, Oxford, Clarendon Press, 1979, 75. Aristotle would entirely disagree.

[20] I ignore the atomists' critique of Aristotle's arguments. See Furley (1967) *op. cit.;* J. Mau, 'Zum Problem des Infinitesimalen bei den antiken Atomisten', *Deutsche Akad. d. Wiss, z. Berlin, Institut für hellenistisch-römisch Philos. Veröffentlichung, Berlin*, 1954.

[21] *Cf. e.g.* C. B. Boyer, *The History of the Calculus and Its Conceptual Development*, New York, Dover, 1959; chapter II.

[22] For the use of *'apeiron'* in Anaximander, Homer and other early Greek writers, see the appendix on the *apeiron* in C. H. Kahn (1960) *op. cit.*

[23] It is well known that Aristotle tried to present his philosophy as embodying that which was correct in the philosophies of earlier thinkers, also that he was often unfair in his portrayal of others' thoughts. *Cf.* H. Cherniss, *Aristotle's Criticism of Presocratic Philosophy*, New York, Octagon, 1976; G. E. L. Owen, *'Tithenai ta phainomena'*, S. Mansion (ed.) *Aristote et les Problèmes de Méthode*, Louvain, 1961.

[24] Aristotle says both that time is a number of change (219b1–2) and a measure of change (220b32–221a1). I have had to suppress a discussion of the distinction between numbering and measuring, but see J. Annas,

O

'Aristotle, Number and Time', *Philosophical Quarterly*, 1975, and D. Bostock 'Aristotle's Account of Time', unpublished mss. *Cf. Met.* X,1–2.

²⁵ Motion (*phora*) is a particular type of change, a change of place. *Cf.* 226a32ff.

²⁶ Simplicii, *In Aristotelis Physicorum, Commentaria in Aristotelem Graeca*, v. IX, H. Diels (ed.), Berlin, 1882, 494–5.

²⁷ J. E. McTaggart, 'The Unreality of Time, *Mind*, 17, 1908; M. Dummett, 'A Defense of McTaggart's Proof of the Unreality of Time', *Truth and Other Enigmas, op. cit.* See also, J. Perry, 'The Problem of the Essential Indexical', *Noûs*, XIII, 1979. I certainly am not claiming that Aristotle had made the distinctions involved in A-series and B-series. See G. E. L. Owen, 'Aristotle on Time', in J. Barnes et. al. *Articles on Aristotle*, v.3, London, Duckworth, 1979.

²⁸ I. Kant, *Critique of Pure Reason* (N. K. Smith, translator), New York, St. Martin's Press, 1965, 396–7. *Cf.* D. H. Sanford, 'Infinity and Vagueness', *Philosophical Review*, 84, 1975

XIII*—'FUNCTIONALISM' IN PHILOSOPHY OF PSYCHOLOGY

by Norman Malcolm

I

The expressions 'functionalism', 'functional analysis' and 'functional explanation', have been used to refer to several different ideas. The notion of a 'functional explanation' has been employed in anthropology, physiology, and psychology. One starts with the idea of 'a system'. A 'system' has parts or component elements, or exhibits certain processes or activities. According to Carl Hempel,[1] there is a notion of 'functional explanation' that is roughly the following: the 'function' of some part of a system is that it provides a necessary condition for the stability, health or survival of the system. Hempel gives these examples: in anthropology the function of the rain-making ceremonies of the Hopi Indians has been deemed to be the preservation of the tribe; in human physiology the function of the kidney has been taken to be the preservation of the health of the organism by discharging waste; in psychoanalysis the function of neurotic compulsive washing has been held to be the prevention of outbreaks of anxiety (Hempel, 307). A system is observed to have a certain part, or to exhibit some process or activity. The question is raised, what is the 'purpose' of this part, process or activity? This is regarded as coming to the same as the question, what would be the effect on the survival, stability, or health of the system if this part, process or activity did not exist? As far as I can see, *this* notion of 'functional explanation' is *not* what I shall be concerned with in the present paper.

II

A second notion of 'functional analysis' or 'functional explanation' occurs in the writing of B. F. Skinner. The systems he is dealing with are animal or human 'organisms'. What is to be

---

* Meeting of the Aristotelian Society held at 5/7 Tavistock Place, W.C.1 on Monday, June 2, 1980 at 6.30 p.m.

explained is the 'behaviour' of a system. Skinner's mode of
explanation does not appeal to 'inner' states, processes or events,
whether physical or mental, but to 'external variables'. He says:

> The objection to inner states is not that they do not exist,
> but that they are not relevant to a functional analysis. We
> cannot account for the behaviour of any system while
> staying wholly inside it; eventually we must turn to forces
> operating upon the organism from without.[2]

Skinner's 'functional analysis' undertakes both to explain and
to predict behaviour in terms of 'external variables' or 'environmental variables'. The general slogan is: "Behaviour is a function of the environment". Skinner says:

> The external variables of which behaviour is a function
> provide for what may be called a causal or functional
> analysis. We undertake to predict and control the behaviour
> of the individual organism. This is our 'dependent variable'
> —the effect for which we are to find the cause. Our 'inde-
> pendent variables'—the causes of behaviour—are the
> external conditions of which behaviour is a function. Rela-
> tions between the two—the 'cause-and-effect relationships'
> in behaviour— are the laws of a science (*ibid.*).

Skinner's brand of 'functional analysis' (sometimes called 'peripheralist' theory as contrasted with 'centralist' theory) has been
heavily criticised by many writers. I do not wish to add anything here to that mass of writing.[3]

III

A third viewpoint, also called 'functionalism', is currently put
forward by various authors. My exposition of this version of
'functionalism' is drawn largely from a work entitled *The Formal
Mechanics of Mind* by Stephen Thomas.[4] Here again we have
the notion of a 'system'. A typewriter, a computer, a human
being, are examples of systems. A system receives 'inputs' and
produces 'outputs'. Thomas introduces the notion of a 'functional state' of a system. A functional state (F-state) is not
defined as a physical part of a system. Instead it is defined as
a relationship between 'input' and 'output'. For example, a

manual typewriter is so constructed that when a key bearing
the label 'a' is struck (input), the machine prints the letter 'a'
(output). An electric typewriter may exhibit the same input-
output relationship, although the electric machine operates on
different physical principles and has a different internal physical
arrangement, than does the manual machine. But since in both
machines there is this same input-output relationship, both
machines are said to exhibit the same F-state. F-states 'are
defined in terms of external *functional* rather than internal
structural distinctions' (Thomas, 124).

We now come to the notion of 'a functional state table' (FST).
An FST is a list of the F-states of a system. It is a description
of the 'operational properties of a system in abstraction from
its internal concrete structure' (*ibid.* 125). If an FST for a
certain system were both true and complete, it would list all
of the F-states, and only the F-states, that hold for that system.
It would be a complete description of the input-output characteristics of the system.

As applied to human beings, 'an FST of the postulated sort
takes as "inputs" different possible environmental situations and
describes as "outputs" various pieces of behaviour' (*ibid.* 135).
An FST for a person will list not only actual responses to actual
environmental situations, but also what the person's responses
would have been in hypothetical situations.

> For an FST describes not only a person's actions in the
> situations that were actualized, but also what the person
> would have done in other circumstances. The hypothesis,
> in other words, has a monopoly on all relevant behaviour,
> actual or possible (*ibid.* 150).

This thesis makes one wonder whether there is such a thing as
a complete FST for a human being. But before going into this
let us note the relationship that Thomas asserts to hold between
the functional states and the mental states of a person. Thomas's
functionalist hypothesis does not assert, and indeed, denies, that
mental states are identical with F-states (*ibid.* 139).

> The hypothesis is only that F-states *determine* mental states
> (that is, for each ordinary-language mental state, being in
> certain F-states is alleged to be a logically sufficient condi-

tion for being in that mental state). The postulated relationship between mental states and F-states is not one-to-one,
but many-to-many. To each ordinary-language mental-state
predicate . . . in general there will correspond (perhaps
infinitely) many F-states that determine it, and each of
these F-states, in general, simultaneously will determine
(perhaps infinitely) many separate and distinct mental
states. So the postulated relationship is a complex many-
to-many correlation, and *not* identity between the states
(ibid. 139–140).

Mental states are logically determined by functional states. But
since functional states are defined solely in terms of input-output
characteristics, and entail nothing whatever about the internal
structures or mechanisms of a system, the same holds true for
mental states : 'the applicability of mentalistic descriptions is
logically independent of the nature of the particular mechanisms
that enable subjects to realize these states' (ibid. 145).

Thomas says that his functionalism is *compatible* with the
assumption that a human being contains an immaterial soul or
mind. His functionalism does require that the inputs to and
outputs from a system are physical; but it does not require 'that
realizations of FSTs determining mental descriptions are entirely
constituted of physical parts' (*ibid.* 160). The possibility that
a system might contain nonphysical components is not, however, taken seriously. Thomas says that his functional state
model

may be transformed into a completely materialistic theory
of mind simply by adding to it the very plausible assumption that in humans the postulated FSTs are entirely
realized by the nervous system and associated bodily
mechanisms (ibid. 161).

When Thomas adds to his functionalism this 'very plausible
assumption' the resulting view is called 'physicalistic functionalism' or 'functional-state materialism'. This view is not,
however, to be identified with the 'central-state materialism'
of, for example, David Armstrong. Whereas central-state
materialism holds that the mental states of a material system
are identical with some of its internal physical states, functional-

state materialism rejects this view (as we have already noted) and holds instead that the mental states of a material system are logically determined by its functional states; but the mental states are neither identical with the functional states, nor with the internal physical states of the system which 'realize' the functional states.

The relation of Thomas's 'physicalistic functionalism' to behaviourism is intriguing. The two forms of behaviourism that are of main philosophical interest, I think, are (1) Skinner's version of 'functional analysis', and (2) the view that is often called 'analytic' or 'logical' behaviourism. Both of these forms of behaviourism have declined in popularity in recent years. Some philosophers have, in the last few years, set forth views to which they have given the name 'functionalism', and which they have regarded as opposed to behaviourism. Not so with Thomas. Although Thomas rejects Skinner's position, for reasons that I won't go into, he does endorse 'analytic' behaviourism. Indeed, he considers analytic behaviourism to be *entailed* by his own version of 'functionalism'. Thomas says:

> My functionalist hypothesis entails that for each pure mental predicate, there exists some description of behaviour whose satisfaction is a logically sufficient condition for that predicate's ascription (ibid. 226).

The thesis that is said here to be entailed by Thomas's 'functionalism' is the thesis that Thomas labels 'analytic' behaviourism. Thomas is well aware that there has been considerable disagreement as to what exactly should be understood by the name 'analytic behaviourism'—whether, for example, it is supposed to mean that a behaviouristic analysis of a mental predicate provides both necessary and sufficient conditions for its true application, or just necessary conditions, or just sufficient conditions (ibid. 263–264). Thomas chooses the latter definition:

> Analytical behaviourism claims that for each mental predicate, 'M', there exists some description, 'Φ', expressed solely in terms of descriptions of behaviour or dispositions to behaviour, that specifies logically sufficient conditions for the application of 'M' (ibid. 270).

Now the 'functionalism' that Thomas espouses holds that 'for each pure mental predicate, 'M', there exists an FST containing an F-state, S, such that being in this F-state is a logically sufficient condition for the true application of the mental description' (ibid.). Since an F-state just is a particular grouping of input-output or stimulus-response characteristics, it would seem that Thomas's functionalism really does entail analytic behaviourism, as this latter is defined by Thomas.

Previously I merely raised the question as to whether there is a complete FST for a human being. Let us return to this question. Remember what an FST is:

> An FST is an abstract 'input-output' characterization that delineates or individuates 'states' of a system exclusively in terms of the system's input-output characteristics (ibid. 218).

Presumably, a 'complete' FST for a particular human being, John Robinson, would individuate *all* of the functional states of Robinson. Now could anyone discover by careful observation and experiments what Robinson's complete FST is? Apparently not. Thomas himself says that 'there is no procedure by which others can *conclusively* ascertain a subject's F-state (and hence, his mental state) by any amount of behavioural or input-output observation' (ibid. 149fn). If this is true of a single F-state then, *a fortiori,* it is true of a complete FST. And Thomas says this too: 'no series of behavioural observations conclusively establishes someone's FST or functional state' (ibid. 159). And again:

> Regardless of the extremes to which their behavioural experimentation is carried, psychologists never will find it possible to ascertain with logical certitude the functional state table or functional state of any system they study (ibid. 269).

The philosophical inclination to say that it is impossible to *'conclusively* establish', or to ascertain 'with logical certitude', any person's 'mental state', is something that is, or should be, familiar to all of us. What usually lies behind this inclination is a temptation to impose upon such phrases as 'conclusively establish' and 'with logical certitude' a self-contradictory requirement. I think enough has been said elsewhere about that confusion; so I won't try to add anything further to it here. But

of course, in the everyday use of the word 'know' we often
do know what some person's 'mental state' is, e.g. that the
person is anxious, surprised, or irritable.
    Now what about a person's 'functional state'? Do we ever
know *that*, in the ordinary use of 'know'? I should think not.
We may indeed know that when Robinson saw the bill for
his automobile insurance, he turned pale and said 'Oh, no!'.
But we must remember that, according to Thomas, Robinson's
'functional state', or at least his 'functional state table', includes
not only his actual behaviour when presented with an actual
stimulus 'input', but also what Robinson's behaviour *would
have been* 'under various unrealized hypothetical conditions'
(ibid. 150). Would anyone know whether Robinson would have
turned pale and said 'Oh, no!', *if* his bank account had contained twice as much money as it actually did?; or *if* Mrs.
Robinson had seen the bill first and had exclaimed in Robinson's
hearing, 'This is dreadful! What shall we do?'? And so on,
with an indefinite number of unrealized possibilities? A functional state table for a particular person is supposed to
include 'all relevant behaviour, actual or possible' (ibid.). We
certainly do not ever have knowledge of that kind.
    Do we have *any reason at all* for believing that functional
states and functional state tables for human beings *do exist*?
Thomas certainly would deny that any have been discovered.
He speaks more than once of our not 'possessing' a 'complete'
FST for a person (ibid., e.g. 153, 154fn). He even expresses
some doubt as to whether there even *exists* a 'complete' FST
for a person—that is, an FST that would show 'what that system
would do for every possible 'input'' (ibid. 290). At the same
time, Thomas frequently asserts *the existence* of FSTs. He says,
as previously noted, that for each mental predicate 'there exists
an FST containing an F-state' such that being in this F-state
is a logically sufficient condition for the true application of the
mental predicate (ibid. 270). And Thomas declares that 'an
FST describes not only a person's actions in the situations that
were actualized, but also what the person would have done in
other circumstances'. An FST 'has a monopoly on all relevant
behaviour, actual or possible' (ibid. 150). Thus Thomas seems
to be in an inconsistent position regarding the existence of a
complete FST for any person. He both affirms it and doubts it.

Leaving this inconsistency aside, by far the main thrust of Thomas's book is to assert the existence of a complete FST for each human being. Or rather, instead of flatly asserting that human FSTs exist, it would be more accurate to say that Thomas speaks of the existence of FSTs as being his 'hypothesis' or his 'postulation'. Now why should Thomas even *postulate* the existence of a human FST? He says: 'Although the hypothesis does not actually supply the FSTs it posits, the postulate of their existence is of fundamental importance to the scientific investigation of mind' (ibid. 140). Why is the hypothesis of fundamental importance? For one thing, according to Thomas, 'it assures researchers that they can gain access to everything relevant to an organism's mental phenomena simply by attending to its functional characteristics' (ibid. 141). For another thing, or perhaps it is the same thing, the hypothesis is supposed to solve a long-standing philosophical problem:

> If my functional hypothesis is true, it indeed solves the classical mind-body problem. For the hypothesis entails that a neural network (plus associated bodily mechanisms) can be in the mental or psychological states determined by the implemented FST. So the theory explains how a completely physical or material structure could undergo mental states, including any state of consciousness. The theory's ability to explain how a purely physical system could be the subject of any mental state shows that it indeed solves the 'mind-body problem' as traditionally conceived (ibid. 164–165).

But since none of us knows of the existence of even a single human F-state, let alone of a complete human FST, how can the mere postulation of the existence of FSTs 'assure' those engaged in research on human psychology of anything at all? Furthermore, it is actually an *understatement* to say that 'we do not know' of the existence of any of the postulated human F-states or FSTs. Remember that the description of an F-state consists exclusively of a description of environmental physical 'inputs' and of physical behavioural 'outputs'. The claim is made that for any particular mental description, 'M', there is an F-state description which *entails* that mental description. When, however, we are presented with any description that merely enumerates physical 'inputs' and physical 'outputs', and which *does not include any mental terms*, we can, with a little reflection and imagination, think of various countervailing circumstances, such that 'M' would *not* be true even if the 'input-output' description were true. Thus no entailment holds. And we get no closer to an entailment by piling on more details of 'input-output'. Thomas could not remove this difficulty by stipulating that the complete F-state description would *include a denial* of each such countervailing circumstance (for example, that the person was pretending, spoofing, play acting, or engaged in some unsuspected enterprise, and so on). This device would not be available to Thomas because, first, it would bring mental terms, such as intentional descriptions, into the F-state description, which is not legitimate; and, second, because there is no finite number of possible countervailing circumstances: which means that the F-state description could not be completed.

We can see, therefore, that an F-state *description*, with the desired entailment property, cannot be produced! This being so, it is quite meaningless to postulate the existence of these imaginary functional states, or to declare that *if* the postulation of their existence is true then some classical philosophical problem is solved. The postulated functional states are merely a phantasy, indulged in by a number of philosophers.

IV

I come now to the fourth and final version of 'functionalism' or of 'functional analysis' that I will consider. This version has been called, by K. V. Wilkes, 'structural-functional analysis'.[5] This functionalist view 'takes for granted the assumption that physicalism is in fact true' (Wilkes, 45). By 'physicalism' is understood the following: 'it is the attempt to correlate explanations of actions couched in psychological terms with descriptions and explanations of cerebral states, events, and processes couched in neurophysiological terms' (ibid. 29). According to Wilkes, structural-functionalism is not 'reductionist' (ibid. 66). This means that it does not try to find neurophysiological descriptions and explanations that are equivalent in meaning to, or paraphrases of, mental or psychological descriptions and explanations. Nor does it accept 'radical behaviourism', which is the view 'that behaviour can be described and explained with no reference whatever to non-physical terms' (ibid. 10).

The method of structural-functionalism is divided into two stages. The first stage is to consider some characteristic activity of a system—for example, the memory-behaviour of people and animals. At this stage the activity under consideration is analysed into functional parts, in terms of some theory of scientific psychology. Let us suppose that in the example of memory-behaviour there is a theory that analyses this phenomenon into the following functional parts: an input of information from learning or perception, encoding of the information, storage, decoding, retrieval, behavioural output. In other words, memory-behaviour is divided, according to the theory, into a sequence of 'functions'. The second stage of the method is to try to locate, for each of these functions, a physical part of or physical process in the organism, which 'realizes' or carries out that function. In this method the sciences of psychology and neurophysiology work hand in hand. Psychology tries to identify functions; neurophysiology tries to find the physical states or processes that carry out those functions.

As J. A. Fodor puts it, stage one requires a psychological theory that provides functional characterizations of the mechanisms responsible for the production of behaviour. For example, there might be a psychological hypothesis that not only does memory require the 'storage' of memory 'traces', but furthermore that *failures* of memory are due to the 'decay' of memory traces. The second stage of explanation will consist in 'the specification of those biochemical systems that do, in fact, exhibit functional characteristics enumerated by phase-one theories'.[6] When applied to the hypothesis about memory, stage two would involve a search for a sub-system of the organism that has the two properties of 'storage' and 'decay'.

According to Daniel Dennett in his book *Brainstorms,* structural-functionalism pictures a person 'as analogous to a large organization, with intercommunicating departments, executives, and a public relations unit to "speak for the organization" '.[7] This type of explanation of human behaviour consists in 'analysing a person into an organization of sub-systems . . . and attempting to explain the behaviour of the whole person as the outcome of the interaction of these sub-systems' (ibid. 153).

This branch of functionalism is called 'centralist' (in contrast with a 'peripheralist' theory, such as Skinner's), and is also called 'cognitive' theory.

Although Dennett favours a functionalist theory of mind, he is acutely aware that it runs the risk of circularity. For example, it would be circular, and so non-explanatory, to attempt to explain human memory by postulating a sub-system that is itself endowed with memory; or to explain how a person chooses between alternative courses of action by positing an internal state or process that does the choosing. Dennett formulates this difficulty in general terms:

> A non-question-begging psychology will be a psychology that makes no ultimate appeals to unexplained intelligence, and that condition can be reformulated as the condition that whatever functional parts a psychology breaks its subjects into, the smallest, or most fundamental, or least sophisticated parts must not be supposed to perform tasks or follow procedures requiring intelligence (ibid. 83).

How can a psychology that is 'cognitive', 'centralist', or 'functional', avoid question-begging circularity? This is a serious problem. The Cambridge psychologist, F. C. Bartlett, was one of the earlier proponents of the notion of a 'cognitive structure', which he called a 'Schema'. He was concerned to understand how a tennis player, for example, is able to make the quick, efficient movements that are required for skill in tennis. This cannot be explained in terms of a series of learned reflexes, since the *novelty* of the situations and of the responsive bodily movements that occur in tennis play, cannot be accounted for in this way. Bartlett's theory was that all of the past training, actions and reactions, in playing tennis, combine to form 'an active, organized setting' (a 'Schema'), which directs the bodily movements of subsequent play. Skill in driving a car would involve a different Schema; skill in playing the piano still another Schema; and so on. In tennis play each 'new sensory impulse' joins up with the already present tennis Schema. Bartlett says:

> What, precisely, does the 'schema' do? Together with the immediately preceding impulse it renders a specific adap-

tive reaction possible. It is, therefore, producing an orientation of the organism towards whatever it is directed to
at the moment.[8]

Bartlett's solution gives rise to puzzling questions. In the first
place, every normal person has a large number of skills, and
therefore a large number of Schemata. Also, there will presumably be, at any moment, a large number of different 'sensory
impulses'. Now how does an incoming sensory impulse manage
to join up with the *right* Schema? Does the impulse *know* which
Schema to attach to? Or does a Schema *know* which impulses
belong to it? In the second place, how does a Schema succeed
in producing an appropriate 'orientation of the organism'? How
does the tennis Schema manage to produce the right postures
and movements? Does the theory 'explain' skilful play by postulating a skilful Schema? Or are the skilled responses of a
Schema to be accounted for by proposing a second-order Schema
that directs the responses of the first one? Does the very ability
or skill that was to be explained have to be invoked at another
level? I offer this as an example of the threat of circularity,
or of infinite regress, that confronts cognitive and functionalist
theories.

The proponents of structural-functionalism are alert to this
danger. They are aware that a large part of human behaviour
is described in ordinary life by what they call 'intentional' (or
'intensional') descriptions—that is, descriptions that imply
something about what the behaviour *meant*, or what the person's intention, goal, aim or purpose was. At the beginning of
their attempt to explain intentional behaviour, the functionalists
may postulate sub-systems that are themselves characterised in
intentional terms. Because of their commitment to physicalism,
however, they realize that they cannot stop there. Their conception is that the functional analysis will continue downward.
The operation of the sub-systems that have been characterised
in intentional language, will in turn be subjected to functional
analysis. The hope is that finally the course of explanation will
terminate at 'the micro-level', where there are only chemical
processes or the firings of neurons, and where (as Wilkes put
it) 'we find no intentionality at all' (Wilkes, 65). The functionalist
methodology does not seek to *translate* intentional descriptions

into extensional descriptions. What it does hold is that at the end, when the functional analysis is completed, intentionality will have 'vanished' (Wilkes, 66).

In his book *Content and Consciousness,* Dennett says:

> There should be possible some scientific story about synapses, electrical potentials and so forth that would explain, describe and predict all that goes on in the nervous system. If we had such a story we would have in one sense an extensional theory of behaviour, for all the motions (extensionally characterized) of the animal caused by the activity of the nervous system would be explicable and predictable in these extensional terms, but one thing such a story would say nothing about was *what the animal was doing.* This latter story can only be told in Intentional terms, but it is not a story about features of the world *in addition to* the features of the extensional story; it just describes what happens in a different way.[9]

Dennett seems here to have the idea that the two modes of description, intentional and extensional, are describing *the same thing.* As he puts it, both are describing *what happens*; they only describe it 'in different ways'. A similar thought seems to be expressed in another of Dennett's comments. Having remarked that there is a 'lack of theoretically reliable *overt* behavioural clues for the ascription of Intentional expressions', Dennett goes on to say that

> This leaves room for *covert,* internal events serving as the conditions of ascription. We do not ordinarily have access to such data, so they could not serve as ordinary criteria for the use of ordinary Intentional expressions, but this is just a corollary of the thesis that our ordinary language accounts of behaviour are Intentional, and says nothing about the possibility in principle of producing a scientific reduction of internal states. Could there be a system of internal states or events, the extensional description of which could be upgraded into an Intentional description? (*Content and Consciousness,* 39–40).

Dennett is inclined to think that the answer is, yes. In speaking of the 'reduction' of Intentional expressions to extensional expressions Dennett did not, I think, wish to say that correlated expressions in the two modes of description have the same meaning, but instead that they equally describe *what happens,* and further that the extensional description of internal physio- logical states and events is theoretically more reliable, and also more fundamental, than is the Intentional mode of description.

What are we to think of the programme of structural-func- tionalism? How would it apply, for example, to human speech? People say things in conversation and sometimes their remarks are witty, ironic, sarcastic, boring, superficial, acute, angry, in- sensitive, rude, tender, and so on. Suppose that Mr. A had made an engagement to meet Mrs. A at a certain time in a downtown store. Mrs. A is on time but Mr. A is twenty minutes late. When he finally does arrive Mrs. A says, with irritation, 'Why have you kept me waiting?'. Mr. A responds sarcastically, 'Are you always on time?'. Let us suppose that there is a structural-functional analysis of oral speech-behaviour. At the first stage there is a psychological theory that divides up oral speech, we may imagine, into components such as pitch, stress, speed, volume, intonation, resonance, and so on. These would be aspects or functions of vocalization. The second stage would be the attempt to locate physical parts of or physical processes in the organism, that control pitch, stress, speed of utterance, and so on. We may suppose that this physiological investigation is successful. Not only is the process in speech musculature that controls pitch, for example, picked out, but further the neural sub-system that controls this musculature is identified. This would be excellent progress. A psychological theory has divided utterances into certain aspects, dimensions or functions; and then neurophysiological investigation has dis- covered the neural sub-systems and associated musculature that control those functions.

So far, so good. But there is more to be done. A complete functional analysis of speech-behaviour will want to take into account not merely the physical dimensions of utterances (pitch, speed, stress, etc), but also the 'psychological' dimensions, such as sarcasm, wit, rudeness, superficiality, and so on. Mr. A's retort was delivered not only with a certain pitch and with a certain pattern of stress (e.g. 'Are *you* always on time?'), but his utterance was also *sarcastic.* Suppose that the psychologist speaks to the neurophysiologist in the following way : 'Sir, you have done splendid work in locating the neural processes that control pitch and stress. Can you now do the same for sarcasm?'. What should one think of this request? Is an intelligible undertaking presented here to the neurophysiologist? If there is a neural sub-system (a 'structural realization') for the pitch of utterances, might there also be a neural sub-system for the sarcasm of utterances—a sarcastic sub-system?

Mr. A's utterance ('Are you always on time?') could of course be produced in circumstances in which it was not sarcastic. For example, Mr. A has a colleague, Mr. X. To Mr. A it appears that Mr. X is habitually punctual in keeping engagements. Mr. A finds this astonishing and impressive. One day he says to Mr. X, with admiration, 'Are you always on time?'. Here is the same sequence of words, delivered with the same pitch, stress, and intonation. But when this utterance was delivered to Mrs. A it was sarcastic, when delivered to Mr. X it was admiring. Could this difference be assigned to different neurophysiological sub-systems?

When Mr. A delivered his retort to Mrs. A he might have produced a different sequence of words, e.g. 'I suppose you are never late?'. Presumably there would be some differences in the neurophysiological processes that produced the two different vocal sequences. But the two utterances would be equally sarcastic. Could there be a cerebral process that was correlated with *just* the sarcasm?

Wilkes says that the functionalism she espouses is committed to physicalism, and (as already noted) she describes physicalism as 'the attempt to correlate explanations of actions couched in psychological terms with descriptions and explanations of cerebral states, events, and processes couched in neurophysiological terms' (Wilkes, 29). Dennett says that 'functionalist theories' are theories of 'the sub-personal level'. He says further that 'Sub-personal theories proceed by analysing a person into an organization of sub-systems . . . and attempting to explain the behaviour of the whole person as the outcome of the interaction of these sub-systems' (Dennett, *Brainstorms,* 153).

Now Mr. A's sarcastic retort to Mrs. A. was a piece of behaviour of 'the whole person' Mr. A. Both Wilkes and Dennett conceive of Mr. A as an organization of sub-systems,

P

and both of them presumably think that the functionalism they
favour would attempt to explain the behaviour of uttering a
sarcasm as the result of the interaction of some of those sub-
systems. I am ready to acknowledge that there may be
sub-systems for pitch or stress, but not that there may be a
sub-system for sarcasm.

The characterization of an utterance as sarcastic would be
called by both Wilkes and Dennett, an 'intentional description'.
The aim of functionalism is to correlate intentional descriptions
of behaviour with extensional descriptions stated in the language
of neurophysiology. The characterization of a remark as sarcastic
is, of course, a description of ordinary language. And Wilkes
declares that the project of physicalism (and therefore of functionalism) has 'nothing to do' with the descriptions of ordinary
language (Wilkes, 41). Functionalism does not seek to correlate
the intentional terms of ordinary language with neurophysiological terms; the correlation it seeks is between the terms and
descriptions of some *theory* of scientific psychology, and the
terms and descriptions of neurophysiology.

Would the term 'sarcasm' be included in the conceptual
apparatus of a psychological theory? Who knows? There might
be a psychological theory that proposed an 'analysis' of the
term 'sarcasm' into other terms; so the term 'sarcasm' would
not belong to its basic conceptual apparatus. Whether any such
analysis was correct or even intelligible, could not be determined until it was laid before us.

Anyway, Wilkes does hold that 'whatever the detailed content of the conceptual apparatus employed by a psychological
theory may prove to be, we must find there some intensional
terms' (ibid. 44). The idea, I think, is that intentional descriptions are required to characterize the *meaning* of behaviour.
Dennett expresses the same idea in saying that a description
of events in the nervous system could account for the *motions*
that a person made but not for *what the person was doing*.
'This latter story can only be told in Intentional terms' (*Content
and Consciousness,* 78). So the descriptions of a psychological
theory, since the theory is concerned with the meaning of behaviour, will have to contain some intentional terms or other,
But the neurophysiological explanations of 'motions' will contain no intentional terms.

What I find surprising is that the friends of structural-functional analysis believe, or hope, that this impasse can be overcome. They think that an extensional description of internal, neurophysiological, states, and events, can be *upgraded,* as Dennett puts it, into an Intentional description (ibid. 40). But how could this possibly be? The 'motions' can be exactly the same but the *meaning* different. On two occasions Mr. A made the same utterance. The physical dimensions, such as pitch, stress, and speed of utterance, could have been the same. Yet the meaning of the utterance was different on the two occasions. Once it was sarcastic; once it was admiring. How could a neurophysiological account of chemical changes at synapses, electrical potentials, and so on, be 'upgraded' into an explanation of how this utterance was sarcastic on one occasion and admiring on another? It would be unsatisfactory for the functionalists to object that the terms 'sarcastic' and 'admiring' will probably not belong to 'the conceptual apparatus' of a psychological theory. For, first, the functionalists concede that if those particular terms do not belong to the apparatus, some other intentional terms will: and so the same difficulty will present itself with those latter intentional terms, whatever they are. Second, Wilkes admits that when interesting and true descriptions of human behaviour occur at the level of ordinary language, 'these must become part of the subject matter of psychology, a part it can reasonably be challenged to explain' (Wilkes, 47). So it would seem that structural-functionalism cannot be indifferent to the interesting fact that an utterance can have a striking difference in meaning on two occurrences, although having identical physical properties. And structural-functionalism can be 'reasonably challenged' to explain how the differences in the meaning of the utterance could be accounted for by some story about neural firings or electrical potentials.

My own belief is that the proponents of structural-functionalism have set themselves a problem that cannot be solved. There is no way in which neurophysiological descriptions can be 'upgraded' into explanations of meaning. That is simply looking in the wrong place. One understands that Mr. A's utterance to his wife was sarcastic, and why it was sarcastic, by knowing or surmising something of the previous course of their lives together. Probably Mrs. A had herself been late for engagements with Mr. A on several past occasions, and probably this had produced some irritation in Mr. A, consciously or unconsciously. So when on this occasion she rebukes him for being late, this evokes from him a response the meaning of which is easily understood in terms of that known or surmised background. This understanding, this explanation, of Mr. A's behaviour, does not in any way relate that behaviour to neural processes or structures.

The functionalists concede that understanding of this sort can be valuable at the level of ordinary language and thought. But they want something better; more scientific. What would this better explanation lay hold of? Well, it would lay hold of the actual processes in the physical organism which cause behaviour. When Mr. A came out with his sarcastic retort, he had almost certainly not reviewed in his mind Mrs. A's past tardiness and his own past irritations. But the structural-functionalists believe that a record of her tardiness and his irritations must have been 'stored' in his nervous system. Mr. A did not consciously think of those past incidents and feelings; nor did he consciously conclude that a sarcastic rejoinder would be appropriate. No: he just came out with the sarcasm, 'spontaneously' (as we say). But a complete, scientific, explanation of the production of that behaviour, would say how that knowledge of the past was 'stored' in Mr. A's brain, how it was brought out of storage into the 'operational area', and how his actual response was 'selected' from innumerable other possible responses.

Dennett neatly expresses this functionalist view when he says: 'We do many things without thinking about them, but surely we do not do these things without the brain's controlling them?' (*Content and Consciousness*, 123). This remark illustrates the impasse from which functionalism cannot escape. For *what* does the brain 'control'? Does it control merely the physical dimensions of behavioural output? Or does it also control the meaning of behaviour? Mr. A might have made an apologetic response to his wife instead of a sarcastic one. Did Mr. A's *brain* choose a sarcastic reply in preference to an apologetic one? To talk in this way would be to apply an intentional description to the brain. Functionalism does not mind doing this *provisionally.* But it holds that when the functional analysis is *completed*, intentional description will have 'vanished'. Would not this imply, however, that functionalism's attempt to explain the meaning of human behaviour will also have vanished?

Structural-functionalism is engaged in the amusing game of thumb-catching. The thumb is behaviour at the intentional level; behaviour that is meaningful and not just 'motions'. The catching-movement consists of neurophysiological descriptions and explanations. But neurophysiology cannot capture that thumb.

NOTES

¹ Carl C. Hempel, "The Logic of Functional Analysis", in Hempel, *Aspects of Scientific Explanation* (Free Press: New York, 1965).

² B. F. Skinner, *Science and Human Behaviour* (Macmillan: New York, 1953), 35.

³ I addressed myself to Skinner's behaviourism in "Behaviourism as a Philosophy of Psychology", (*Thought and Knowledge,* Cornell: Ithaca and London, 1977).

⁴ Stephen N. Thomas, *The Formal Mechanics of Mind,* (Cornell, Ithaca, 1978).

⁵ K. V. Wilkes, *Physicalism,* (Routledge & Kegan Paul: London, 1978), 54–55.

⁶ J. A. Fodor, *Psychological Explanation* (Random House: New York, 1968), 108–109.

⁷ Daniel C. Dennett, *Brainstorms* (Harvester: Hassocks, Sussex, 1979), 152.

⁸ F. C. Bartlett, *Remembering,* (Cambridge: London, 1932), 207–208.

⁹ Daniel C. Dennett, *Content and Consciousness,* (Humanities Press: New York, 1969), 78.

XIV*—SCEPTICISM AND NATURAL KNOWLEDGE

by Michael Woods

In this paper, I examine what I shall, rather sweepingly, call traditional epistemology, in the light of the conception of epistemology described by Quine and others in recent writings. By traditional epistemology, I understand what is now sometimes called *foundationalist* epistemology. Of course, not all attacks on the view that human knowledge has foundations have explicitly argued for a novel conception of the enterprise urged by Quine. My concern will be exclusively with the implications for scepticism of naturalised epistemology. Traditional, foundationalist epistemology conceived its task to be the rational defence of the body of human knowledge against various kinds of sceptical challenge. The topic of this paper is precisely what the appropriate response should be to such sceptical challenges. In speaking of scepticism I have in mind exclusively scepticism about human empirical knowledge.[1]

Epistemology becomes naturalised when it conceives its task to be the examination of human knowledge, its character, acquisition and structure, making use of all the findings of natural science, and aiming to explain rather than justify the corpus of human knowledge. Its aim is, not so much to show that, broadly, we possess the knowledge that we think we have, but to explain how we come by it, given that we do have it. Naturalised epistemology regards human knowledge as one natural phenomenon among others, to be studied as part of the natural world and located within it. Epistemology on this model is contrasted with a traditional view of it as supplying the foundations for human knowledge—as a study in some sense prior to natural science.[2] Writers in the older tradition aimed to provide a rational justification of human knowledge— for example to justify our knowledge of the physical world from a suitably thin epistemic base. Quine and others reject the whole idea of philosophy as somehow supplying the foundations of the

* Meeting of the Aristotelian Society held at 5/7 Tavistock Place, W.C.1, on Monday, 16 June, 1980 at 6.30 p.m.

knowledge of common sense and natural science. That is a general thesis about the nature of philosophy and not just about the province of the theory of knowledge. It is not that the very idea of a theory of knowledge is rejected; the thesis is rather, that its role has been misconceived. Whereas the traditional epistemologist attempted to justify our belief in the physical world without appeal to anything that itself presupposed beliefs about the external world, on the grounds that any such appeal would beg the question, the task that Quine and others recommend for the theory of knowledge is that of *describing*, and producing an adequate theory of, the manner in which human beings are able, as a result of their interaction with the environment, to arrive at the sophisticated and mutually supporting system of beliefs that they have. Thus the epistemologist, instead of being required to forswear all appeal to the findings of natural science, on pain of arguing in a circle, is expected to make use of all the scientific knowledge relevant to the enterprise in carrying out his task of explanation. His role is one of producing a causal theory, philosophical on account of its generality, rather than providing a rational reconstruction of natural knowledge.[3]

If it is objected to this that epistemology therewith ceases to be philosophy, the answer would be that philosophy is not to be distinguished by subject matter or method but by generality : questions about how knowledge is acquired of sufficient generality are philosophical questions, just as questions about what there is in the universe that reach a sufficient degree of generality are questions of philosophy. So there is no reason to refuse to allow this particular enterprise to count as a *philosophical* theory of knowledge in the only sense in which a *philosophical* account of knowledge is possible. And of course the denial of any *first* philosophy is simply one aspect of the denial of any special subject matter to philosophy.

This attitude to traditional conceptions of the theory of knowledge may be illustrated also by what Quine says about the problem of induction. That problem, as traditionally conceived, and as it was posed by Hume, was seen as the problem of justifying our practice of generalising from the observed to the unobserved, or taking the fact that a pattern has been observed to hold in a sufficiently large sample of observed instances as good grounds for believing that the pattern will be detectable outside that sample. Hume's answer was that no rational justification can be given. To him, our belief in induction is not founded on reason : all that we can say is that human beings are so constituted that they have the habit of generalising, and indeed one of the things that we learn by induction is that they could not survive if they did not do so. The habit of extrapolating from the observed to the unobserved can be described as a natural phenomenon, but not given a rational justification.

Quine commends Hume for reaching the right conclusion, given his conception of the enterprise, but he thinks the task was misconceived from the start. Hume was a victim of the illusion that there could be a first philosophy prior to science. Quine wants to replace the old problem of induction, the problem of justification, with a new one, that of explaining why the generalisations that we hit on coincide, most of the time, with those that turn out correct, even though an indefinitely large number of alternative generalisations are compatible with any limited sample of observations. The explanation that he gives is that our tendency to classify objects for the purposes of generalisation in ways that turn out correct has survival value, and hence may be supposed to be an inherited characteristic, the product of natural selection.[4]

The question that I want to raise is where this leaves the programme of answering the sceptic of the traditional kind. Does the 'liberated epistemologist' regard himself as equipped with an answer to scepticism of the traditional sort? Or does he, rather, hold that, from the vantage point of naturalised epistemology, we can see that traditional scepticism is incoherent? Or is the position, rather, that we can still raise all the old sceptical questions, but that we can see that no answer will be forthcoming, and hence, to continue with the attempt is a barren pursuit, to be abandoned in favour of the different sort of enterprise that Quine favours.[5] Plainly, someone who holds that the investigator of human knowledge ought to study it as a natural phenomenon is not obviously precluded from allowing that sceptical questions of the traditional kind still remain, though it is clear that Quine, at least, thinks that the attempt to answer traditional scepticism does not remain as a fruitful line of enquiry. So it is not quite clear why the new enterprise should supersede the old.

In what follows, I shall be having something to say about three forms of traditional scepticism; two of them I have mentioned already, namely scepticism about the physical world and about induction; I shall also mention scepticism about memory. I begin by asking what arguments there are for recommending the naturalisation of epistemology. On what does this view of the province of the theory of knowledge rest? It is clear that this recommendation rests upon a group of connected doctrines that are forms or aspects of holism: holism about meaning and holism about knowledge. (I do not mean to suggest that these last two can really be separated; they represent different aspects of a single picture. Nor do I attempt to give a general definition of 'holism'. I think I can discern two arguments for naturalised epistemology, that start from the holistic picture, and in elaborating them I hope I shall make it clear exactly what is to be understood by that term).[6]

The aspects of holism that I want to distinguish that are relevant are, first, the view mentioned already, that philosophy is continuous with science, and second, the view that all statements, or very nearly all, are theory-impregnated. I will take these in turn. The bearing on the naturalisation of epistemology is rather different. Not all those who espouse holism to the extent of accepting that even the statements of common sense are theory-impregnated go along with Quine in holding that scepticism cannot be answered and that it is futile to try.[7]

If one takes the view that experience is relevant to our beliefs as a body, so that none of them is immune to revision, and which of them we revise when a revision is called for will depend upon holistic considerations, this has to be applied across the board, and in particular to our philosophical beliefs. There will be no room for distinctively philosophical propositions, about whose truth we can decide by purely conceptual arguments. Philosophy will have to be continuous with the empirical knowledge of common sense. What this means is that there is no room for the preliminary, *a priori* sort of enquiry that has been engaged in by those who have sought to provide an answer to scepticism about knowledge. If experience bears on our beliefs as a body, there is no room for a class of beliefs that are capable of being adjudicated on independently of experience. In Quine's words, 'there is no place for a prior philosophy'. What this means is that if we take the view that our beliefs have to be seen as a body, without discontinuities, there is no available position from which the traditional epistemology can be carried on. For the sceptic attempts to take up a vantage point outside science and empirical knowledge in general apart from the basic data which he takes to supply the foundations, and then ask how the body of knowledge that we think we have is to be justified. But if any enquiry has to take place *from within* our system of beliefs, making adjustments to the totality in the light of experience, there will be no room for the attempt to find a reply to philosophical scepticism about human knowledge. Quine has often quoted Neurath's famous image of the sailors required to mend their boat on open sea while still remaining afloat in it. If any enquiry has to take place in a setting in which the body of our beliefs is taken as given, and we examine some of our beliefs in the light of experience, together with the rest of the corpus, there is no room either for raising or for answering doubts about human knowledge as a whole, nor accepting any of our beliefs that prove open to doubt.[8]

We have here the suggestion that traditional scepticism was deluded in thinking that it was examining human knowledge from an external vantage point; its delusion becomes apparent once it is seen that in raising the sceptical challenge,—for example to our knowledge of the external world—it is covertly relying on the empirical knowledge that is supposedly being subjected to challenge. The position that the sceptic thinks he is occupying is simply not available to him. To appeal to a knowledge of how human beings interact with their environment, to the knowledge they have of how information reaches us through our sense organs would be condemned as circular by traditional epistemology. The argument now under discussion purports to show that the very same charge can be laid against the traditional sceptic—he is making use of the very knowledge that he is supposed to be renouncing all appeal to in developing his argument. That he is guilty of this circularity is a reflexion of the lack of discontinuity between philosophy and science that is one aspect of the holistic view of human knowledge and belief. I shall be returning to this argument later.

I now want to turn to the second aspect of holism that I mentioned—what might be called holism about meaning, as contrasted with holism about knowledge: what I called the view that all statements are theory-impregnated, or putting it another way, that the unit of meaning is not an individual sentence, but a whole theory.[9] This aspect of holism is, of course, very close to something stressed by Duhem, one of the precursors of contemporary holism. The relevance of this holistic view to traditional scepticism is as follows. If we hold that empirical import cannot be parcelled out sentence by sentence, then we must also hold that no kind of phenomenalistic reduction is possible. For the driving force behind phenomenalism is the thought that there cannot be anything more to the meaning of an empirical statement than what its truth would imply for the course of our experience—its truth and falsehood cannot, for an empiricist, consist in anything more than our experience's being thus and so. So some sort of phenomenalistic reduction ought to be possible, which would spell out the experiential import of our statements. This view can be presented as a form of verificationism.[10] But someone who espouses holism of the sort now under discussion will claim that, whatever other reasons there may be for rejecting phenomenalism, it must be rejected on the ground that it takes an unacceptably atomistic view of the meaning of empirical statements. If even ordinary statements about physical bodies are theory-impregnated, it is useless to analyse them one by one in a phenomenalistic fashion. Now one of the standard methods of supplying an answer to traditional scepticism about the external world was to propose a phenomenalistic reduction of statements about physical objects to statements about sense data, or whatever. If phenomenalism is in principle impossible, at least that way of answering scepticism is ruled out.[11]

This second argument from holism to naturalised epistemology seems to me to have a much more restricted scope than the first. In the first place, it has an evident bearing only on scepticism about the external world, and not, as the first argument did, on traditional scepticism in general. Secondly, it seems to be an argument against epistemology as traditionally conceived only in so far as it purports to show that one method of answering scepticism is closed. It attempts to block the use of phenomenalistic reduction as a means of disposing of scepticism. But not all attempts to answer the traditional sceptic in the theory of knowledge have taken that form, and Russell, for example, later abandoned his version of phenomenalism in favour of a view that made the physical world something of which we knew by a species of causal inference. More recently, Hilary Putnam,[12] though plainly committed to some form of holism, has argued that the belief in an external world is justified as being the best possible explanation of the course of our experience—or rather the only explanation that is seriously in the field.

Having sketched the ways in which the rejection of epistemology, as traditionally conceived, is related to the adoption of holism, I now go on to ask where this all leaves traditional scepticism. If the first of the two arguments I have outlined is correct, then, if holism is true, traditional epistemology is not a possible enterprise; but can we appeal to holism in trying to deal with the traditional sceptic? For he will plainly wish to challenge any holistic position that is appealed to in trying to dislodge him from his external vantage point. Is there any way in which scepticism can either be answered or shown to be incoherent, without begging the question? One possible reaction of someone who espouses holism is to turn away from the project of answering scepticism, without claiming to show, in terms that the sceptic will himself accept, that the project is misconceived. However, it may be thought that we ought if possible to aim at something more ambitious than that, and actually confront scepticism on its own terms.

Any argument for the view that naturalised epistemology ought to supersede the traditional enterprise must proceed, it seems to me, in one of two ways. Either it must be argued that, although scepticism cannot be refuted, it can safely be ignored, and naturalised epistemology is available as a new alternative. We start from the body of scientific knowledge that we have, and argue that this itself shows that the old enterprise is impossible, so that any success it had would be self-undermining. Alternatively, and more ambitiously, it may be claimed that scepticism, as traditionally conceived, is incoherent, because sceptical questions about human knowledge can only be raised by someone who accepts at least some of the truths that are supposed to have been called in question, and to argue this without presupposing, in a circular fashion, the general truth of holism.[13] It is, of course, quite consistent to adopt both : to claim that traditional scepticism can safely be ignored, and that it is actually incoherent.

An argument of the less ambitious sort might be along the following lines : Among the most general facts about human psychology and physiology is the fact that when we perceive the world, our sense organs are stimulated in a certain way, and they in turn affect our brain in certain ways. We learn from physiology that whatever experiences occur when we are perceiving an object of a certain sort could have been produced by artificial stimulation of the brain, and hence, if no other knowledge or beliefs are assumed, other than beliefs about the character of our experience, we can have no rational ground for inferring anything at all about the character of the world external to ourselves. So the attempt to provide a rational justification of our beliefs about the external world on the basis of the patterns that an individual discerns in his experience is doomed to failure. Again, we can take the example of memory. What we know about the physiology of memory tells us that it is possible that the traces that are produced by a remembered past event should be capable of being artificially caused, and in such cases someone will have an apparent memory that is totally delusive. But if so, any attempt to answer scepticism about memory in a totally *a priori* fashion must fail. This argument involves no circularity : it will have a form reminiscent of Russell's famous argument against Naive Realism—'Naive Realism leads to physics. And if physics is true, Naive Realism is false. Therefore it is false'. The argument will be simply that any answer to scepticism on its own terms will just give us knowledge that will, in its turn, undermine our answer. Given what we know about the world, there is no rational ground anyone could have for inferring the existence of the external world from his experience alone.[14] If the question whether the edifice of human knowledge is an edifice built on foundations is allowed to be answered *a posteriori,* the answer can only be that it is not like that.

But having noted that an argument of this form could be

developed, we are naturally led on to consider what I called
the more ambitious argument—the argument that the sceptic
can be caught out, as it were—he can be shown covertly to
presuppose some of the knowledge that is supposed to have been
called in question. One suggestion might be that, in appealing
to such phenomena as illusion, the sceptic is presupposing our
ordinary knowledge of the external world, because illusions
can only be detected against a background of veridical perception. Indeed, such an argument was once widely deployed as
a way of refuting general scepticism of a Cartesian kind about
the external world. But it has now for long been accepted that
an argument of that kind will not do as it stands. It is true
that a sceptic about the external world cannot claim to *identify*
cases of illusion with certainty without assuming a background
of knowledge about the external world, contrary to the sceptical
enterprise, but there is no need for him to do so. All that the
sceptic needs to do is to point to the *possibility* that any individual's experience should have been just the way it is, without
correspondence to an external reality. Similarly, in the case of
memory, it is irrelevant, and indeed quite inappropriate, for
a sceptic to appeal to cases in which our memories have actually
played us false, for such an appeal presupposes the correctness
of memory; what the sceptic needs to do is to appeal to the
possibility that we should have all the apparent memories that
we actually have without any correspondence between them
and the past. And this may be thought to remove the force of
the argument that the very occurrence of illusions is part of
our natural knowledge of the world, and therewith the very
distinction between reality and illusion. For there need be no
appeal to the actual occurrence of illusion, but only to its
possibility.

It is here that the sceptic seems to be in his strongest position,
against Quinean holism, at least with respect to the claim that
his question can at least be raised. How can it be claimed that
'the sceptical challenge springs from science itself', or again
'the epistemologist is confronting a challenge to natural science
that arises from within natural science'? As traditionally presented, philosophical scepticism appeals simply to logical possibilities, to what we can recognise as such in a purely *a priori*
fashion. It seems clear, then, that if a naturalised epistemologist

is to take a more ambitious line with the sceptic, and actually convict him of begging the question, he must show that the sceptic cannot appeal to these possibilities without making assumptions about what we can know that are inconsistent with the position of a sceptic. That seems to be the point of saying that the sceptical challenge arises from within science. In order to show that the sceptical position is actually incoherent, it is necessary to challenge the view that these possibilities that the sceptic appeals to can be recognised as such in a purely *a priori* fashion.

Earlier, we saw that someone who takes the less ambitious line with the sceptic may draw on the natural knowledge we have about knowledge itself, and the manner in which human beings acquire it, to argue that the sceptic cannot be answered and therefore that the old epistemological enterprise is futile: he can appeal to the mechanism involved in perception and memory and so on. He is then appealing to causal possibilities, but the traditional sceptic claims to appeal to no more than bare logical possibility.

What I want is to sketch a way in which I think that the more ambitious challenge to the sceptic can succeed. I consider first the case of scepticism in regard to knowledge of the external world. The sceptic here begins with the thought that any individual human being is confronted with a pattern of experience —a stream of sense-impressions exhibiting recurrent patterns from which the individual constructs or infers the external world. The challenge made by the sceptic was to show that this inference or construction can be justified. The problem comes when the attempt is made to describe the possibility that the sceptic wishes to exploit,—to spell out what is claimed to be a logical possibility without begging any questions. And here the difficulty arises; crucial use has been made of the notion of *experience*, where this is conceived of as a stream of presentations in the traditional Humean fashion. These, it is claimed, could occur in just the manner that they do occur in the experience of an individual even if there were no external world.

Here, two things should be said by way of qualification. First, of course, that what I have called the notion of experience need not be specifically that; reference may be made to sensory states, or some such, but something must be brought in to play the systematic role that is most naturally played by the notion of sensory experience.

Secondly, there is the point, stressed by Strawson and others,[15] that the beliefs we have about external reality are partly constitutive of experience's having the character it does, so that there is no question of our experience's having the character it has independently of the inference that scepticism invites us to justify. But then the traditional sceptic need not deny that our experience is indeed impregnated with our beliefs about external reality.

That traditional scepticism has to make systematic use of the notion of subjective experience, or some variant of that, in presenting its challenge, is reasonably clear, for only in this way can the possibility that he wishes to invoke be stated. I earlier argued that we can indeed make sense of this possibility from within the context of naturalised epistemology, since we can give content to this idea by introducing the causal facts of perception; we know, in general terms, how external objects impinge upon our sensory surfaces and causally affect the brain. This enables us to give *one* reasonably clear interpretation of the notion of experience, and give content to the possibility that our experience should have the character it does have even though no external world corresponded to it. What I want to challenge is the notion that scepticism can make use of the notion of experience in a systematic way without begging any questions.

I shall not, of course, attempt to survey exhaustively all the ways in which the notion of experience may be introduced to play this important systematic role. In the present century, the notion of a sense-datum has played an important part, but even since the notion of a sense-datum has fallen out of favour, some have still regarded the traditional enterprise with favour. So what I want to do is to appeal to certain general considerations. Clearly, any attempt to characterise the notion of experience in purely causal terms is going to invite the charge of begging the question against scepticism.

I want to suggest that any attempt to present the logical possibility that the sceptic wishes to exploit must introduce the crucial notion of experience in an epistemic fashion—that is, in terms of certainty. Often, it has been claimed that the reports of immediate experience are peculiarly certain, or at least incorrigible; but it is not necessary to claim that they are absolutely certain in order to identify these favoured sentences. What is required is that our confidence in their truth should in no way be undermined by anything that might prove to be the case about the external world. The belief in the existence of sentences satisfying this minimal condition might indeed be regarded as constitutive of foundationalist epistemology. Sense data, sensory states or whatever one wishes to call them, can then be introduced as what forms the topic of such favoured sentences—as that, the occurrence of which is required for their truth.

Now I think that this programme can be challenged at two points: first, I think that it is an error to suppose that there are in fact any sentences satisfying the required conditions; and second, I think that if one makes use of the notion of experience generally in that way, it cannot be regarded as an evident possibility that what is reported in statements of immediate experience could occur independently of the external world. The causal possibility that I mentioned earlier, of perceptual experience the same in character as that which occurs when someone is perceiving an object of a certain kind in the absence of the object, clearly does not presuppose anything at all about the possibility of experience in the absence of physical objects, since the causal facts as presented are compatible with the identification of mental states with physical. If perceptual experience is introduced by a sceptic as the topic of certain first-person reports, identified epistemically, he is entitled to assume *nothing whatever* about the ontological status of what is reported, and, in particular, about the possibility of the occurrence of experience in the absence of a physical world.

At this point, I ought to make clear what I take the dialectical position to be. I am not claiming that we can appeal to the truth of physicalism to refute the sceptic about the external world. Such an argument would indeed be circular. What one can do, however, is to claim that, in presenting his position, he makes certain assumptions that he is not in a position to make from his sceptical standpoint. If it is allowed that it is at least epistemically possible that what his favoured sentences reporting immediate experience in fact report is certain physical occurrences then the possibility that he takes to be evident will not be a real one.

I have challenged the view that the possibility that the sceptic about the external world takes to be evidently a real one, is one that he is entitled to take for granted. In arguing this, I have, for the moment, left unchallenged the supposition that the relevant class of sentences can be defined in a purely epistemic fashion. But I want to challenge that also, on the ground that it is mistaken in principle to attempt to define a class of epistemically basic statements in advance of a general theory of human knowledge. Quine, in his discussion of naturalised epistemology, brings in the psychological and physiological knowledge that we have in order to define the relevant sort of epistemological priority. Quine suggests that 'A is epistemologically prior to B if A is causally nearer than B to the sensory receptors'. Whether or not we find that particular way of defining epistemological priority satisfactory does not matter for our immediate purposes. What is important is the question whether there is any way of defining priority that does not bring in natural knowledge of this sort. I want to argue that there is no way of defining a class of epistemologically basic sentences in terms solely of the notions of certainty and incorrigibility. My argument is that the application of epistemic notions like certainty ought to depend on a thoroughgoing theory of what human knowledge is and what its various sources are. A fully developed theory of human knowledge, exploiting psychological knowledge and what we know of the way in which human beings interact with the world cannot fail to make a difference to what we regard as the relative certainty of statements in different classes.

To take this point of view is, of course, to take up the standpoint of naturalised epistemology; and it may be thought that such an appeal will beg the question against scepticism. But for present purposes it is enough to point out that the traditional sceptic cannot remain neutral on the issue of the character of human knowledge, and this is enough to show his position is untenable. I am suggesting that the traditional sceptic can be attacked by what might, in a suitably broad sense, be called a transcendental argument. For it will show that it is not possible to identify a class of epistemologically basic statements without prejudging what human knowledge eventually turns out to be.

I have argued, then, that in two distinct ways, traditional scepticism takes up a stand on issues that it is not in a position to prejudge from the sceptical position. Firstly, it prejudges what we might wish to say, on the basis of naturalised epistemology, about the possibilities of falsification of first-person statements about our experience, in identifying a certain set of statements as epistemically basic. Second, it assumes that certain possibilities exist whose existence is not independent of the identity of the events that form the topic of these basic statements, supposing that we could identify them. What is regarded as a basic statement will, of course, be relative to the particular sort of sceptical challenge that is under consideration.

It will be apparent that I am assuming that the truth of the thesis that true identity statements are necessarily true, in speaking, as I have done, of real possibilities; it is not possible, here, to offer a defence of that thesis, and the arguments for it are now familiar. I am assuming that if the experiences that form the topic of the basic statements, that traditional epistemology relies on so heavily, were in fact certain physical states or occurrences, then it could indeed be impossible for them to occur without certain occurrences in the public physical world. Traditional epistemology, in other words, derives its plausibility from taking what appears to be an epistemic possibility to be a real one. In saying this, I am not attempting to refute traditional epistemology from the position of materialism or physicalism; what I am claiming is that traditional epistemology cannot avoid taking up a position on the subject of the identity or non-identity of mental states with physical states; and this shows that there is no position available for traditional epistemology to occupy.

The position with scepticism over memory is similar, and a parallel argument can be developed. There is this difference, that the apparent memories that the sceptic takes as his starting point do not have the problematic status of reports of sense-data. But, in an important respect, the situation is parallel. What the sceptic claims to be a possibility is that we might have had all the apparent memories that we do have without the past history that they purport to be memories of, and, once again, this is something that he is not entitled to assume. Just what memory is is one of the questions that form part of naturalised epistemology. And the answer to that question will in its turn have implications for the identity of apparent memories. If apparent memories can only count as such if they have a certain causal ancestry, there will still be no room for the sceptical doubts about memory to be raised without begging the question. Precisely what is compatible with the apparent memories that we actually have is something that the sceptic is in no position to prejudge.

One objection that may be raised to my argument is that I have been accusing the traditional sceptic of a confusion that I have made myself, namely a confusion of epistemic and real possibility. I have claimed that the sceptic has to claim to be a real possibility something that he is not entitled to assume is one from his sceptical standpoint—namely that subjective experience should occur in the absence of any physical world. It may be argued against this that all he wishes to insist on is an epistemic possibility, namely that, given his experience, for all he knows, there may be no external world. What is being demanded is a rational justification of the knowledge that we habitually claim, and to show that that demand is in place it is enough to point out that a certain epistemic possibility exists. Thus, it may be said by the sceptic that, given what we know, or can be certain of, about our experience, it is still epistemically possible that there should be no external world. To say that, for a person A, it is epistemically possible that P, is to say that P is compatible with all that A knows. Applying that to the present case, if it is claimed by the sceptic that the falsehood of all our beliefs about the external world is compatible with all that we know from immediate experience, then we can once again accuse him of begging the question. For we can say that he is not entitled to assume, from his sceptical standpoint, that the falsehood of all his beliefs about the external world *is* compatible with what he learns from immediate experience. The argument here is that precisely what we do know or are certain of, and therefore what is compatible with what we know, is not to be prejudged in advance of a general theory of human knowledge. That is the consequence of taking seriously the fact that the acquisition of knowledge by human beings is part of the natural world.

Against this whole line of argument, it may be objected that, even if it is conceded that the sceptic is not entitled to make any claim about what we know or are certain of, on pain of prejudging issues that must not be prejudged, he can retreat to a higher order, and persist in his scepticism there. Even if he is not in a position to say that a certain class of statements are more certain than the rest, or that our knowledge is less extensive than it has been commonly held to be, he can still say that we do not know just how extensive our knowledge is. However, such a retreat would not provide room for the old epistemological enterprise; for that depended upon the possibility of identifying a class of favoured epistemologically basic statements. The retreat to a higher order will leave the sceptic not saying anything.

Finally, I make some brief remarks about the application of this to traditional scepticism about induction. In a passage from *The Roots of Reference* (pp. 19-20), Quine, after mentioning his view about the source of our disposition to extrapolate from observed regularities in ways that prove fruitful, says 'These thoughts are not meant to *justify* induction. For that purpose, the appeal to a law of natural selection would be unwarranted, since that law rests in turn on induction'. Nonetheless, we might still ask whether the position of one who questions induction is an entirely coherent one. For we can at least ask how much of what the inductive sceptic does know he can claim to know with prejudging the question whether the laws to which he extrapolates do hold in the physical world. If the description of the observations made itself embodies a set of beliefs about what the physical world contains, we can no longer allow the sceptic to describe the limited sample of observations he has made without accusing him of begging the question. From the position of naturalised epistemology, there is no separating the premisses of inductive inference from all the knowledge that is required by the use of inductive reasoning.

NOTES

[1] The work of Quine that I have particularly in mind is, of course, 'Epistemology Naturalised', in the collection *Ontological Relativity and Other Essays* (New York, 1969) but I make use also of some observations

about induction in the essay 'Natural Kinds' in the same volume, and, more important, I refer to certain things Quine says about epistemology in general in the opening pages of *The Roots of Reference* (la Salle, Illinois, 1973).

2 This tradition, which is commonly traced back to Descartes, is represented, in this century, most powerfully in the writings of Russell and Ayer.

3 As Quine says in 'Epistemology Naturalised' (op. cit. p.83) 'The old epistemology aspired to contain, in a sense, natural science; it would construct it somehow from sense-data. Epistemology in its new setting, conversely, is contained in natural science, as a chapter of psychology, and hence of natural science. It studies a natural phenomenon, viz. a physical human subject. The subject is accorded a certain experimentally controlled input—certain patterns of irradiation in assorted frequencies, for instance—and in the fullness of time the subject delivers as output a description of the three-dimensional world and its history. Epistemology just investigates how the input and output are related. Our liberated epistemologist ends up as an empirical psychologist, scientifically investigating man's acquisition of science.'

4 As he says in 'Natural Kinds' (op. cit. p.126): 'Creatures inveterately wrong in their inductions have a pathetic but praiseworthy tendency to die before reproducing their kind'. Or again, in *The Roots of Reference* (p.20): 'In the matter of justifying induction we are back with Hume, where we doubtless belong. Asking for a justification of induction is like asking for a first philosophy in support of science. What natural selection, rather, . . . supplies, is a reason why induction works, granted that it does'.

5 A reading of Quine may suggest reason for attributing all three of these positions to him.

6 I should also add that the basing of the naturalisation of epistemology on holism may be thought to show that the issue has a more general interest than might have been thought. We may wish to accept some degree of holism without going as far in that direction as Quine.

7 Hilary Putnam has attempted to offer a reply to scepticism about the physical world, as well as about other worlds, although he accepts holism so far as the all-pervasiveness of theory is concerned. See, for example, 'Other Minds' in *Philosophical Papers*, vol. 2 (London, 1975).

8 Compare Quine in *The Roots of Reference*: 'Ancient skepticism challenged science from within. The skeptics cited familiar illusions to show the fallibility of the senses; but this concept of illusion itself rested on natural science, since the quality of illusion consisted simply in deviation from external scientific reality.' (p.2–3). 'The skeptical challenge springs from science itself and that in coping with it we are free to use scientific knowledge'. (p.3).

9 Cf. 'Epistemology Naturalised', p.79: 'The typical statement about bodies has no fund of experiential implications it can call its own'.

10 In Russell, it tends to appear as a doctrine about what we can justifiably claim to know: if we can justifiably claim to know empirical truths about bodies, they had better be construed phenomenalistically.

11 This line of argument is to be found in 'Epistemology Naturalised' when Quine discusses various attempts of Carnap to translate the sentences of science into observation terms. These attempts were unsuccessful, and if one gives up all hope of providing a translation, an empiricist is conceding that 'the meanings of typical statements about the external world are inaccessible and ineffable.' This inaccessibility is in its turn explained by

the holistic view that 'the typical statement about bodies has no fund of experiential implications it can call its own'.

¹² op. cit.

¹³ There are certainly signs of the latter, more ambitious, way of dealing with sceptic in the passages that I have quoted from the first four pages of *The Roots of Reference*, but there are also signs, elsewhere in Quine's writings of the less ambitious line of thought.

¹⁴ I am not suggesting that an argument of this sort is actually to be found in Quine; but this argument does consort well with Quine's remark that, in regard to traditional scepticism, we are, and belong, where Hume left us.

¹⁵ See, for example, P. F. Strawson, 'Perception and Imagination', in Lawrence Foster and J. W. Swanson (ed.): *Experience and Theory*, (London, 1970).